D0295329

The Encyclopedia of

US MILITARY AIRCRAFT

US MILITARY AIRCRAFT

Martin W. Bowman

USAF
a&ap
Arms and Armour Press
A Bison Book

First published in 1980 by
Arms and Armour Press
Lionel Leventhal Limited
2–6 Hampstead High Street, London NW3 1PR

Produced by Bison Books Limited
4 Cromwell Place, London SW7

British Library Cataloguing in Publication Data:
Bowman, Martin
The encyclopedia of US military aircraft.
1. Airplanes, Military
2. Aeronautics, Military – United States
I. Title
623.74'6'0973 UG1203

ISBN 0 85368 383 2

Printed in Singapore

Designer: David Eldred
Editor: Catherine Bradley
Indexer: Susan Piquemal

Half title and title pages: General Dynamics F-16 Multi-role Fighters.
***Right:* A US Marine pilot poses on the front of his Vought F8U-1 Crusader.**

Contents

Author's Preface

This encyclopedia of US military aircraft is a complete, popular analysis of the most important aircraft made in the United States and, occasionally, in other countries used by the US Air Force, US Navy, US Marines and US Army Air Corps from earliest times to the present. Since no aircraft for specific military use were built in the US until 1918, and since none of these were used in World War I, the period from 1930 has been analyzed far more extensively than the previous period. It was not until 1934, with the advent of the B-17 design, that American aviation really took off.

Chronology proved as difficult as deciding which aircraft to portray and how? Under headings like Helicopters, Bombers, Trainers, Fighters etc? Fighters for instance, have been called pursuit and Bombers have been known as attack but how does one define a trainer? Aircraft like the Skyhawk can operate equally well in both the trainer and fighter roles. Finally I decided to break the book down into four main periods of American military aviation history although there is no fixed rule governing the sections in which aircraft appear. The C-47 for instance, is featured in the World War II section although this remarkable piston-engined aircraft, like many others, was still in service in Korea and Vietnam. Generally, all aircraft have been categorized in the era when they showed their greatest elan. For this reason, an aircraft like the Invader does not appear in the World War II section but later, when it did sterling service in Korea.

The chronology of this book has been divided into four

An Air-launched Cruise Missile (ALCM), designated AGM-86B by the USAF, is released from the belly of a B-52. The B-52 is capable of carrying 12 ALCMs on its wings and eight internally.

sections. The first covers the period leading up to and including World War II. The second covers the postwar era during the height of the Cold War and includes the Korean War period. The third period, 1961–69, covers the new technology mingled with the old during the Vietnam War build up. The final period covers the new aircraft brought into use at the end of the Vietnam War and the planes the United States will introduce in large numbers in the 1980s.

The result is a book which I believe to be the first to feature the most well-known American military aircraft from the late 1930s to the present day in one publication. Apart from the famous and the not so famous, also featured are less well known, sometimes obscure aircraft, which nevertheless made their contribution to American military aviation. Therefore, aircraft like the B-23, which was the first American bomber to feature a tail-gun position, the XB-43, America's first jet bomber, and the Lockheed XFV-1 vertical take-off aircraft, have been included.

I am eternally grateful to all the Aircraft companies listed in the photograph credits for such a glittering array of illustrative and technical material. My deepest thanks too go to Mike Bailey for his customary kindness in granting all my requests for photographs and technical expertise.

Martin W. Bowman
Norwich, January 1979.

Introd

North American B-25 Mitchell, one of the USAAF's most outstanding bombers in World War II.

American aviation began in 1898 when the US Army invested 50,000 dollars in the development of a man-carrying airplane. It failed and it was not until 1908 that the Army accepted a tender of 25,000 dollars from the Wright brothers to build a military biplane capable of carrying two airmen at 40 mph. In August 1909 the Aeronautical Division of the US Army, formed two years before, accepted the Wright Model B and it remained the only aircraft on the inventory for two years. On 26 September 1910 the US Navy appointed Captain W I Chambers to deal with all naval aviation matters. Chambers chose Glenn Curtiss to build an A-1 Triad, which was first flown on 1 July 1911, and arranged for Eugene Ely, a Curtiss demonstration pilot, to take-off and land on special platforms aboard US Navy ships in 1910 and 1911.

During January and February 1913 an embryo Naval aviation unit participated in Fleet exercises off Cuba and seven Naval aircraft took part in the Mexican crisis with the Atlantic Fleet a year later. By March 1913 the 1st Air Squadron, equipped with Curtiss R-2 biplanes, had formed the nucleus of the first American Army aviation unit.

But progress was slow. By early 1917 the Aviation Section of the Signal Corps, which had been vested with all responsibilities for US Army flying on 18 July 1914, could only boast seven squadrons throughout the USA, Panama and the Philippines. It was not until 1 July 1915 that the Navy Department finally recognized aviation when an Office of Naval Aeronautics was established.

When America entered World War I on 6 April 1917 her military air arms were in an even more perilous state than those of the European powers had been in 1914. In April 1917 the Naval Flying Corps could only muster 54 aircraft and 48 qualified and student pilots.

Of all the aircraft flown by the American Expeditionary Force in World War I, none were American built. However, America moved quickly, designing and developing the mighty Liberty engine and making plans for a vast expansion of its ailing aircraft industry. On 3 April 1918 the 94th Pursuit Squadron, resplendent with its famous 'Hat-in-Ring' insignia, became the first American trained pursuit squadron in action on the Western Front. Captain Eddie V Rickenbacker had joined the squadron a month before and was to finish the war as America's top 'ace' with 26 'kills.' The Americans' greatest test and success came in the Battle of St Mihiel where the US commander, Brigadier General William 'Billy' Mitchell, had amassed over 1500 aircraft for the big American push in August 1918.

When the Armistice was signed in November 1918 America possessed 45 Army squadrons and 200,000 personnel but by June 1920 this had dropped to only 10,000 personnel. World War I had also seen a vast expansion of the Naval Flying Corps. By November 1918 the Navy's aircraft strength stood at 2107 with over 37,000 officers and enlisted men and almost 2500 officers and enlisted men in the Marine Corps. But the Navy and Army Air Corps suffered severe cutbacks in the 1920s and by 1926 what was left of the Army air squadrons were placed under the new command of the US Army Air Corps.

Military progress between the world wars was slow. Allied governments decided that their forces would have to continue using weapons they had used in France. Uncertainty in the role of military air power also played its part. But the Navy steered clear of Government wrangles and forged ahead with its dynamic leader from 1921 to 1933, Rear Admiral W A Moffett, at the helm. Moffett laid the foundations for the great Naval air arm that was to emerge in World War II. He was ably supported by Admiral W S Sims, a staunch advocate of aircraft carriers. However Congress were still to be convinced. By the end of 1929 America boasted only three aircraft carriers and one of these was an old sea dog.

Below: **Lockheed RF-80A as used in the Korean War.**
Right: **P-61B Black Widow night fighter of World War II.**

My Miss Carole B.
FT-260

USAF

U.S. AIR FORCE
14262

Exciting developments in the field of Naval aircraft continued to be made. In the late 1920s naval dive bombers were of stressed-skin construction and built to withstand the extreme stresses of 75 to 90 degree dives; features which put them among the world's elite during 1928–1950.

But while the US Navy tried to stay out of the Government's way interservice rivalry with the Army was often bitter. It was not until the Pratt-MacArthur agreement of 9 January 1931, which defined the US Navy Flying Corps as an element of the Fleet, and as such, separate from the total defense strategy. US Navy admirals were eager to prove to the young 'upstart' AAS that no bomber could sink a battleship. But the Army, led in 1921 by Brigadier General Mitchell, was out to disprove such a theory. Mitchell wanted to bomb one of Germany's largest World War I battleships, the *Ostfriesland*, at anchor off the Capes of Virginia after the surrender. It had been widely proclaimed as unsinkable but on 21 July 1921 Mitchell's eight Martin MB-2 bombers only needed to drop seven bombs to capsize and sink her. It was a milestone in US Army aviation history but Mitchell was later court-martialled for his uncompromising campaign on behalf of strategic bombing.

The dawning of the mid-30s, especially after the announcement of German re-armament, spawned a whole host of new military aircraft. Boeing and Martin developed the first all-metal American monoplane bombers, the B-9 and B-10 respectively, as private ventures. In 1933 Boeing followed up with the P-26A, the first all-metal monoplane fighter.

In 1934 the Army ordered a design study to determine the feasibility of an extremely heavy bomber. Boeing designed the XB-15, a massive four-engined bomber weighing over 70,000lbs and armed with six machine guns. It was so large that passageways were built inside the wing to enable the crew to make minor engine repairs in flight. Unsuitable for combat, it was converted to a cargo carrier and used in World War II. Undismayed, Boeing continued, in August 1934, with the Model 299, later to gain fame as the B-17 Flying Fortress.

Meanwhile the Curtiss P-36 and the Republic P-35 were the first single-seat Army pursuit monoplanes to incorporate retractable undercarriages and enclosed cockpits. Although neither type was produced in large numbers they did bridge the gap between the old generation of biplane fighters and the high-performance monoplanes of World War II.

When civil war broke out in Spain in 1936 the Luftwaffe and the Regia Aeronautica took advantage of the situation to test their new aircraft in combat. Few American types, like the Grumman GE-23, took part, but Martin B-10s, Curtiss BT-32 Condors and Hawk III biplane fighters were among those which participated in the Sino-Japanese conflict on the Chinese side when full-scale war erupted in 1937.

In 1939 America added another notable bomber, the B-24 Liberator, to its growing pre-eminence in four-engined bombers. This remarkable aircraft was designed in January that year and incorporated the famous Davis high aspect ratio wing. On 30 March 1939 a contract was awarded for a single prototype and in October the wing and fuselage were married together to form the basis for one of the best bombers of World War II. The B-24 and the B-17 helped give the USA a world lead in four-engined heavy bomber design.

The same could not be said of the United State's front-line fighters. When World War II broke out in Europe in September 1939 the principal American fighters were the Curtiss P-36 and P-40 and the Navy's Grumman F2F biplane. But the Bell Airacobra and the Mitchell bomber were ordered that year while the US Navy forged ahead with the Grumman F4F, which entered service in 1940 and proved one of the most outstanding Naval fighters of the war. The standard torpedo bomber in 1939 was the ineffective Douglas TBD-1 but it was to be replaced by the highly successful SBD Dauntless in 1941. Although America was no more prepared for war in 1939 than any of the European nations outside Germany, she had developed aircrew oxygen supply, superchargers to boost high-altitude performance, the costly but effective Norden bomb-sight, and by 1940, standard .5 inch machine-gun armament. When the time came these innovations would prove invaluable.

That time came on the normally peaceful Sunday morn-

Lockheed T-33A trainers of the USAF. They also served with the US Navy and Marine Corps, as the T-33B (TV-2), and with 23 other nations.

Above: **USAF Tactical Air Command's F-104C streaks towards its target in a simulated combat mission.**
Below: **F-104G Starfighters of the Belgian Air Force.**

ing of 7 December 1941. Waves of Japanese dive bombers, fighters and torpedo bombers attacked the US Pacific fleet at Pearl Harbor in Hawaii, killing more than 2000 personnel and decimating the fleet of battleships. But they failed to destroy the entire carrier fleet which was fortunately at sea on maneuvers. The following day the USA and Britain declared war on Japan.

At that time the air arms of the US Navy and Marine Corps could muster 5233 aircraft of all types and 5900 pilots and 21,678 enlisted men. The USNAF, in fulfillment of its primary mission of supporting the fleet, became heavily involved in the war against Japan in the Pacific. At home American bomber and fighter units prepared to move to Britain to begin the concerted fight against the Axis.

B-17s and B-24s flew the Atlantic ferry routes and were joined by P-38 Lightnings, Republic P-47 Thunderbolts and finally P-51 Mustangs. The American bomber crews' brief to bomb in daylight, without escort if necessary and from high-altitude, astounded RAF Chiefs. The RAF had incurred heavy losses using similar tactics and so had the Luftwaffe in the Battle of Britain. Both had later switched to night bombing. But the high-flying B-17s and B-24s, equipped with heavy armament and precision bombsights, would have been useless at night. Unfortunately, the clear skies of the North American continent, which were ideal for 'pickle barrel' accuracy, were not often to be found in Europe. American losses were catastrophic in the early part of the war, especially at Schweinfurt and Regensburg on 14 October 1943 when over 60 B-17s were shot down.

The round-the-clock bombing, with the RAF by night and the American Eighth and 15th Air Forces by day, finally turned the tide in Europe. It was the introduction of the P-51 Mustang in December 1943, with its ability to escort the 'heavies' to their targets and back, which finally tipped the balance of air power in the Allies' favor. The installation of the Merlin engine at a vital stage in the Mustang's development helped it become the greatest fighter of the war.

In the Far East and Pacific theaters the US Navy fought an uncompromising and implacable Japanese enemy on land and sea and in the air. During the latter half of the war the US Navy could call upon some of the best aircraft of the war. The F4U Corsair, issued to Navy and Marine squadrons in 1942, proved one of the most outstanding Navy fighters of the war. By VJ-Day, Corsairs had destroyed over 2000 enemy aircraft. Other superb Navy fighters, like the Grumman Hellcat, entered the fray while the excellence of the SBD Dauntless dive bomber, which knocked out and disabled four Japanese heavy carriers at the Battle of Midway in June 1942, was only improved upon by the Curtiss SB2C Helldiver.

Mitchells had also played their part in the Pacific. As

early as 18 April 1942 B-25s took off from the carrier *Hornet* and dropped the first Allied bombs on Tokyo. B-29s brought further retribution with mass air strikes on Japan, culminating in the dropping of two atomic bombs in August 1945.

US Navy aircraft strength reached its peak in 1945 with almost 41,000 on its inventory. By VJ-Day Navy and Marine Corps units had sunk, in actions independent of ground or sea forces, over 600 Japanese warships and merchant vessels as well as 63 U-Boats and 15,000 enemy aircraft.

At its wartime peak in March 1944 the USAAF comprised 78,757 aircraft and almost 2.5 million personnel, but by May 1947 this had dwindled to only 303,614 men. On 18 September 1947 the National Security Act created the United States Air Force and a gradual build-up in aircraft and personnel began again. The USAF had already been subdivided in March 1946 into Strategic, Tactical and Air Defense Commands. US Strategic Air Forces Europe, created in January 1944, continued under the title, US Forces Europe Air with its counterpart, the Far East Air Force, in the Pacific.

With World War II at an end the Cold War set in between East and West. In the summer of 1948 the Soviet Union imposed the Berlin blockade, preventing food and supplies reaching 2.5 million Berliners in the Western-controlled part of the city. The Soviets hoped to gain a moral victory and win for Communism the whole of Eastern Germany. On 25 June all roads, railroads, and canals, on the inter-zonal frontier were closed and Berlin, already in ruins, became a beleaguered city, incapable of supporting itself.

But the Western powers refused to give in. On 26 June 1948 America mounted 'Operation Vittles' when a C-54 Skymaster flew in with a priority cargo. RAF DC-3s and C-47s also began flying in supplies along four 20-mile wide corridors. Despite Russian interference the US, RAF and Commonwealth air forces maintained a regular supply to Berlin for 10.5 months, transporting a total of 1,583,686 short tons and over 160,000 tons of material to build and improve airfields. On 11 May 1949 the Soviets lifted the blockade and air power alone had prevented World War III. Without it the only course open to the Allies would have been military confrontation.

If the same situation occurred today the average daily airlift into Berlin of more than 5000 tons could be handled by 20 C-5 Galaxys, operating only six hours a day.

One of the outcomes of the Berlin blockade and the Russians' obvious intention of prolonging the Cold War was American development of purpose-built heavy transport aircraft like the Douglas C-124 Globemaster II and in the long term, the formation of the NATO alliance on 4 April 1949.

East and West vied for postwar superiority in jet fighter aircraft with America's first operational jet aircraft, the Lockheed 'Shooting Star' first appearing in 1944 with a British turbojet. The most famous swept-wing jet fighter to appear outside the Soviet bloc in 1947 was the F-86 Sabre, which, although conceived during the closing stages of World War II, benefited from the release of German research data after hostilities.

The Sabre and Shooting Star formed the backbone of the US Far East Air Force which supported the United

Above: **A B-52C with enlarged wing tanks.**
Below: **Ground crew about to prepare an F-94B Starfire for a flight over Korea.**

AS
USS INTREPID
CVSG-52
152798
NAVY
VS-31
31

An S-2E Tracker ASW aircraft of VS-31 is craned aboard the carrier USS *Intrepid*.

Nations' forces when war broke out in Korea in June 1950. The Communist advance into South Korea caught the West unawares and unprepared. By November 1950 the North Korean army had infiltrated as far south as the small region around Pusan. Western forces faced their first defeat at the hands of the Communists, with only two crowded airstrips in Pusan itself and one at Taegu. America's Japan-based fighter force was anything up to 500 miles away, severely restricting combat time over Korea. This first military confrontation between East and West had sinister implications. In the background was the threat of global confrontation on a nuclear scale.

Postwar recession in the West had resulted in no urgent steps being taken to build many new types of aircraft. Unfortunately, the new types that were built, like the USAF's Sabre, Shooting Star and Thunderjet and the US Navy and Marine Corps' F9F Panther and F2H Banshee, were often ill-suited for the immediate task of providing close-support for United Nations' troops. All were designed to operate from paved airstrips at least 6000 feet long or from aircraft carriers, which in the Korean War could not sail nearer than about 70 miles from the coast because of the shallow sea-bed.

Mustangs and Corsairs soon joined with other piston-engined aircraft like the Skyraider to provide close-support from the short, improvised Korean airstrips. The Skyraiders were very successful but their pilots were often so exhausted after a straight ten hours in the air that they had to be lifted bodily from the cockpit. Several American fighter squadrons even traded in their F-80s during the early months of the war for the old piston-engined P-51 Mustang.

And so the strange war in the air continued. Jet fighters, expected to join in dogfights at 30,000 feet, buzzed over the Korean landscape at 1000 feet desperately trying to provide ground support. In the Pentagon staff worked overtime to discover the right aircraft for the task. But the war would be over before Ed Heinemann, designer of the Skyraider, could produce the A-4 Skyhawk. Piston-engined aircraft remained the order of the day with many of wartime vintage carrying wartime stocks of ammunition and ordnance. Martin Mariners were only later supplemented by the Lockheed Neptune on ocean patrol while Boeing C-97s and Douglas C-124 Cargomasters ferried in troops and supplies. Helicopters came into their own, picking up downed crews and operating from all kinds of rough terrain.

During the fall of 1950 United Nations' air support contributed to the breakout from the Pusan perimeter. Meanwhile unopposed Superfortresses made precision attacks on strategic targets in North Korea. In the north the Chinese crossed the Yalu river and Soviet-built MiG-15's began to appear in November 1950. Only the Sabres could compete with the MiG-15 on level terms, mainly because of the American pilots' combat inexperience.

War in Korea swiftly turned to one of basics. Sabre pilots tore out every complicated piece of equipment, like the APG-30 gunsight, that was not firmly screwed down, in an effort to reduce weight. The MiG-15 was a straightforward jet with a simple optical reflector sight. MiGs were constantly in the air while American jets were grounded with all sorts of unserviceable equipment that pilots did not want anyway. Radar carrying aircraft like the F3D Skynight were often grounded because of equipment malfunctions.

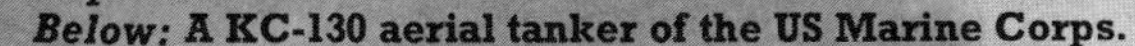

Above: **A Lockheed SP-2H, the final production version of the Neptune.**
Below: **A KC-130 aerial tanker of the US Marine Corps.**

A Douglas C-133A of the Military Air Transport Service.

Korea proved the wrong place to deploy advanced combat aircraft. The terrain was tough and uncompromising and in summer tens of thousands of troops were put out of action by sunstroke and almost as many by frostbite in winter. When the war ended in July 1953 the Communists heeded the many lessons learned in Korea but America, save from Kelly Johnson's F-104 Starfighter and Ed Heinemann's Skyhawk, continued spending most of its defense budget on nuclear strategic weapons better suited to a totally different kind of war.

By 1951 the B-50 had replaced the B-29 in most front-line SAC bomber squadrons while the B-47 became the standard SAC medium bomber. The huge B-52, which entered SAC service in 1955, enjoyed a better fuel economy and is still in widespread service today. Meanwhile, in 1956, the US Navy was issued with the first of their long-range carrier-borne strategic bombers, the A-3 Skywarrior, each capable of carrying an H-bomb.

Continued improvements in performance enabled the USAF to reduce its combat wings from 137 in mid-1957 to 96 in the mid-60s (93 of which were manned aircraft) without losing its combat effectiveness. By late 1961 SAC, the major USAF deterrent force, could call upon almost 1500 jet bombers and over 260,000 personnel. By the end of 1961 the USAF had no less than 16 major commands in deterrent, defensive and support roles from Alaska to the Pacific.

The year before, American reconnaissance aircraft hit the world headlines when a U-2 spyplane was shot down over Russia. In 1962 LTV RF-8A Crusader photographic—reconnaissance aircraft flying from US Navy carriers discovered Russian-built long-range missiles in Cuba. It was mainly due to the statesmanship of President Kennedy and Krushchev and the US Naval blockade that prevented the situation escalating into a full-scale nuclear war between the superpowers. Krushchev withdrew the missiles and the nuclear deterrent, for all its high cost, had been seen to be effective.

In 1963 President Diem of the corrupt and tottering regime in South Vietnam was assassinated. Three years before he had appealed for US military aid to prevent the Vietcong taking over his country. America had sent 'advisers.' In March 1965 President Johnson sent in American Marines after repeated attacks on US installations in South Vietnam. Air strikes from three carriers in the Bay of Tonkin were also made and a squadron of F-105 Thunderchiefs was dispatched from Thailand. Chairman Mao said that if America's special warfare in South Vietnam could be overcome, then it could be defeated anywhere in the world. Johnson had called Mao's bluff.

Vietnam turned out to be no Korea. The conflict escalated and soon US forces were consuming ordnance on a scale four times faster than in Korea. But this time the right aircraft were available. Helicopters, flying 13 hours a day in some cases, were used in rescue and gun-ship roles. The unique Bronco LARA/COIN (Light Armed Reconnaissance Aircraft, Counter-Insurgency) with STOL performance, was developed and incorporated the lessons learned in 'brushfire' wars of the 1960s. Old aircraft like Dakotas, Skyraiders, and Invaders again made their presence felt. Unusual aircraft like the Cessna 0-2 joined the wide range of aircraft flown and tested over the war-torn terrain of Vietnam. The superb multi-role F-4 Phantom's capability was enhanced with a Gatling gun and wing slats while others, like the Northrop F-5 remained operational for a very limited period and F-111s were soon grounded after early crashes. The Boeing B-52s, which had operated from Guam and Thailand almost unopposed until high losses in mid-1972, brought about an urgent rethink and were hurriedly armed with SRAM missiles. The F-100 Super Sabres and F-105 Thunderchiefs aquitted themselves well in fighter and ground attack roles while the venerable Voodoo supplemented the Phantom on most battlefield reconnaissance missions.

The US Navy's Grumman A-6 Intruder proved the only aircraft capable of striking at pin-point targets in all weathers by day and night. Carrier-borne RA-5C Vigi-

Above: **An F-111B in US Navy markings, although the Navy later cancelled its order for the fighter.**
Below: **A USAF Phantom of the Black Knights based in Iceland.**

The Boeing CH-47B Chinook.

RR
NAVY
720
RR
NAVY
727
RR
7224
NAVY
726
RR
8914
NAVY

850
TA-4F

lantes, the most sophisticated reconnaissance aircraft to serve in the conflict, provided instantaneous and total multi-sensor surveillance of targets.

Transports too proved very adaptable. Fairchild Providers were used to defoliate forests with sprays to prevent them being used by the Vietcong for cover. Starlifters and the redoubtable Hercules handled logistics and tactical supplies to earn the respect of all who flew in them, including battlefield casualties brought back on return trips.

By January 1973 the feared B-52s had ripped the heart out of North Vietnam but at high cost. Almost 30 B-52s were lost in the three months beginning November 1972. This resulted in urgent discussions on the role of ECM and anti-SA-3 missile devices. Despite the losses full-scale raids helped sap the North's ability to wage lasting war and East and West gathered around the conference table.

Against a background of wholesale destruction and bloodshed on a scale never envisaged even after Guernica, the Blitz or the Hamburg fire raids, air power had not only been deemed effective but also cost-effective and that is what matters in the technology-oriented air arms of the 1970s and 1980s.

Today's aircraft, which are literally capable of 'sniffing' out the enemy, will soon be part of aviation history. Satellites even now, capable of photographing Moscow street signs, will eventually replace all conventional manned reconnaissance aircraft while the strategic bomber has probably gone for ever. The cancellation of the B-1 in 1977 has put it out of economic reach. But Russia continues to pose an alarming threat behind the facade of detente, constantly building up its already considerable military might on land, sea and air. In October 1978 US Intelligence sources announced that the Soviet Union was increasing production of its Tupolev Backfire-B bomber from 30 to 36 aircraft per year. Despite Soviet denials it is considered an inter-continental not a peripheral weapon.

Hopefully, there will be no more wars on the scale of Korea, Vietnam or the Arab-Israeli conflict. The absence of such wars has led to full-scale mock wars involving no civilian casualties. Annual 'Red Flag' (curiously named because recent NATO exercises do not mention this color in keeping with detente) exercises involving US aircraft over the Nevada desert, insure that pilots can at least gain simulated battle experience. 'Red Flag' was launched as a result of USAF losses in Vietnam, caused partly through pilot inexperience. The greatest loss rate occurred during a pilot's first ten missions. The exercises enable a pilot to fly ten simulated combat missions so that he might have the edge on day one of any other war.

Aircraft flying at high speed at low level on 'Red Flag' exercises are proving highly successful against simulated Soviet Atoll missiles, exemplifying once again the continued need for manned aircraft.

Left: **Grumman E1-B Tracers, or Willy Fudds as they are called by their crews, of the USS *Ticonderoga***
Below: **The TA-4F two-seat trainer version from the successful Skyhawk stable.**

Part One

1941

1945

The Night Lightning saw service during the last weeks of the Pacific War. Its double mission was to seek and destroy Japanese aircraft and serve as a nocturnal prowler armed with machine guns, cannon and rockets on inverted 'Christmas tree' launchers under each wing.

Bell P-39 Airacobra

Manufacturer: Bell Aircraft Corporation, Buffalo, New York.
Type: single-seat pursuit and advanced trainer.
Crew: pilot only.
Specification: P-39Q.
Power Plant: one 1200 hp V-1710-85.
Dimensions: span, 34 ft; length, 30 ft 2 in; height, 12 ft 5 in; wing area, 213 sq ft.
Weights: empty, 5645 lb; gross, 8300 lb.
Performance: maximum speed, 385 mph at 11,000 ft; initial climb, 4.5 min to 15,000 ft; service ceiling, 35,000 ft; range, 650 miles.
Armament: one 37 mm gun; four 0.50 in guns; one 500 lb bomb.

The P-39 was designed to accommodate the nose-mounting of the American Armament Corporation's 37 mm T-9, around which the whole design was drawn. Bell had seen the gun demonstrated in 1935 and it was decided to locate it on the aircraft centerline in the nose for optimum effect. This dictated the engine position, buried in the fuselage section aft of the cockpit. This in turn dictated the tricycle undercarriage arrangement; the engine being the center of gravity. Ample stowage was still afforded the nose wheel under the cannon. The Air Corps contracted for a single XP-39 prototype on 7 October 1937 – the first tricycle single-engined fighter yet ordered by that body. In April 1939 12 YP-39s and one YP-39A (with no turbo-supercharger) were ordered. Meanwhile a number of design changes were made and the XP-39B, incorporating wing root radiators, main wheel doors and deletion of the turbo-supercharger among others, flew on 25 November 1939. In January 1940 the Army abandoned the turbo-supercharger and jeopardized any future success at high altitude. The P-39 went into full production in August 1939 and by 1944 nearly 10,000 Airacobras had been built. In April 1940 the British Purchasing Commission ordered 675 Bell Model 14s (similar to the P-39D but with a 20-mm gun) but many were lost at sea during delivery and only one squadron ever became operational with the RAF. Over 4700 were sent to the USSR. The Russians employed them with deadly effect against armor and other ground targets. Crew chiefs in the North African desert, where it fought with distinction, and in Europe welcomed the easy access to engine and armament.

Below: **Bell Airacobra.**
Bottom: **A P-39N of the Italian Co-Belligerent force.**

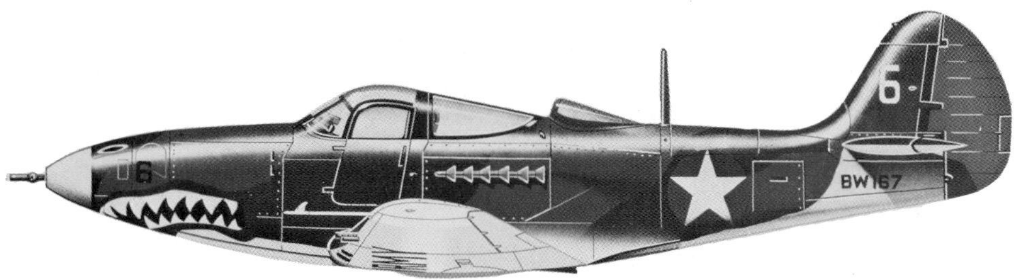

Bell P-63 Kingcobra

Manufacturer: Bell Aircraft Corporation, Buffalo, New York.
Type: fighter and fighter bomber; RP-63, target aircraft.
Crew: pilot only.
Specification: P-63A.
Power Plant: one 1325 hp V-1710-95.
Dimensions: span, 38 ft 4 in; length, 32 ft 8 in; height, 12 ft 7 in; wing area, 248 sq ft.
Weights: empty, 6375 lb; gross, 10,500 lb.
Performance: maximum speed, 408 mph at 24,450 ft; cruising speed, 378 mph; initial climb, 7.3 min to 25,000 ft; service ceiling, 43,000 ft; range, 450 miles.
Armament: P-63A-10, one 37 mm and four 0.30 in guns and three 500 lb bombs.

Several fighter designs reached the preliminary flight stage after the USA entered World War II, but only the P-63 entered large-scale production because it was not a new design but a development of the P-39. Three XP-39Es were built during 1941 using P-39D fuselages. By September 1942 orders to commence production to succeed the P-39 were given and deliveries of the P-63A began 13 months later. Bell built 1725 P-63As but only a few reached USAAF units, the bulk went to the USSR. The P-63C was predominantly supplied to the Soviet Air Force and France, which received 300. Outperformed at altitude by the P-51 and P-47 it was relegated to training. During 1943 the Kingcobra was developed for use as a manned target aircraft which could actually be fired at. This is considered unique in aviation and was made possible by having all armament and armor removed and in its place, a toughened skin was used on all surfaces to withstand the impact of special frangible bullets. Hits were indicated by a red light which blinked at the wing tip and became known as the 'pinball' version. Kingcobra production ceased in 1946 by which time 3300 models had been produced with the Soviet Air Force taking delivery of 2000 P-63s.

Boeing P-12

Manufacturer: Boeing Airplane Company, Seattle, Washington.
Type: single-seat pursuit.
Crew: pilot only.
Specification: P-12E.
Power Plant: one 500 hp R-1340-17.
Dimensions: span, 30 ft; length, 20 ft 3 in; height, 9 ft; wing area, 227.5 sq ft.
Weights: empty, 1999 lb; gross, 2690 lb.
Performance: maximum speed, 189 mph at 7000 ft; cruising speed, 160 mph; service ceiling, 26,300 ft.
Armament: two 0.30 in guns.

The Boeing P-12 was developed from the private venture Boeing models 83 and 89 built in 1928. The first prototype was flown on 11 April 1929. It was one of the most well-known Air Corps fighters to serve between the wars. Purchased by the US Navy in June 1929, the Army Air Corps followed up with an order for an equivalent version without first evaluating a prototype.

Boeing P-26

Manufacturer: Boeing Airplane Company, Seattle, Washington.
Type: pursuit.
Crew: pilot only.
Specification: P-26A.
Power Plant: one 500 hp R-1340-27.
Dimensions: span, 27 ft 11.5 in; length, 23 ft 10 in; height, 10 ft 5 in; wing area, 149.5 sq ft.
Weights: empty, 2271 lb; gross, 3012 lb.
Performance: maximum speed, 234 mph at 7500 ft; cruising speed, 199 mph; initial climb, 2360 ft per min; service ceiling, 27,400 ft; range, 360 miles.
Armament: two 0.30 in guns; 112 lb bombs externally.

The 'Peashooter,' as it was affectionately called by its pilots, was evolved during 1931, using similar design techniques applied to the Boeing B-9. After testing as the XP-936, the US Army bought all three prototypes as XP-26. These were called Y1P-26 for service test and finally, P-26. The XP-936 first flew on 20 March 1932 and the first P-26As were delivered on 16 December 1933. It was the first monoplane fighter developed for the US Army Air Corps and the first of all metal construction. One of a group of P-26As turned over to the Philippine Army late in 1941 was one of the first Allied fighters to shoot down a Japanese aircraft during their attack on the Philippines.

Neatly stacked formation of P-26As. The 'Peashooter' was the USAACs first monoplane fighter and the first of all-metal construction.

The skeletal beginnings of a P-12 undergoing assembly in February 1929.

Curtiss P-36 Hawk

Manufacturer: Curtiss Airplane Division of Curtiss-Wright Corporation, Buffalo, New York.
Type: single-seat pursuit and advanced trainer.
Crew: pilot only.
Specification: P-36G.
Power Plant: one 1200 hp R-1820-95.
Dimensions: span, 37 ft 4 in; length, 28 ft 10 in; height, 9 ft 6 in; wing area, 236 sq ft.
Weights: empty, 4541 lb; gross, 5750 lb.
Performance: maximum speed, 323 mph at 15,100 ft; cruising speed, 262 mph; service ceiling, 32,700 ft; range, 1000 miles.
Armament: six 0.30 in guns.

Work began on the Model 75 monoplane in November 1934. The Air Corps held design competitions in 1935-6 which led to P-36 orders being placed. The P-36 was first delivered to the USAAF in April 1938.

With the Seversky P-35, the P-36 was the first single-seater monoplane pursuit to incorporate a retractable undercarriage, enclosed cockpit and other modern features. On 7 December 1941 four P-36As of the Hawaii-based 46th Pursuit Squadron shot down two Japanese bombers in the second phase of the attack on Pearl Harbor.

Curtiss P-40 Warhawk.

Curtiss P-40 Warhawk

Manufacturer: Curtiss-Wright Corporation, Airplane Division, Buffalo, New York.
Type: single-seat pursuit, ground-attack reconnaissance and advanced trainer.
Crew: pilot only.
Specification: P-40N-20.
Power Plant: one 1360 hp V-1710-81.
Dimensions: span, 37 ft 4 in; length, 33 ft 4 in; height, 12 ft 4 in; wing area, 236 sq ft.
Weights: empty, 6000 lb; gross, 8850 lb.
Performance: maximum speed, 378 mph at 10,500 ft; cruising speed, 288 mph; climb, 6.7 min to 15,000 ft; service ceiling, 38,000 ft; range, 240 miles.
Armament: six 0.5 in guns and one 500 lb bomb.

After evaluation trials in May 1939 in competition with other pursuit prototypes, the XP-40 was declared the most acceptable and an order for 524 P-40s was placed. Production continued with the P-40B, similar to the British Tomahawk II. The P-40B introduced armor protection for the pilot and doubled the wing firepower from two to four .30 inch guns, in addition to two .50 inch guns mounted on the engine cowling. Curtiss built 131 P-40Bs in 1941 before going over to P-40C production with improved self sealing fuel tanks. On 7 December 1941 a few P-40s managed to get into the air at Pearl Harbor and joined in scoring the first American fighter kills on Japanese aircraft. Although short on performance compared with other American fighters in service at the outbreak of war, the P-40 was available in large numbers with highly trained pilots to fly them. It earned its fame through the activities of less than 100 aircraft flying in China with the American Volunteer Group, the 'Flying Tigers' commanded by General Claire Chennault. Operating in a hostile environment using equipment inferior to the enemy, the P-40s with their red and white shark teeth emblems on the nose, went into combat two weeks after Pearl Harbor and, before being disbanded in 1942, shot down 286 Japanese aircraft for the loss of only eight.

Below and bottom: **The Hawk 75A was supplied to the French Armée de l'Air and to the RAF as the Mohawk.**

Right: **Some of the first P-40s used in combat were flown in China.**

Curtiss produced 13,783 P-40s in various configurations known as the Warhawk, Kittyhawk and Tomahawk. These fighters served throughout the war on every front with no less than 28 Allied nations. No other fighter during the war saw wider service.

Lockheed P-38, F-4, F-5 Lightning

Manufacturer: Lockheed Aircraft Corporation, Burbank, California. Consolidated Vultee, Nashville.
Type: single-seat pursuit and long-range escort; two-seat night fighter (P-38M only); unarmed photographic reconnaissance (F-4 and F-5); advanced trainer.
Crew: pilot only (P-38M) with radar operator in tandem.
Specification: P-38L.
Power Plant: two 1475 hp V-1710-111/113.
Dimensions: span, 52 ft 0 in; length, 37 ft 10 in; height, 9 ft 10 in; wing area, 327.5 sq ft.
Weights: empty, 12,800 lb; gross, 21,600 lb.
Performance: Maximum speed, 414 mph at 25,000 ft; cruising speed, 290 mph; climb, 7 min at 20,000 ft; service ceiling, 44,000 ft; range, 450 miles.
Armament: one 20 mm and four 0.5 in guns and two 1600 lb bombs.

One of the best-known and most easily recognizable fighters of the war, the P-38 was already in mass production before the outbreak of hostilities. Designed in 1937 as a long-range tactical fighter its development was delayed because of the prevailing belief that American heavy bombers could defend themselves on long missions over Europe. The P-38 began to be deployed in large numbers in the European Theater by mid-1942 when it was evident that long-range fighters would after all be required. The first German aircraft destroyed by the USAAF was a FW200 Condor shot down near Iceland by two P-38s and a P-39. The Germans soon called the Lightning, the Fork-Tailed Devil, and the Japanese too learned to hate it. The P-38 registered more Japanese kills than any other American aircraft and the two leading American aces, Major Richard Bong and Major Tom McGuire (40 and 38 kills respectively) flew P-38s in the Pacific. Lightnings were also responsible for shooting down Admiral Yamamoto, mastermind of the Japanese attack on Pearl Harbor. From 1940–45 Lockheeds built almost 10,000 P-38s which served in fighter and bomber configurations and provided the most widely used photo-reconnaissance aircraft of the war.

The XP-38 prototype Lightning first flew on 27 January 1939.

12670

Below: Two drawings of Lockheed Lightnings.

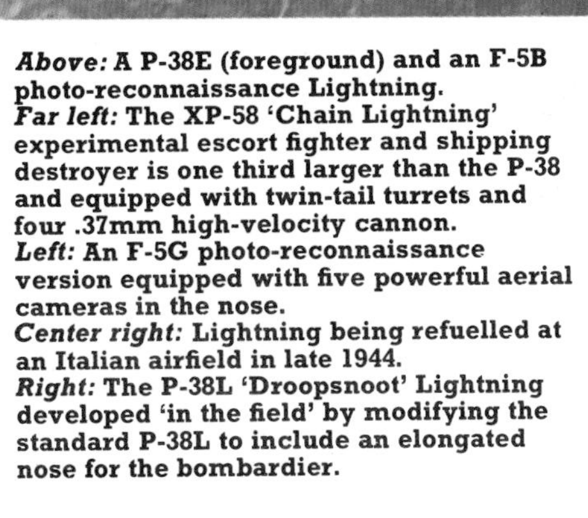

Above: **A P-38E (foreground) and an F-5B photo-reconnaissance Lightning.**
Far left: **The XP-58 'Chain Lightning' experimental escort fighter and shipping destroyer is one third larger than the P-38 and equipped with twin-tail turrets and four .37mm high-velocity cannon.**
Left: **An F-5G photo-reconnaissance version equipped with five powerful aerial cameras in the nose.**
Center right: **Lightning being refuelled at an Italian airfield in late 1944.**
Right: **The P-38L 'Droopsnoot' Lightning developed 'in the field' by modifying the standard P-38L to include an elongated nose for the bombardier.**

North American P-51, A-36, F-36 Mustang

Manufacturer: North American Aviation, Incorporated, Inglewood, California, and Dallas, Texas.
Type: single-seat fighter ground attack and long-range escort; unarmed reconnaissance and two-seat trainer.
Crew: pilot only (pilot and instructor in tandem in TP-51).
Specification: P-51H/M.
Power Plant: one 1380 hp V-1650-9.
Dimensions: span, 37 ft 0 in; length, 33 ft 4 in; height, 13 ft 8 in; wing area, 233 sq ft.
Weights: empty, 6585 lb; gross, 11,054 lb.
Performance: maximum speed, 487 mph at 25,000 ft; cruising speed, 380 mph; climb, 12.5 min at 30,000 ft; service ceiling, 41,600 ft; range, 850 miles.
Armament: six 0.5 in and two 1000 lb bombs or ten 5 in RP.

One of the greatest fighters of the war, it was one of the very few aircraft types conceived during the hostilities to see large-scale service. The P-51 was originally designed as a long-range wing mate to the depleted RAF Spitfire and Hurricane squadrons. A 120-day limit was imposed on North America to build a prototype but the company delivered it in 117 days. The

Right: **The P-51H, the final and fastest of all the Mustang models.**
Far right, top: **A P-51 undergoes a refit at the Eighth AF repair center in England.**
Far right, bottom: **A P-51B in 1943.**
Below: **A P-51 Mustang of the Italian Co-Belligerent Air Force.**

NO SMOKING

37116

Right: **RF-51D at an airfield in Japan during the Korean War.**
Below: **Interior of a P-51.**

model's first flight was in October 1940 and the first production models were delivered a year later to the RAF, who christened it Mustang. It was obvious an improved engine was needed to achieve greater high-altitude performance and a Rolls-Royce Merlin installation was proposed in Britain. From then on the P-51 never looked back. Flight tests in late 1942 increased its maximum speed from around 390 mph to 441 mph at optimum altitude. Delivery to the 8th AF began on 1 December 1943 and these P-51s flew their first mission 12 days later. Their range of 2080 miles, achieved by the use of wing drop tanks, was far in excess of that available in other fighters of the day. In March 1944 P-51Bs flew to Berlin and back for the first time, escorting B-17s and B-24s to their targets. By the end of the war the P-51 equipped all but one of the 8th AF fighter groups. The Mustang went through a number of major modifications during its production run of over 9000. It went on to serve in Korea and the airframe design survived as the Cavalier F-51D, a US tactical support aircraft of the late 1960s and a civilian sport aircraft.

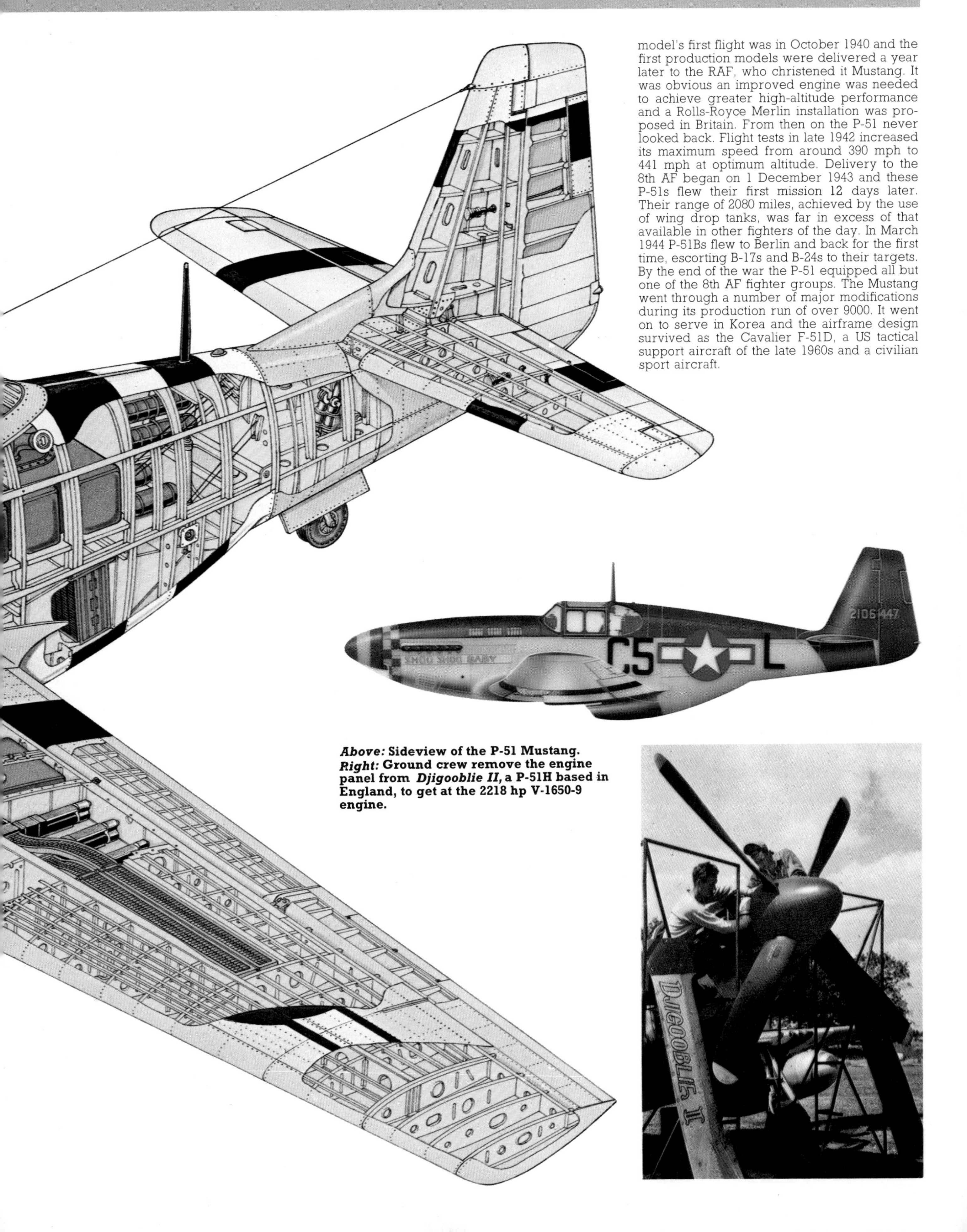

Above: **Sideview of the P-51 Mustang.**
Right: **Ground crew remove the engine panel from *Djigooblie II*, a P-51H based in England, to get at the 2218 hp V-1650-9 engine.**

Northrop P-61 Black Widow

Manufacturer: Northrop Aircraft Incorporated, Hawthorne, California.
Type: Night fighter.
Crew: Three (pilot, radar operator and gunner in central nacelle).
Specification: P-61B.
Power Plant: two 2000 hp R-2800-65.
Dimensions: span, 66 ft; length, 49 ft 7 in; height, 14 ft 8 in; wing area, 664 sq ft.
Weights: empty, 22,000 lb; gross, 29,700 lb.
Performance: maximum speed, 366 mph at 20,000 ft; climb, 12 min to 20,000 ft; service ceiling, 33,100 ft; range, 3000 miles.
Armament: four 0.5 in and four 20 mm guns and four 1600 lb bombs.

The P-61 was the first USAAF aircraft designed from the outset as a night fighter and was the standard front-line night fighter by the end of World War II. Design work commenced in 1940 at the time of continued RAF night bombing raids on occupied Europe. Northrop incorporated many of the lessons learned on the other side of the Atlantic. European experience revealed that the ideal night fighter should have heavy armament and armor, good endurance, advanced radar and provide a steady gun platform. The resultant design, the XP-61 signalled urgent production orders. The Army contracted for 13 YP-61s in March 1941, 150 more six months later and 410 in February 1942. Over 600 were on order before the first prototype flew in May 1942. After successful trials, delivery of the production aircraft began in the second half of 1943. The first of these P-61As had a remotely controlled turret with four .5 inch guns but problems arose in service and the majority had the turret deleted. In July 1944 'Black Widows' first flew on operations, recording their first victory in the South Pacific and destroying four Japanese aircraft in their first combat. P-61s were also employed as intruders and provision was made for long range fuel tanks or bomb loads. The last versions, the F-15A Reporters, were built in 1946 and retired from service by 1952.

Below: **Northrop P-61 Black Widow.**
Bottom: **Deliveries of the P-61B began in July 1944. This version could carry either four 1600 lb bombs or 300-gallon drop tanks under the wings.**

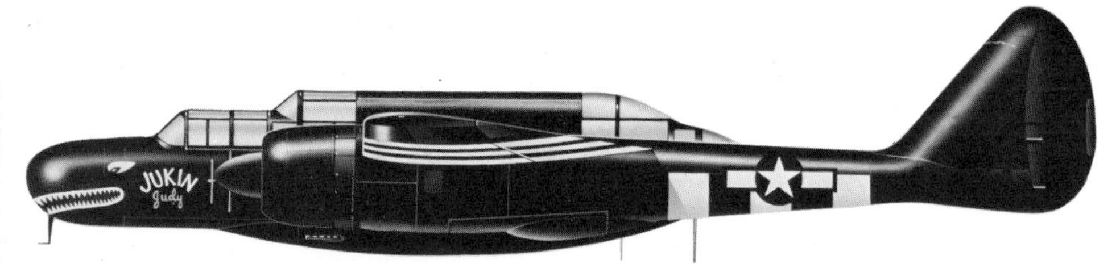

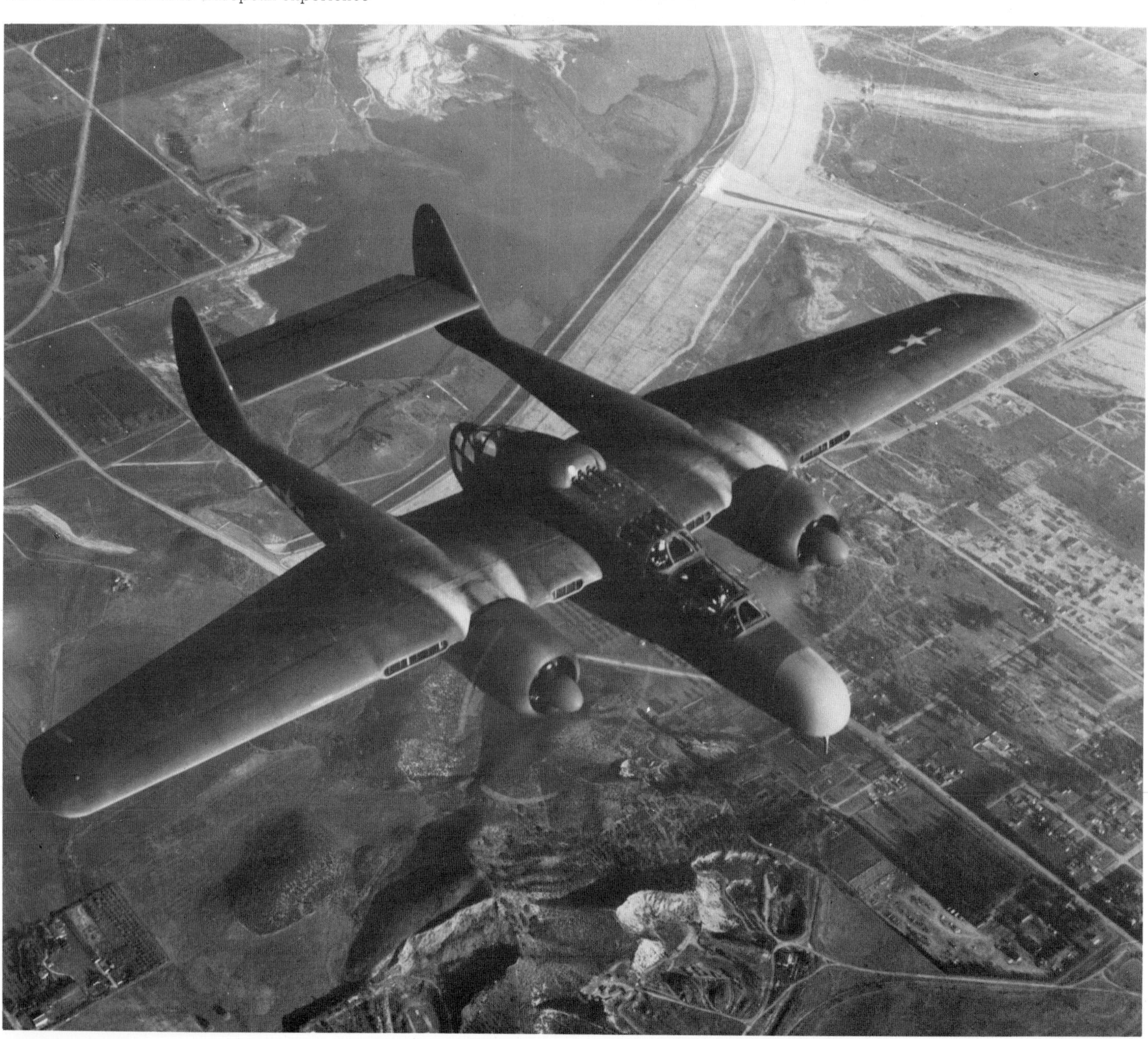

Above: **Thunderbolts head for North Luzon.**
Left: **A Republic P-43.**
Below: **A P-47N of the Italian Co-Belligerent Air Force.**
Bottom: **The P-47 Thunderbolt.**

Republic P-43 Lancer

Manufacturer: Republic Aviation Corporation, Long Island, New York.
Type: pursuit.
Crew: pilot only.
Specification: P-43.
Power Plant: one 1200 hp R-1830-47.
Dimensions: span, 36 ft; length, 28 ft 6 in; height, 14 ft; wing area, 223 sq ft.
Weights: empty, 5654 lb; gross, 7935 lb.
Performance: maximum speed, 349 mph at 25,000 ft; cruising speed, 280 mph; initial climb, 2850 ft per min; service ceiling, 38,000 ft; range, 800 miles.
Armament: two 0.5 in and two 0.3 in guns.

This aircraft was the slightly improved model of the Seversky XP-41 (see page 46) which was first tested in 1939 and ordered by the Army Air Corps in 1940 as the YP-43. Service deliveries began in 1941. In 1942 most surviving Lancers were converted to a reconnaissance role and some saw action with the Chinese Air Force in the war with Japan.

In parallel with the P-43 design, Republic developed the P-44 which led to the highly succesful P-47 Thunderbolt.

Republic P-47 Thunderbolt

Manufacturer: Republic Aviation Corporation, Long Island, New York; and Evansville, Indiana. Curtiss-Wright Corporation, Buffalo, New York.
Type: single-seat escort fighter and fighter-bomber.
Crew: pilot only.
Specification: P-47N.
Power Plant: one 2800 hp R-2800-77.
Dimensions: span, 42 ft 7 in; length, 36 ft 1 in; height, 14 ft 8 in; wing area, 322 sq ft.
Weights: empty, 11,000 lb; gross, 20,700 lb.
Performance: maximum speed, 467 mph at 32,500 ft; cruising speed, 300 mph; climb, 14.2 min to 25,000 ft; service ceiling, 43,000 ft; range, 800 miles.
Armament: eight 0.5 in and two 1000 lb bombs.

The P-47 Thunderbolt was conceived, tested, produced and flown in combat during World War II. Designed originally as a strategic escort for deep penetration B-17s and B-24s over Europe, the P-47 also served with distinction in the Pacific. Known as the 'flying milk bottle' because of its shape and also nicknamed the 'Jug,' the P-47 could outdive any other fighter,

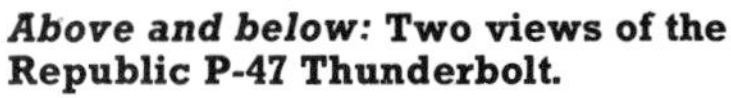
Above and below: **Two views of the Republic P-47 Thunderbolt.**

weighing as it did almost twice as much as any other single-engined aircraft. Despite this it could climb to 15,000 feet in six minutes and utilizing its unique tail mounted turbo-supercharger, the P-47 achieved some excellent capabilities above 30,000 feet. From there it could dive on an enemy at a red line airspeed of 504 mph. From March 1943, when it first began overseas operations, until August 1945 P-47s flew on every front destroying over 7000 enemy aircraft on the ground and in the air. Altogether, 15,579 Jugs were produced and the last were phased out of service in 1955. The P-47 was also noted for being able to sustain battle damage.

Seversky P-35

Manufacturer: Republic Aviation Corporation, Long Island, New York.
Type: pursuit.
Crew: pilot only.
Specification: P-35.
Power Plant: one 1050 hp R-1830-45.
Dimensions: span, 36 ft; length, 26 ft 10 in; height, 9 ft 9 in; wing area, 220 sq ft.
Weights: empty, 4575 lb; gross, 6723 lb.
Performance: maximum speed, 290 mph at 12,000 ft; cruising speed, 260 mph; initial climb, 1920 ft per min; service ceiling, 31,400 ft; range, 950 miles.
Armament: two 0.5 in and two 0.3 in guns; 350 lb bombs.

The P-35 was developed from two privately-financed experimental fighters produced by Seversky in 1935. Later redesign work produced the AP-1 which was submitted to the Army in 1937 and accepted. Seversky delivered 76 P-35s, the last aircraft on the contract, the XP-41, proving the prototype for the Republic P-43.

In February 1940 export versions were purchased by the Royal Swedish Air Force and continued until mid-1940 when all EP-106s, as they were known, were requisitioned by the American Government. By the close of 1941 48 P-35As were stationed in the Philippines and all except eight were destroyed by the Japanese in two days, mostly on the ground.

A P-47 of the 365th Fighter Group prepares for a sortie over occupied Europe.

***Top:* The Y1B-9 military development of the revolutionary Monomail commercial plane which first flew on 13 April 1931. *Above:* The Y1B-9A on an early test flight accompanied by a P-26A.**

Boeing B-9

Manufacturer: Boeing Airplane Company, Seattle, Washington.
Type: light bomber.
Crew: four (pilot, navigator/bombardier, two gunners).
Specification: Y1B-9A.
Power Plant: two 600 hp R-1860-11.
Dimensions: span, 76 ft 10 in; length, 52 ft; height, 12 ft; wing area, 954 sq ft.
Weights: empty, 8941 lb; gross, 14,320 lb.
Performance: maximum speed, 188 mph at 6000 ft; cruising speed, 165 mph; initial climb, 900 ft per min; service ceiling, 20,750 ft; range, 540 miles.
Armament: two 0.3 in machine guns; 2260 lb bomb load.

In 1930 Boeing began work on Models 214 and 215, which became the Army Y1B and YB-9. These were logical military developments of the Monomail, an all-metal, low-wing mail/cargo-plane which had first flown in May 1930. The XB-901 was first flown on 29 April 1931.

Although not ordered in quantity, the B-9 raised the speed of bombers to a point 5 mph above that of contemporary fighters at a time when Air Corps bomber squadrons were equipped with many different types of biplanes with equally differing performance.

***Above:* Boeing SB-17G in Japan during the Korean War.**

Boeing B-17 Flying Fortress

Manufacturers: Boeing Aircraft Company, Seattle, Washington (all variants); Douglas Aircraft Company, Long Beach, California (B-17F and G); Lockheed (Vega) Aircraft Corporation, Burbank, California (B-17F and G).
Type: strategic bomber.
Crew: nine (two pilots, bombardier, radio-operator, five gunners).
Specification: B-17G.
Power Plant: four 1200 hp R-1820-97.
Dimensions: span, 103 ft 9 in; length, 74 ft 4 in; height, 19 ft 1 in; wing area, 1420 sq ft.
Weights: empty, 36,135 lb; gross, 65,500 lb.
Performance: maximum speed, 287 mph at 25,000 ft; cruising speed, 182 mph; climb, 37 min to 20,000 ft; service ceiling, 35,600 ft; range, 3400 miles.
Armament: thirteen 0.5 in guns; 17,600 lb bomb load.

In August 1934 Boeing was invited to participate in an Army competition for a four-engined bomber capable of carrying a bomb load of 2000 lb for between 1020 miles and 2200 miles at a speed of between 200–250 mph. A flying prototype had to be ready for Army trials by August 1935.

To meet the specification Boeing came up with the Model 299, which together with the four-engined transport, the Model 300, had been outlined earlier. Flying Fortress was adopted as the trade mark for the Model 299 because it was conceived for a purely defensive mission: the protection of the American coast-line from foreign surface fleets. It was this function and not the armament that suggested the famous name, Flying Fortress.

Rushed to completion in just a year the 299 was flown to Wright Field from Seattle on 20

S

August 1935, only a month after roll out. It completed the 2100 mile non-stop flight in a remarkable time of nine hours at a then unheard of speed of 252 mph. The competitive testing was almost completed when the 299 crashed on 30 October 1935 following take-off with the controls inadvertantly locked. Although thus disqualified from the competition the demonstration up to that point had been so impressive that the Army placed a service test order for 13 flight articles and a static test model under the designation YB-17. This was changed to Y1B-17 shortly before the first one was flown in December 1936. The major significant change from the 299 was the substitution of Wright 'Cyclone' engines of 1000 take-off horsepower for the original 'Hornets.'

Shortly after the first Y1B-17s entered service the Army ordered the static test aircraft completed as a high-altitude bomber with turbo-supercharged engines. This was duly delivered as the Y1B-17A and resulted in a production order or 39 similar B-17Bs. Twenty aircraft of a 1939 contract for 38 B-17Cs were diverted to the RAF as Fortress Is. High altitude combat missions in 1941 proved the suitability of the super-charged engines but revealed that armament and armor were inadequate. As a result the 42 B-17Ds were built with self-sealing fuel tanks and other minor refinements. The remaining B-17Cs were modified to B-17D standard. Results of European combat experience, especially the requirements for defensive armament were incorporated into extensively improved B-17E models. Really large-scale Fortress production began with the B-17F, which could be outwardly distinguished from the E by a perspex nose. The B-17G, the final production version, was distinguishable with the addition of a chin turret.

In postwar years B-17s carrying droppable lifeboats were designated B-17H. A number were diverted to the US Navy as PB-1W for anti-submarine and weather reconnaissance work and to the Coast Guard as PG-1G. Wartime reconnaissance versions, originally known as F-9 were redesignated RB-17G. After replacement as standard bombers, B-17s remained in service as trainers and VIP transports. Some were converted to radio-controlled targets and the last B-17 in US military service, a QB-17 drone, was destroyed in 1960, ironically, by a Boeing Bomarc missile.

***Left:* Boeing's Model 299 was to become famous as the Flying Fortress.**
***Far left bottom:* B-17s were flown in combat by RAF Bomber Command.**
***Below:* A B-17F on an early test flight.**

Center: **Overhead and sideview cutaways of a B-17G.**
Below: **An oil-stained B-17E *Yankee.* Together the B-17 and B-24 formed the backbone of the USAAF's striking force in Europe.**
Bottom: **A Boeing B-17C of which 20 from a contract of 38 were diverted to the RAF as Fortress Is. High-altitude missions over enemy-occupied Europe proved the suitability of supercharged engines but revealed weaknesses in armament and armor. As a result the remaining B-17Cs were modified to B-17D standard and all 42 B-17Ds were built with self-sealing fuel tanks and minor refinements.**

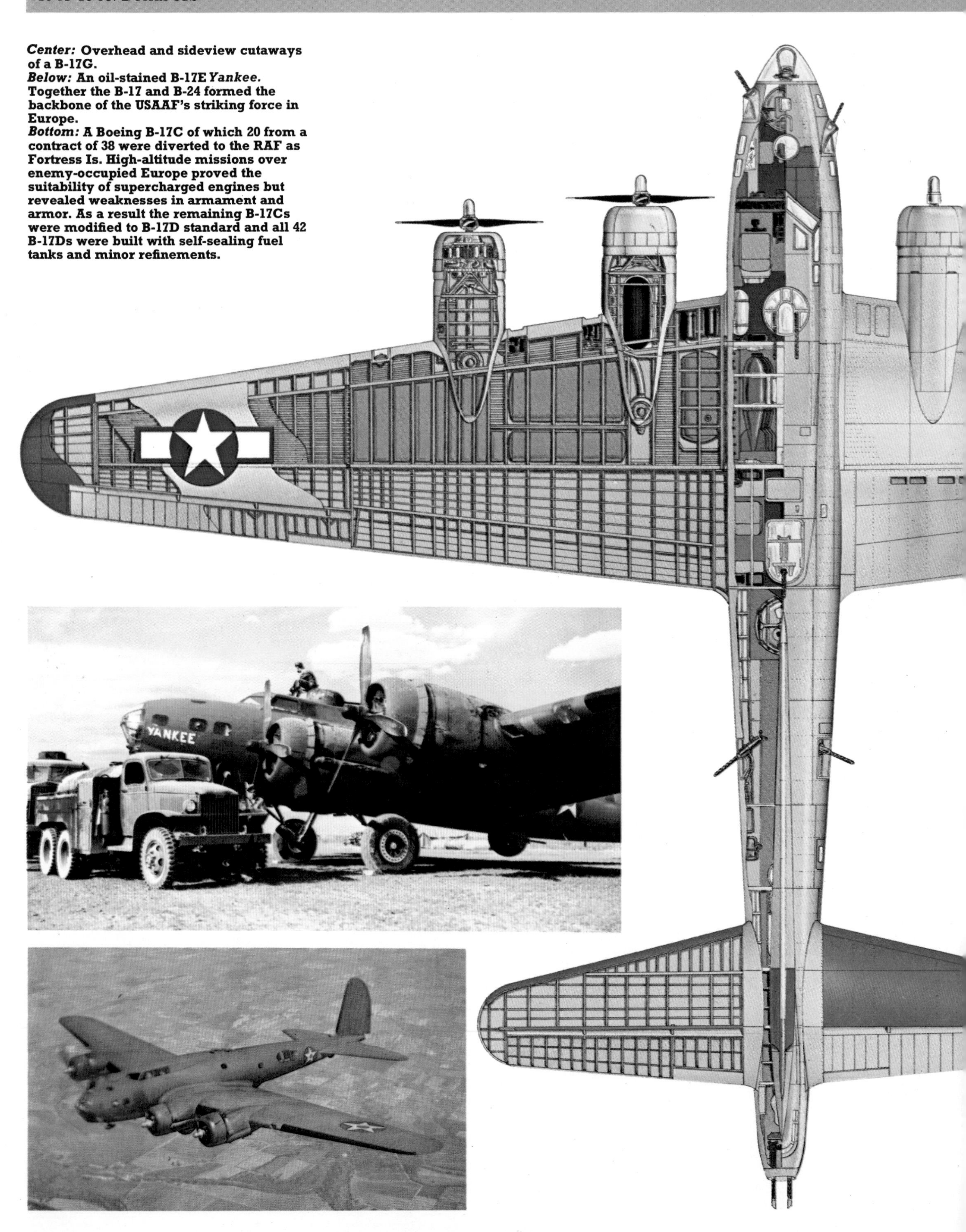

Right: **B-17Gs prepare to release bombs over occupied Europe.**
Center right: **Sergeant Harrell Farrah repairs a Wright-Cyclone engine of a B-17 in England.**

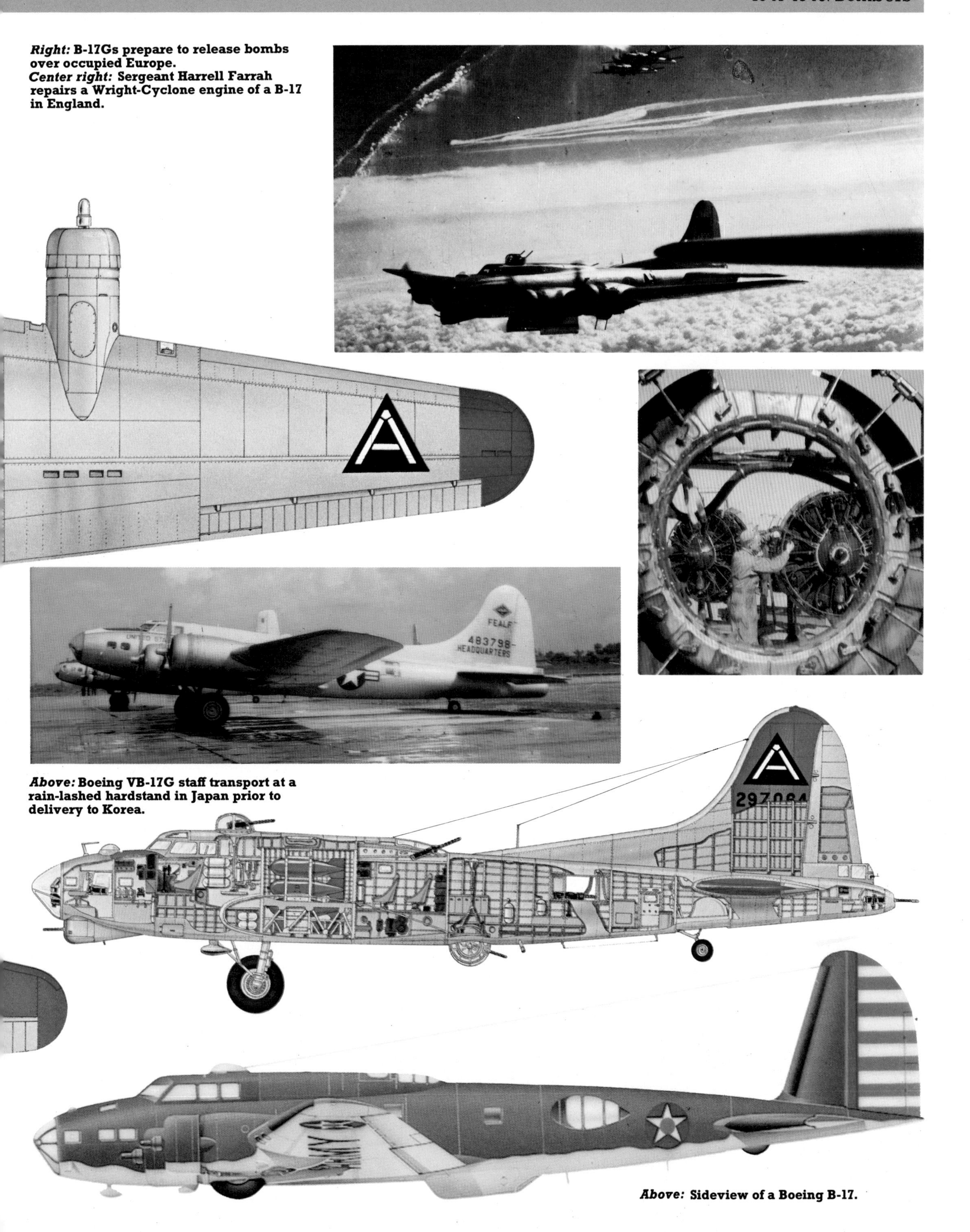

Above: **Boeing VB-17G staff transport at a rain-lashed hardstand in Japan prior to delivery to Korea.**

Above: **Sideview of a Boeing B-17.**

Boeing B-29 Superfortress

Manufacturer: Boeing Airplane Company, Seattle and Renton, Washington; Wichita, Kansas. Bell Aircraft Corporation, Atlanta, Georgia. Glenn L. Martin Company, Baltimore, Maryland.
Type: strategic bomber and reconnaissance aircraft; flight re-fuelling tanker.
Crew: normally, ten.
Specification: B-29B.
Power plant: four 2200 hp R-3350-79 or piston radials.
Dimensions: span, 141 ft 3 in; length, 99ft; height, 29 ft 7 in; wing area, 1736 sq ft.
Weights: empty, 69,000 lb; gross, 137,500 lb.
Performance: maximum speed, 364 mph at 25,000 ft; cruising speed, 228 mph; climb, 38 min to 20,000 ft; service ceiling, 32,000 ft; range, 4200 miles.
Armament: ten 0.5 in and one 20 mm guns and 20,000 lb bomb load.

Initial studies of a Boeing proposal to the Army for an improved B-17 began in 1938 with a pressurized cabin to increase crew efficiency and comfort. There were no military requirements for such a design at that time but Boeing continually updated the design until, in February 1940, an official invitation was received to bid on a high altitude, long-range bomber. After several revisions in design the XB-29 first flew in September 1942. It was far ahead of its contemporaries with ten-gun defensive

Extreme left, top: **Under the designation KB-29M, 72 B-29s were converted to flying tankers.**
Left: **A Lockheed-produced Superfortress.**
Extreme left, bottom: **B-29s *en route* to their target over China.**
Below: **B-29s bombed targets throughout Southeast Asia using staging posts in China.**

armament in four remotely controlled power turrets and a single directly controlled tail turret. The fuselage was divided into three pressurized compartments, two of which were connected by a tunnel over the tandem bomb bays. Even before the prototype was completed the Army ordered full-scale production. The Wichita plant was expanded and Bell and Martin were ordered to build B-29s in two new plants. B-29 production became the largest single aircraft programme of World War II. B-29s first bombed Japan in June 1944 and by the time production ceased, in 1946, 3970 had been built with the end of the war resulting in the cancellation of 5092 more. Postwar B-29s carried lifeboats, and were used on antisubmarine and weather duty. The B-29 served as a flying powerplant laboratory with a retractable jet engine in the bomb bay. P2B-1s were developed to carry supersonic research aircraft that had to be carried aloft for launching. The B-29s served with the RAF after World War II as Washingtons.

Below: **Boeing B-29.**

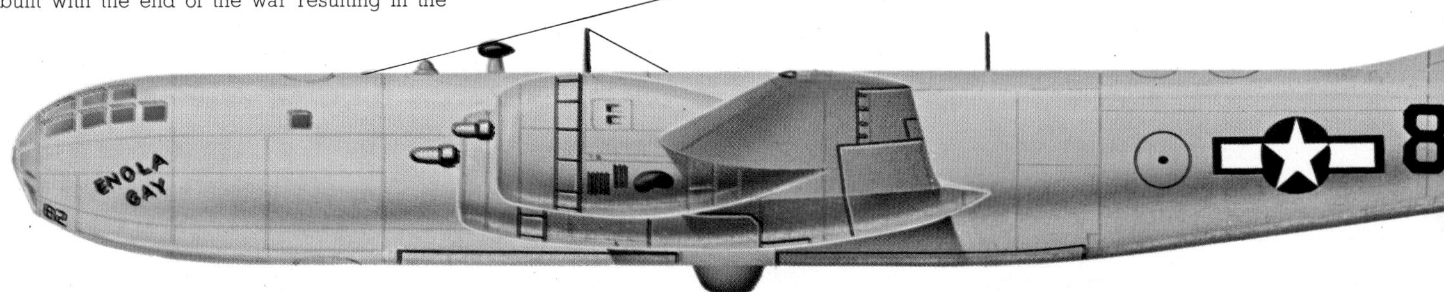

Consolidated B-24 Liberator, PB4Y Privateer

Manufacturer: Consolidated B24/PB47 (later Consolidated Vultee) Aircraft Corporation, San Diego, California (B-24, A, B, C, D, F, J, L, M, P) and Fort Worth (B-24D, E, H, J). Douglas Aircraft Company, Tulsa, Oklahoma (B-24D, E, H, J). Ford Motor Company, Willow Run, Michigan (B-24E, H, J, K, L, M, N, Q). North American Aviation Inc, Dallas (B-24G, J). PB4Y-1, Consolidated (later Consolidated Vultee) Aircraft Corporation, San Diego, California. PB4Y-2, Consolidated Vultee Aircraft Corporation, San Diego.
Type: B-24, strategic bomber; PB4Y-1 and 2, US Navy land-based patrol bomber.
Crew: B-24, eight to ten; PB4Y-1, nine to ten; PB4Y-2, eleven.
Specification: B-24M.
Power Plant: four 1200 hp R-1830-65.
Dimensions: span, 110 ft; length, 67 ft 2 in; height, 18 ft; wing area, 1048 sq ft.
Weights: empty, 36,000; gross, 64,500.
Performance: maximum speed, 300 mph at 30,000 ft; cruising speed, 215 mph; initial climb, 25 min to 20,000 ft; service ceiling, 28,000 ft; range, 2100 miles.
Armament: ten 0.50 in guns and 8800 lb bomb load.
Specification: PB4Y-2.
Power Plant: four 1350 hp R-1830-94.
Dimensions: span, 110 ft; length, 74 ft 7 in; height, 30 ft 1 in; wing area, 1048 sq ft.
Weights: empty, 37,485 lb; gross, 65,000 lb.
Performance: maximum speed, 237 mph at 13,750 ft; cruising speed, 140 mph; initial climb, 1090 ft/min; service ceiling, 20,700 ft; range, 2800 miles.
Armament: twelve 0.50 in and up to eight 1600 lb bombs.

Design work began in 1939 to meet an Air Corps demand for a heavy bomber superior in performance to the B-17, at that time in production.

The XB-24 was first flown on 29 December 1939 and it was first delivered to service in 1941. The B-24 was possibly the most versatile aircraft of World War II. It served in every theater of the war as bomber, supply and VIP transport, gunship, photo-reconnaissance, flying classroom and tanker. In Europe the B-24 rose from obscurity alongside the Flying Fortresses to form a unique and powerful arm of the 8th Air Force. In August 1943 Liberators attacked the Ploesti oilfields in Rumania. In the Far East they hauled supplies across the 'Hump' from India into China, re-supplying B-24 squadrons before they could bomb enemy targets. The Liberator served with distinction with the US Navy and the RAF in the Far East and the Pacific, proving a scourge to Japanese shipping. In August 1944 Liberators in England began conversion to a transportation role in support of the Allied Armies in France which were in urgent need of supplies and fuel. These 'trucking' missions, as they were called, continued until September 1944 when the B-24s supplemented the C-47s in the Market Garden Operation. By the close of World War II more B-24s (18,188) had been built than any other American aircraft of the period.

Center: **B-24 Liberators of the 466th Bomb Group, 8th Air Force, drop their bombs on smoke markers released by the leading element.**
Right bottom: **A consolidated B-24 Liberator.**
Below: **The RAF Convair C-87 transport version of the Liberator at New Delhi, India in 1945. Note the waist windows and the absence of gun turrets.**

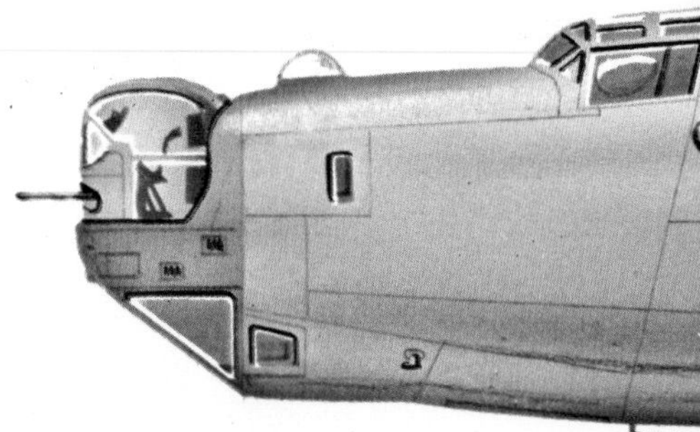

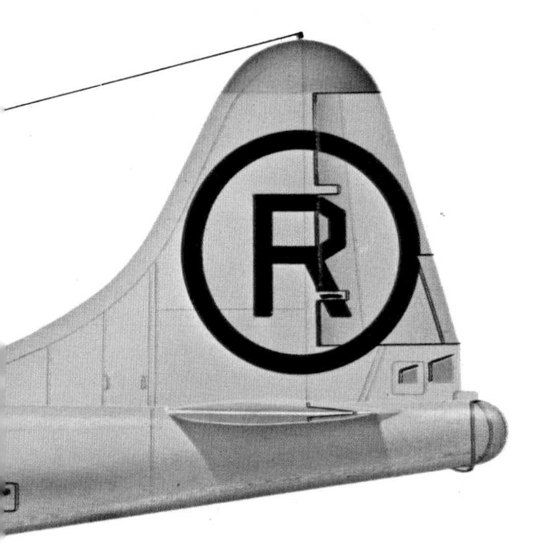

Above: **The B-24D was used on the famous Ploesti raid in August 1943.**
Below: **The Twin-Wasp engine of a B-24 Liberator.**

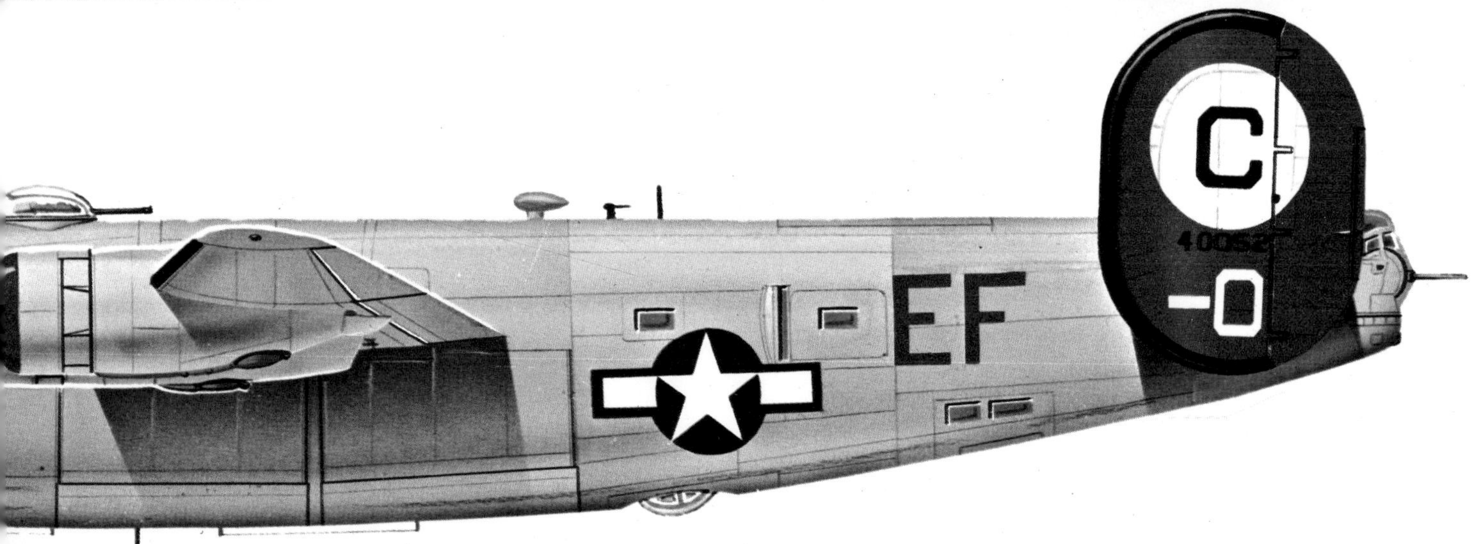

The Dominator only saw very limited action towards the end of World War II. Only 115 had been delivered by VJ Day.

Consolidated B-32 Dominator

Manufacturer: Consolidated Vultee (later Convair), San Diego, California, Fort Worth, Texas.
Type: strategic bomber.
Crew: eight.
Specification: B-321-CF.
Power Plant: four 2200 hp R-3350-23.
Dimensions: span, 135 ft; length, 82 ft 1 in; height, 32 ft 2 in; wing area, 1422 sq ft.
Weights: empty, 60,278 lb; gross, 111,500 lb.
Performance: maximum speed, 357 mph at 30,000 ft; initial climb, 23.5 min to 25,000 ft; service ceiling, 35,000 ft; maximum range, 3800 miles.
Armament: ten 0.5 in machine guns.

The B-32 was developed as a parallel project with the Boeing B-29 as a safeguard against possible delays in production. Prototypes were ordered on September 1940 (ostensibly as replacements for the B-17 and B-24). The first of three XB-32s were flown on 7 September 1942 (two weeks before the XB-29's aerial debut). The second prototype (with stepped-down cockpit) was flown on 2 July 1943. The third prototype (changed from twin to single tail) was flown on 9 November 1943.

Paradoxically, it was the B-32 that was plagued with test and development troubles which delayed its introduction to service until 1945 when 115 saw limited action in the western Pacific. Forty TB-32s were completed for training and 1588 were cancelled.

Douglas B-18 Bolo, Digby

Manufacturer: Douglas Aircraft Company, Santa Monica, California.
Type: medium bomber, anti-submarine and trainer.
Crew: six.
Specification: B-18A.
Power Plant: two 1000 hp R-1820-53.
Dimensions: span, 89 ft 6 in; length, 57 ft 10 in; height, 15 ft 2 in; wing area, 965 sq ft.
Weights: empty, 16,321 lb; gross, 27,673 lb.
Performance: maximum speed, 215 mph at 10,000 ft; cruising speed, 167 mph; initial climb, 1030 ft per min; service ceiling, 23,000 ft.
Armament: three 0.3 in machine guns; 6500 lb bomb load.

The Douglas B-18 was built to meet a requirement from the USAAF in 1934 to replace the Martin B-10 as the standard American bomber.

Production orders were placed in January 1936 and by 1940 B-18s and B-18As were standard equipment.

***Below:* A Douglas B-18A Bolo in flight. The RCAF ordered a batch of 20 which were designated Digby but by 1941 a vast majority of the US Bolos had been replaced by the B-17.**

Douglas B-23, UC-67

Manufacturer: Douglas Aircraft Company, Santa Monica, California.
Type: medium bomber, anti-submarine, transport/glider tug.
Crew: six.
Specification: B-23.
Power Plant: two 1600 hp R-2600-3.
Dimensions: span, 92 ft; length, 58 ft 4 in.
Weights: gross, 30,500 lb.
Performance: maximum speed, 282 mph at 12,000 ft.
Armament: one 0.5 in tail gun and three 0.3 in guns.

The B-23 was developed from the B-18A Bolo and was first flown on 27 July 1939. Initially it served on coastal patrols off the Pacific coast before being relegated to training and other minor roles. It was the first US military bomber to incorporate a tail-gun position.

***Below:* The B-23 Dragon was a direct development of the B-18 but with a considerably modified fuselage.**

Above: **Douglas A-24.**

***Top:* The SBD Dauntless was credited with 40 of the 91 Japanese aircraft lost during the Battle of the Coral Sea.**
***Above:* An SBD-3A (A-24) delivered in 1941.**

Douglas A-24

Manufacturer: Douglas Aircraft Company, El Segundo and Tulsa.
Type: dive bomber.
Crew: two (pilot and gunner).
Specification: A-24.
Power Plant: one 1000 hp R-1820-52.
Dimensions: span, 41 ft 6 in; length, 32 ft 8 in; height, 12 ft 11 in; wing area, 325 sq ft.
Weights: empty, 6265 lb; gross, 9200 lb.
Performance: maximum speed, 250 mph at 17,200 ft; cruising speed, 173 mph; initial climb, 7 min to 10,000 ft; service ceiling, 26,000 ft; range, 1300 miles.
Armament: two 0.5 in guns, two 0.3 in guns; 1200 lb bomb load.

Interest in dive bombers for the USAAF was first aroused by the successes achieved by the Ju 87 'Stuka' in 1940. Dive bombers were already in production for the US Navy and the A-24 was similar to the Douglas Dauntless.

During June–October 1941 A-24s were delivered from the US Navy production line and designated SBD-3A (for Army).

Douglas A-20 Havoc

Manufacturer: Douglas Aircraft Company, Santa Monica, El Segundo and Long Beach, California. Boeing Airplane Company, Seattle, Washington.
Type: medium bomber.
Crew: four (pilot, navigator, bombardier, gunner).
Specification: A-20K.
Power Plant: two 1700 hp R-2600-29.
Dimensions: span, 61 ft 4 in; length, 48 ft 4 in; height, 17 ft 7 in; wing area, 464 sq ft.
Weights: empty, 17,266 lb; gross, 27,000 lb.
Performance: maximum speed, 333 mph at 15,600 ft; cruising speed, 269 mph; initial climb, 6.6 min to 10,000 ft; service ceiling, 25,100 ft; range, 830 miles.
Armament: five 0.5 in guns; 2600 lb bombs.

The Douglas A-20 was the most produced 'attack' category aircraft to see service with the USAAF and the first American aircraft operated by American crews in the bombing of a German target. On 4 July American Independence Day, 1942, six American crews joined with RAF Boston crews in a low-level attack on four Luftwaffe airfields in the Low Countries. Originally designed in 1938 as an attack bomber the A-20 earned a reputation for being a 'jack-of-all-trades' in a variety of missions with the US Army Air Forces, RAF and French Air Force (as the DB-7), and the Soviet Air Force. Initial US Army contracts were for 206 A-20 and A-20A models, both variants of the French DB-7 specification. While generally employed as an extreme low-level attack bomber the A-20 also performed well as a night fighter in RAF service. It is perhaps best remembered for its performance in the North African campaign and in the run up to D-Day when the US 9th AF flew tactical sorties before the Normandy invasion. The US 5th AF also employed the Havoc to great effect during the battle for Dutch New Guinea. Over 7300 A-20s had been built by the time production ceased in 1944.

Below: **Douglas A-20 Havoc.**

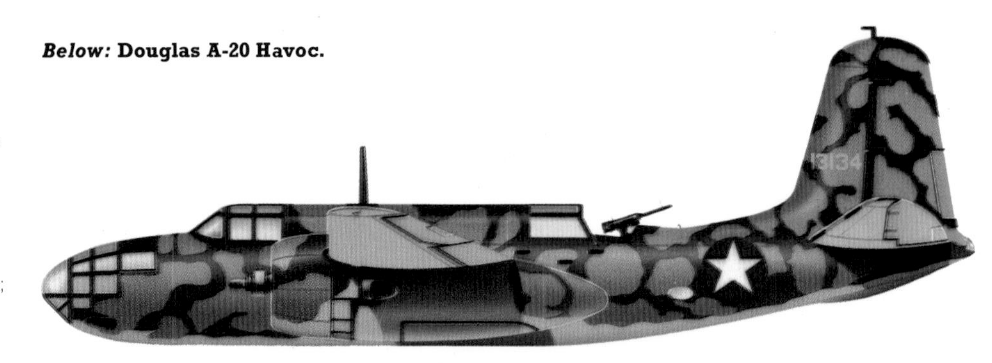

Right: **The A-20 was designed in 1938 as an attack bomber.**
Below: **An A-20 of the 416th BG, 669th Sqn.**
Below center: **An A-20 of No 107 Sqn RAF.**

Lockheed A-28, -29 Hudson AT-18

Manufacturer: Lockheed Aircraft Corporation, Burbank, California.
Type: light bomber, maritime reconnaissance and troop transport.
Crew: four (two pilots, navigator/bombardier and gunner).
Specification: A-29.
Power Plant: two 1200 hp R-1820-87.
Dimensions: span, 65 ft 6 in; length, 44 ft 4 in; height, 11 ft 11 in; wing area, 551 sq ft.
Weights: empty, 12,825 lb; gross, 21.000 lb.
Performance: maximum speed, 253 mph at 15,000 ft; cruising speed, 205 mph; climb, 6.3 min to 10,000 ft; service ceiling, 26,500 ft; range, 1550 miles.
Armament: five 0.3 in guns; 1600 lb bomb load.

The A-29 was developed in 1938 from the Lockheed 14 transport expressly to meet RAF requirements and designated Hudson.

It was first flown on 10 December 1938 and served as a coastal reconnaissance bomber with the RAF. In 1941 the USAAF and then the US Navy employed the Hudson on anti-submarine patrol. The first sinking of a U-Boat by the USAAF, was by a Hudson. Some 2500 were built before production ceased in 1943.

Below: **Lockheed A-29.**

Above: **Hudson Mark Vs of No 608 Squadron, RAF.**
Above right: **A Hudson of No 206 Squadron, RAF demonstrates how effective camouflage could be.**
Below: **The porcine fuselage of the Lockheed Ventura lent its name to the 'Flying Pig' sobriquet.**

Lockheed B-34, B-37, PV-1 Ventura

Manufacturer: Lockheed Aircraft Vega Division, Burbank, California.
Type: medium bomber, anti-submarine and trainer.
Crew: four.
Power Plant: two 2000 hp R-2800-31.
Specification: B-34A.
Dimensions: span, 65 ft 6 in; length, 51 ft 5 in; height, 11 ft 11 in; wing area, 551 sq ft.
Weights: empty, 17,275 lb; gross, 27,250 lb.
Performance: maximum speed, 315 mph at 15,500 ft; cruising speed, 230 mph; initial climb, 8.2 min to 15,000 ft; service ceiling, 24,000 ft; range, 950 miles.
Armament: two 0.5 in guns; six 0.3 in guns; 2500 lb bomb load.

The B-34 resulted from the development of the Lockheed Model 18 to further the Hudson design to meet RAF requirements.

It was first flown on 31 July 1941. All Ventura production switched to the US Navy at the end of 1942 and as the PV-1, continued in production until May 1944.

Lockheed PV-2 Harpoon

Manufacturer: Lockheed (Vega) Aircraft Division, Burbank, California.
Type: patrol-bomber.
Crew: four or five.
Power Plant: two 2000 hp R-2800-31.
Specification: PV-2.
Dimensions: span, 74 ft 11 in; length, 52 ft 0.5 in; height, 11 ft 11 in; wing area, 686 sq ft.
Weights: empty, 21,028 lb; gross, 36,000 lb.
Performance: maximum speed, 282 mph at 13,700 ft; cruising speed, 171 mph; initial climb, 1630 ft per min; service ceiling, 23,900 ft; range, 1790 miles.
Armament: five fixed forward-firing 0.5 in guns in nose; two flexible 0.5 in each in dorsal turret and ventral mount. Up to four 1000 lb bombs internal and two 1000 lb external.

The US Navy requisitioned 27 B-34 Venturas from the Lend-Lease contract with Britain and designated them PV-1. All Ventura production was turned over to the US Navy at the end of 1942 and continued in production until May 1944 with the Navy receiving 1600 in total. The PV-2 was a stop-gap to replace the PV-1 and bridge the gap between the PV-1 and P2V Neptune, then in its preliminary design stage. The PV-2 Harpoon was conceived to remedy the PV-1's shortcomings in range and iron out unwelcome characteristics like ground looping and a high minimum control speed on one engine.

US Navy deliveries of PV-1 began in December 1942 and of PV-2 in March 1944. The PV-2 served mainly in the Pacific theater.

Right: **The Ventura PV-1 saw widespread service in the Pacific from 1943 until the war's end.**
Right, below: **Martin B-10.**

Martin B-10, B-12, B-14

Manufacturer: Glenn L. Martin Company, Cleveland, Ohio.
Type: light bomber.
Crew: four (pilot, radio operator and two gunners).
Specification: B-10B.
Power Plant: two 775 hp R-1820-33.
Dimensions: span, 70 ft 6 in; length, 44 ft 9 in; height, 15 ft 5 in; wing area, 678 sq ft.
Weights: empty, 9681 lb; gross, 16,400 lb.
Performance: maximum speed, 213 mph; cruising speed, 193 mph; service ceiling, 24,200 ft; range, 1240 miles.
Armament: one 0.3 in Browning gun in nose and rear turrets and one in ventral tunnel; 2260 lb bombs.

The B-10, -12, -14 and 139 were designed and built as a Martin private venture.

The US Army prototype, XB-907 was delivered on 20 March 1932 for flight trials which began in July 1932. By October it was achieving 207 mph at 6000 feet in trials, faster than any US fighter then in service. Service deliveries began June 1934 but it had poor service record.

It was the first US all-metal bomber fitted with a gun turret. In February 1938 Martin 139s operated by the Chinese Air Force flew missions against the Japanese mainland. The B-10s, flown by Dutch crews in the Netherlands East Indies, were among the first US bombers flown in combat during World War II.

Right: **At the time of its introduction the B-10 was faster than the majority of contemporary fighters and incorporated such revolutionary features as a retractable undercarriage and stressed-skin construction.**

Martin A-30 Baltimore

Manufacturer: Glenn L. Martin Company, Baltimore, Maryland.
Type: light bomber.
Crew: three (pilot, WOP-AG, bomb-aimer/navigator).
Specification: A-30 Baltimore V.
Power Plant: two 1660 hp R-2600-29.
Dimensions: span, 61 ft 4 in; length, 48 ft 6 in.
Weights: empty, 15,875 lb; gross, 22,622 lb.
Performance: maximum speed, 320 mph at 15,000 ft; cruising speed, 224 mph; service ceiling, 25,000 ft; range, 980 miles with 2000 lb of bombs.
Armament: Martin dorsal turret with two 0.5 in machine guns and four 303s in the wings plus two in ventral position or two 0.5 in machine guns and six 303s in the wings.

The basic Maryland design was completed to fulfill British requirements and was powered by Wright engines. Britain ordered 400 in May 1940 with further orders for 575 more in July 1942. The Model 187B was first flown on 14 June 1941. Like its predecessor the Maryland, the Baltimore never served with US forces. However it served with the Royal Air Force and even in July 1944 with the Italian Co-Belligerent Air Force.

Below: **The Baltimore was the result of improvements carried out to the Maryland. It saw widespread service with the Royal Air Force, the South African Air Force and Italian units in the Mediterranean from El Alamein to Tunisia and in Italy and Sicily. The Italian Co-Belligerent AF used Baltimores against the Axis in Yugoslavia.**

Martin A-22 Maryland

Manufacturer: Glenn L. Martin Company, Baltimore, Maryland.
Type: originally ground attack but later light bomber/reconnaissance.
Crew: three (pilot, WOP-AG, bomb-aimer/navigator).
Specification: A-22 Maryland I.
Power Plant: two 1200 hp S3C4-G.
Dimensions: span, 61 ft 4 in; length, 46 ft 8 in; height, 14 ft 11.75 in; wing area, 538.5 sq ft.
Weights: empty, 10,586 lb; gross, 15,297 lb.
Performance: maximum speed, 304 mph at 13,000 ft; cruising speed, 248 mph; service ceiling, 29,500 ft; range, 1300 miles.
Armament: six 0.3 in machine guns.

In late 1937 the USAAF announced a design competition for a two-engined Attack light bomber. Martin were one of four companies who tendered in July 1938 along with North American's NA-40 (later B-25 Mitchell) and the winning design, the Douglas Model 7B (later DB-7). However, Martin's Model 167W (Army XA-22) received a 115-aircraft order from the French Purchasing Commission in 1939.

The XA-22 was first flown on 14 March 1939 and although it never served in combat with US Forces during World War II, Marylands gained a good reputation fighting in the Western desert with the SAAF and the RAF, who purchased the residue of the French contract after the fall of France. Marylands also did much valuable work on reconnaissance patrols from Malta and a Maryland brought back photographs of the Italian fleet at Taranto in 1940.

Right: **A few Marylands served with the Armée de l'Air before the collapse in 1940 after which the RAF took delivery of all models.**

Martin B-26 Marauder

Manufacturer: The Glenn L. Martin Company, Baltimore, Maryland (all except B-26C) and Omaha, Nebraska (B-26C only).
Type: light bomber.
Crew: seven.
Specification: B-26G.
Power Plant: two 2000 hp R-2800-43.
Dimensions: span, 71 ft; length, 56 ft 1 in; height, 20 ft 4 in; wing area, 658 sq ft.
Weights: empty, 23,800 lb; gross, 38,200 lb.
Performance: maximum speed, 283 mph at 5000 ft; cruising speed, 216 mph; climb, 8 min to 5000 ft; service ceiling, 19,800 ft; range, 1100 miles.
Armament: eleven 0.5 in guns; 4000 lb bomb load.

In January 1939 the USAAF circulated US aircraft manufacturers with a specification for a new high-speed medium bomber. Martin submitted a design in July 1939 together with a guarantee to build a certain quantity in a given period. With World War II imminent the AAF took the unprecedented step of ordering the design without the benefits of prototypes or testing. In September 1939 110 of the type, now numbered B-26, were ordered. Its first flight in 1940 seemed to offer great promise but subsequent testing and training flights resulted in many accidents and earned the B-26 a reputation early in its career as an unsafe aircraft. Deliveries began in 1941 but squadrons were slow to become operational because of the B-26s high landing speed. Crews pointed to its small wing area and said it had 'no visible means of support.' However, the B-26 turned out to be one of the great medium bombers in terms of speed, power, versatility and precision bombing, helped by an increase in wing area and other modifications along the way. By the end of the war 4708 B-26s had been built and had seen service with the USAAF, RAF and many other Allied air forces.

Above: **Marauders of the 416th BG, 668th BS sporting invasion stripes during the softening-up of the Normandy coastline.**
Right: **A sight that was all too common in the ETO as a Marauder goes down in flames.**

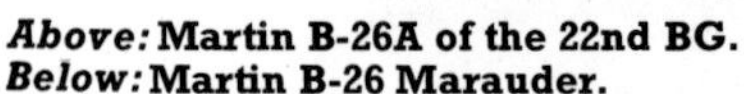

Above: **Martin B-26A of the 22nd BG.**
Below: **Martin B-26 Marauder.**

North American B-25 Mitchell

Manufacturer: North American Aviation Incorporated, Inglewood, California (B-25 A, B, C, E, F, G, H) and Kansas City, Kansas (B-25D, J).
Type: light bomber.
Crew: up to six.
Specification: B-25J.
Power Plant: two 1700 hp R-2600-92.
Dimensions: span, 67 ft 7 in; length, 52 ft 11 in; height, 16 ft 4 in; wing area, 610 sq ft.
Weights: empty, 19,480 lb; gross, 35,000 lb.
Performance: maximum speed, 272 mph at 13,000 ft; cruising speed, 230 mph; service ceiling, 24,200 ft; range, 1350 miles.
Armament: 12 0.5 in; eight 5 in RP; 3000 lb bomb load.

Chosen to bear the name of the late Brigadier General 'Billy' Mitchell, a pioneer advocate of military air power, the B-25 proved to be one of the most outstanding bombers used by the USAAF in World War II. Design work began in 1938 as a light, fast attack bomber. By 1940 the B-25 had matured into a medium bomber and was produced in that configuration, which included a large bomb bay and heavy armament. Very popular with its crews, the B-25 adapted to many combat roles in every theater of the war. Of all its many combat exploits none was perhaps greater than the bombing raid on Japan on 18 April 1942 when 16 B-25s, under the command of Lieutenant Colonel Jimmy Doolittle, were launched from the deck of the carrier *Hornet*. Tokyo was bombed and the B-25s headed for shuttle bases in China although all were lost (most of the crews bailing out before ditching) but the mission was hailed as a great morale boost for a depressed American public. It operated as a bomber in the assaults on the central Pacific chain of islands and proved the scourge of Japanese shipping with its .75 mm cannon and with its 'skip bombing' tactics. The Mitchell also operated in China, Alaska, North Africa and Europe in the colors of the USAAF, USN and Marines, USSR, RAF, Free Dutch and Polish air forces among others. Between 1940–45 almost 11,000 examples were built, of which the USAAF received 9816.

Top: **A TB-25K during the Korean War.**
Above: **A Mitchell prepares for take-off.**
Below: **A North American B-25 Mitchell.**

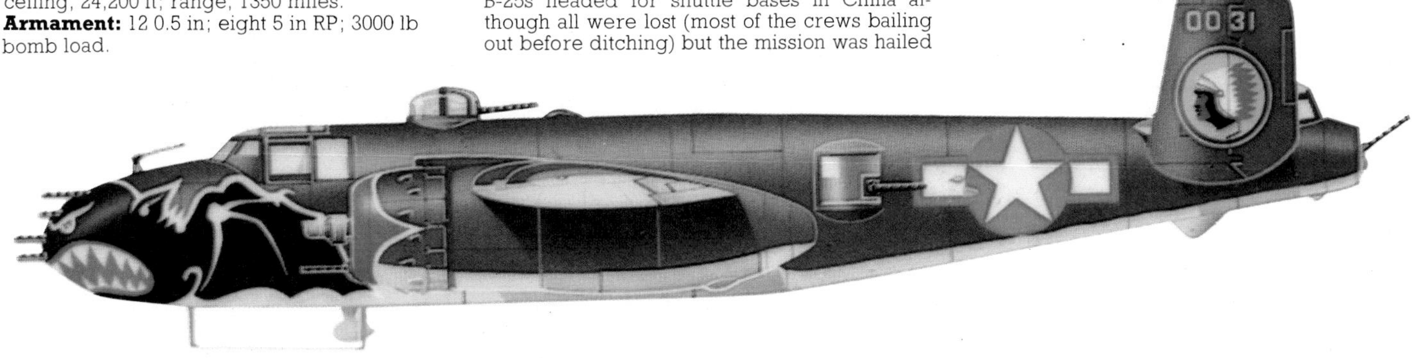

Right: **A B-25J with package guns. Most Js which served with the USAAF later went to the Pacific and the glasshouse in the nose was modified to a solid configuration because the bombardier was not needed on low-level attacks.**
Below: **B-25 Mitchells were used to great effect in the Pacific where they replaced the B-26, making low-level 'masthead' attacks like this one on enemy shipping.**

Vultee A-31, A-35 Vengeance

Manufacturer: Vultee Aircraft, Incorporated, Nashville and Northrop Aircraft, Hawthorne, California.
Type: dive bomber.
Crew: two (pilot and gunner).
Specification: A-35B.
Power Plant: one 1700 hp R-2600-13.
Dimensions: span, 48 ft; length, 39 ft 9 in; height, 15 ft 4 in; wing area, 332 sq ft.
Weights: empty, 10,300 lb; gross, 16,400 lb.
Performance: maximum speed, 279 mph at 13,500 ft; cruising speed, 230 mph; initial climb, 11.3 min to 15,000 ft; service ceiling, 22,300 ft; range, 2300 miles.
Armament: six 0.5 in guns; 2000 lb bomb load.

The Vultee A-31 was ordered by the British Purchasing Commission in 1940 before it had been procured by the US Army Air Corps. The latter placed an order in March 1941.

Although the Vengeance saw extremely limited action with the US Army Air Corps, many being relegated to target-towing duties, it gave sterling service with the RAF and Indian Air Force in support of troops in Burma.

Above: **The Vengeance served with distinction on the Burma Front.**
Below: **Vultee Vengeance.**

Left: **Brewster Buffalo.**
Right: **Because of its protracted development the Helldiver was long in arriving but when it did, in November 1943, it was so successful that it remained in service with the US Navy for several years after the war.**
Below: **The Curtiss SB2C Helldiver.**
Bottom, center: **An SB2C-4 displays its neatly folded wings.**

Brewster F2A Buffalo

Manufacturer: Brewster Aeronautical Corporation, Long Island City, New York.
Type: carrier-borne fighter.
Crew: pilot only.
Specification: F2A-3.
Power Plant: one 1200 hp R-1820-40.
Dimensions: span, 35 ft; length, 26 ft 4 in; height, 12 ft; wing area, 209 sq ft.
Weights: empty, 4732 lb; gross, 7159 lb.
Performance: maximum speed, 321 mph at 16,500 ft; cruising speed, 161 mph; initial climb, 2290 ft per min; service ceiling, 33,200 ft; range, 965 miles.
Armament: four 0.5 in guns.

The US Navy placed an order for a prototype of the Brewster F2A Buffalo on 22 June 1936. The prototype XF2A-1 was first flown on December 1937 and the first F2A-1s were rolled out in June 1939. It is included in this encyclopedia because it was the first monoplane fighter to equip a US Navy squadron.

Curtiss SBC Helldiver

Manufacturer: Curtiss-Wright Corporation, Curtiss Airplane Division, Buffalo, New York.
Type: carrier-borne scout-bomber.
Crew: two (pilot and observer/gunner).
Specification: SBC-4.
Power Plant: one 950 hp 1820-34.
Dimensions: span, 34 ft; length, 28 ft 4 in; height, 12 ft 7 in; wing area, 317 sq ft.
Weights: empty, 4841 lb; gross, 7632 lb.
Performance: maximum speed, 237 mph at 15,200 ft; cruising speed, 127 mph; initial climb, 1860 ft per min; service ceiling, 27,300 ft; range, 590 miles with 500 lb bomb.
Armament: two 0.3 in guns; one 500 lb or 1000 lb bomb load.

In June 1932 the US Navy contracted the Curtiss company to produce a two-seat, parasol-wing carrier-borne fighter with retractable undercarriage.

The resulting prototype was first flown in 1933 and the completed SBC-4 Helldiver was delivered in March 1939. It was the last combat biplane produced in the US.

Curtiss SB2C Helldiver

Manufacturer: Curtiss-Wright Corporation, Airplane Division, Columbus, Ohio; Canadian Car & Foundry Company Limited, Montreal; and Fairchild Aircraft Limited, Longueuil, PQ, Canada.
Type: carrier-borne scout-bomber.
Crew: two (pilot and observer).
Specification: SB2C-4.
Power Plant: one 1900 hp R-2600-20.
Dimensions: span, 49 ft 9 in; length, 36 ft 8 in; height, 13 ft 2 in; wing area, 422 sq ft.
Weights: empty, 10,547 lb; gross, 16,616 lb.
Performance: maximum speed, 295 mph at 16,700 ft; cruising speed, 158 mph; initial climb, 1800 ft per min; service ceiling, 29,100 ft; range, 1165 miles with 1000 lb bomb load.
Armament: two 20 mm cannon; two 0.3 in guns. Up to 1000 lb bombs internal and 1000 lb external.

The 'Big-Tailed Beast,' as its less endearing crewmembers nick-named the SB2C, was first planned in 1938. It was the Curtiss company's first monoplane bomber and the last to carry the title Helldiver. It was ordered on 15 May 1939, while the SBC Helldiver biplane was still in quantity production. The prototype XSB2C-1 first flew on 18 December 1940 but prolonged and troubled development resulting in 800 major design changes postponed its entry into service until the battle of Rabaul in early 1943.

Throughout 1944 the SB2Cs replaced the Dauntlesses as the US Navy's standard dive bomber. More than 7200 SB2Cs were built including 1194 in Canada. Helldivers were the last pure dive bombers to serve with the US Navy.

Below: **Curtiss SBC-3 Helldiver.**

Above: **TBD-1s in formation during a training flight in June 1941.**

Douglas TBD Devastator

Manufacturer: Douglas Aircraft Company, El Segundo, California.
Type: carrier-based torpedo-bomber.
Crew: three (pilot, torpedo officer/navigator, gunner).
Specification: TBD-1.
Power Plant: one 900 hp R-1830-64.
Dimensions: span, 50 ft; length, 35 ft; height, 15 ft 1 in; wing area, 422 sq ft.
Weights: empty, 5600 lb; gross, 10,194 lb.
Performance: maximum speed, 206 mph at 8000 ft; cruising speed, 128 mph; initial climb, 720 ft per min; service ceiling, 19,500 ft; range, 716 miles with 1000 lb bomb.
Armament: two 0.3 in guns; 1000 lb torpedo.

This new torpedo bomber was developed in 1934 to meet the needs of a new generation of aircraft carriers for the US Navy.

The XTBD-1 prototype was first flown on 15 April 1935. The TBD-1 was delivered to the US Navy on 5 October 1937 and remained operational until after the Battle of Midway when TBD-1 Squadrons were decimated. The remaining Devastators were used for training.

Its development marked the point of change from biplane to monoplane torpedo bombers.

Douglas SBD Dauntless

Manufacturer: Douglas Aircraft Company, El Segundo, California, and Tulsa, Oklahoma.
Type: carrier-borne scout/dive bomber.
Crew: two (pilot and observer/rear gunner).
Specification: SBD-5.
Power Plant: one 1200 hp R-1820-60.
Dimensions: span, 41 ft 6.25 in; length, 33 ft 0.1 in; height, 12 ft 11 in; wing area, 325 sq ft.
Weights: empty, 6675 lb; gross, 10,855 lb.
Performance: maximum speed, 245 mph at 15,800 ft; cruising speed, 144 mph; initial climb, 1190 ft per min; service ceiling, 24,300 ft; range, 1100 miles.
Armament: two 0.5 in guns; two 0.3 in guns; 1925 lb bomb load.

At the time of the Japanese attack on Pearl Harbor this easy to fly and maintain aircraft was the US Navy's standard carrier-borne reconnaissance/dive bomber. Production orders had

Below: Douglas Dauntless.
Right: A Dauntless skirts an island in the Pacific.

been placed in April 1939 for 57 SBD-1s and 87 SBD-2s. Production, stepped up after 7 December 1941, totalled 584 and by the end of the year the SBD-3 was already equipping units on four carriers. At the Battle of Midway in June 1942 the Dauntless reigned supreme, sinking the Japanese heavy carriers, *Akagi*, *Kaga* and *Soryu* and putting the *Hiryu* out of action. It was Japan's first major naval defeat in 300 years and marked the beginning of the end of their brief reign in the Pacific. The SBD served in every key Pacific battle until it was phased out during the Philippine campaign in 1944. Some 5936 SBDs were built but today only three are known to have been preserved.

Grumman FF and SF

Manufacturer: Grumman Aircraft Engineering Corporation, Bethpage, Long Island, New York.
Type: carrier-borne fighter.
Crew: two (pilot and observer/gunner).
Specification: FF-1.
Power Plant: one 700/750 hp R-1820-78.
Dimensions: span, 34 ft 6 in; length, 24 ft 6 in; height, 11 ft 1 in; wing area, 310 sq ft.
Weights: empty, 3221 lb; gross, 4800 lb.
Performance: maximum speed, 207 mph at 5300 ft; service ceiling, 22,000 ft; range, 647 miles.
Armament: three 30-cal machine guns.

The FF was one of the first aircraft produced by the Grumman Aircraft Engineering Corporation and it was test flown on 29 December 1931. The XFF-1 was such a good design that the US Navy ordered 27. With the Wright R-1820-78 and the new retractable landing gear and covered cockpits, production FF-1s could exceed 200 mph at a time when the F4B-4 could reach 188 mph. Thirty-four similar SF-1 scouts were ordered by the US Navy for 1934.

Right: SBD-5s head out over the Pacific.
Below: An SF-1 Scout developed from the FF-1.
Center bottom: A Grumman XSF-1 on the USS _Saratoga_.

***Above:* A civil F3F-2 owned by Windward Aviation and built in June 1938.**

Grumman F2F, F3F

Manufacturer: Grumman Aircraft Engineering Corporation, Bethpage, Long Island, New York.
Type: carrier-borne fighter.
Crew: pilot only.
Specification: F3F-3.
Power Plant: one 950 hp R-1820-22.
Dimensions: span, 32 ft; length, 23 ft 2 in; height, 9 ft 4 in; wing area, 260 sq ft.
Weights: empty, 3285 lb; gross, 4795 lb.
Performance: maximum speed, 264 mph at 15,200 ft; initial climb, 2750 ft per min; service ceiling, 33,200 ft; maximum range, 980 miles.
Armament: one 30-cal and one 50-cal machine guns.

On 15 October 1934 Grumman was contracted to design the XF3F-1, an improved version of the F2F-1 but with the same Pratt and Whitney R-1535 engine. In August 1935 54 production F3F-1s were ordered. The advantages the F3F had over the F2F were greater maneuverability and better directional stability. The F3F-1 could take off within 200 feet and despite higher weight and larger dimensions was equally fast as the earlier model. An improved prototype the XF3F-2, with a 1000 hp Wright Cyclone, was delivered to the Navy on 27 July 1936 and in March 1937 Grumman received a contract for 81 production F3F-2s. In 1938 the 'Flying Barrel' was further modified and the resulting F3F-3 was considered a pleasure to fly. By mid-1939 all first-line US Navy and Marine Corps squadrons flew Grumman fighters. The last Grumman biplane fighter left service in November 1943.

Grumman F4F Wildcat

Manufacturer: Grumman Aircraft Engineering Corporation, Bethpage, Long Island, New York.
Type: carrier-borne fighter.
Crew: pilot only.
Specification: F4F-4.
Power Plant: one 1200 hp R-1830-86.
Dimensions: span, 38 ft; length, 28 ft 9 in; height, 11 ft 10 in; wing area, 260 sq ft.
Weights: empty, 5785 lb; gross, 7952 lb.
Performance: maximum speed, 318 mph at 19,400 ft; cruising speed, 155 mph; initial climb, 1950 ft per min; service ceiling, 34,900 ft; range, 770 miles.
Armament: six 0.5 in guns.
Specification: FM-2.
Manufacturer: General Motors Corporation, Eastern Aircraft Division, Trenton, New Jersey.
Power Plant: one 1350 hp R-1820-56.
Dimensions: length, 28 ft 11 in; height, 11 ft 5 in.
Weights: empty, 5448 lb; gross, 8271 lb.
Performance: maximum speed, 332 mph at 28,800 ft; cruising speed, 164 mph; initial climb, 3650 ft per min; service ceiling, 34,700 ft; range, 900 miles.
Armament: four 0.5 in guns. Two 250 lb bombs or six 5 in rockets.

This is one of the most outstanding naval fighters of the war and the Grumman company's first monoplane. Design began in 1935 and by the time of the Japanese attack on Pearl Harbor in December 1941, the Wildcat was the standard US Navy carrier-borne fighter. It remained as such until 1943 when the Corsair and Hellcat

***Below:* The Grumman F4F-4 Wildcat.**

Above: **An early 1942 F4F-4 with large fuselage stars which were altered to avoid confusion with Japanese insignia.**
Below: **Grumman F4F Wildcat.**

became operational. Although slowest of all American fighters and out-performed by the Japanese Zero, the F4F still managed an impressive combat record mainly because of its rugged construction and the skill of its pilots. The Wildcat averaged almost seven enemy aircraft shot down to every one F4F lost. One of the most memorable claims to fame occurred when Navy Lieutenant Commander Edward 'Butch' O'Hare singlehandedly saved his carrier, *Lexington*, in the battle for Bougainville by breaking up an attack by nine Japanese bombers and downing five of them in six minutes. Some 8000 F4F Wildcats were built from 1939 to 1942. The F4F also served with the Royal Navy as the Martlet.

Below: **F6Fs were vital in the Philippine Sea in 1944.**

Grumman F6F Hellcat

Manufacturer: Grumman Aircraft Engineering Corporation, Bethpage, Long Island, New York.
Type: carrier-borne fighter.
Crew: pilot only.
Specification: F6F-5.
Power Plant: one 2000 hp R-2800-10W.
Dimensions: span, 42 ft 10 in; length, 33 ft 7 in; height, 13 ft 1 in; wing area, 334 sq ft.
Weights: empty, 9238 lb; gross, 15,413 lb.
Performance: maximum speed, 380 mph at 23,400 ft; cruising speed, 168 mph; initial climb, 2980 ft per min; service ceiling, 37,300 ft; range, 945 miles.
Armament: six 0.5 in guns (or two 20 mm and four 0.5 in).

Work began on the F6F during 1941 and was a logical extrapolation of the F4F Wildcat. Pilot experience and feedback of existing Naval fighters influenced Grumman's designers and it was apparent that the Navy needed a fighter able to cope with the fast and highly maneuverable Japanese Zero. The designers even had at their disposal a captured Zero with which to compare their Hellcat design. The operational use of the Hellcat began in August 1943 during the attack on Marcus Island in the Pacific. Re-equipment of F4F squadrons began during 1943 and by mid-1944 the Hellcat and the Corsair had become standard equipment in the US Navy throughout the Pacific. In 1944 during the Marshall Islands campaign, Hellcats and dive bombers attacked the island of Truk, considered impregnable by the Japanese, destroy-

Below: **Grumman F6F Hellcat.**
Bottom: **Hellcats freezing over, off Newfoundland during shipment to Britain.**

ing 50 Zeros in the air and another 150 on the ground for the loss of only four F6Fs. Hellcats shot down almost 5000 enemy aircraft by the end of the war. This constituted almost 75 percent of all US Navy's air-to-air victories against Japanese aircraft. More than 12,000 Hellcats were built, including 252 F6F-3s and 930 F6F-5s delivered to the Royal Navy. The F6F-5s and F6F-5Ns remained in service after World War II and some continued in service in the Korean Conflict.

Modified F6F-5K pilotless drones, each carrying a 2000-lb bomb, were launched from the USS *Boxer* against North Korean targets, beginning on 28 August 1952.

Grumman TBF, TBM Avenger

Manufacturer: Grumman Aircraft Engineering Corporation, Bethpage, Long Island, New York.
Type: torpedo bomber.
Crew: three (pilot, gunner, radar operator).
Specification: TBF-1.
Power Plant: one 1700 hp R-2600-8.
Dimensions: span, 54 ft 2 in; length, 40 ft; height, 16 ft 5 in; wing area, 490 sq ft.
Weights: empty, 10,080 lb; gross, 15,905 lb.
Performance: maximum speed, 271 mph at 12,000 ft; cruising speed, 145 mph; initial climb, 1430 ft per min; service ceiling, 22,400 ft; range, 1215 miles.
Armament: two 30-cal and one 50-cal guns; 1600 lb bombs or torpedo.
Specification: TBM-3E.
Manufacturer: General Motors Corporation, Eastern Aircraft Division, Trenton, New Jersey.
Type: torpedo bomber.
Crew: three (pilot, gunner, radar operator).
Power Plant: one 1900 hp R-2600-20.
Dimensions: span, 54 ft 2 in; length, 40 ft 11.5 in; height, 16 ft 5 in; wing area, 490 sq ft.
Weights: empty, 10,545 lb; gross, 17,895 lb.
Performance: maximum speed, 276 mph at 16,500 ft; cruising speed, 147 mph; initial climb, 2060 ft per min; service ceiling, 30,100 ft; range, 1010 miles.
Armament: two 0.5 in guns; one dorsal 0.5 in; one ventral 0.3 in. Up to 2000 lb in bomb-bay.

Grumman received a contract from the US Navy for two prototypes of a torpedo bomber in April 1940 and although they had no previous experience of such a type they had been specializing for several years in the design of Navy fighters. The first flight of the XTBF-1 occurred on 1 August 1941 and the first production TBF-1 appeared in January 1942. In the first six months of 1942 Grumman delivered 145 Avengers. Six were checked out and flown to Pearl Harbor where they were destined for the USS *Hornet*, but the ship was already at sea. They flew on across the Pacific and arrived just in time for the Battle of Midway on 4 June 1942. However five failed to return and the sixth was severely damaged. From that moment on though, the Avenger never looked back. It proved its excellence against Japanese shipping for the remainder of the war. Two of its victims were the battleships *Yamato* and *Musashi*, the latter sinking after only three solid hits. The Avenger remained in operational Fleet service in a variety of roles until 1954. Of nearly 10,000 produced some 1000 served with the Royal Navy.

***Top right:* Early TBF-1 Avenger in green and light gray camouflage.**
***Center right:* Tight-knit formation of Avengers over the Pacific.**
***Right:* Grumman TBF Avenger.**

***Below:* Vought SB2U Vindicator.**

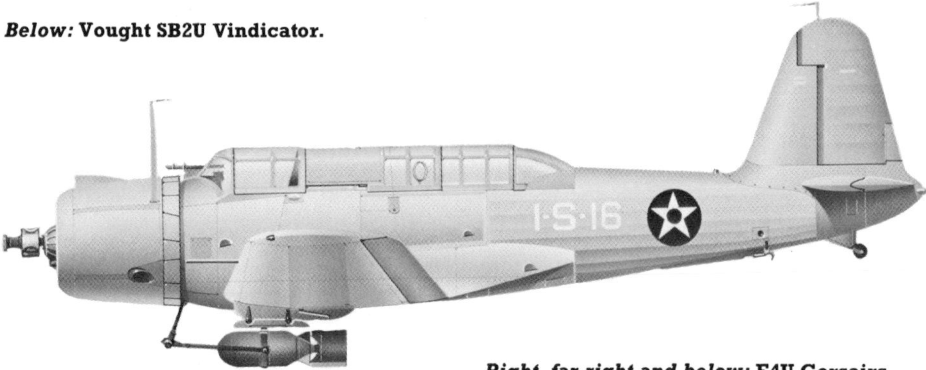

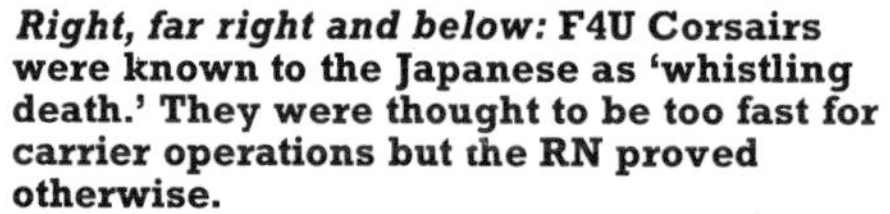

***Right, far right and below:* F4U Corsairs were known to the Japanese as 'whistling death.' They were thought to be too fast for carrier operations but the RN proved otherwise.**

Vought SB2U Vindicator

Manufacturer: Vought-Sikorsky Division, United Aircraft Corporation, Stratford, Connecticut.
Type: carrier-borne scout/dive bomber.
Crew: pilot and observer/gunner.
Specification: SB2U-3.
Power Plant: one 825 hp R-1535-02.
Dimensions: span, 42 ft; length, 34 ft; height, 10 ft 3 in; wing area, 305 sq ft.
Weights: empty, 5634 lb; gross, 9421 lb.
Performance: maximum speed, 243 mph at 9500 ft; cruising speed, 152 mph; initial climb, 1070 ft per min; service ceiling, 23,600 ft; range, 1120 miles with full bomb load.
Armament: two .50-cal machine guns, one belly-mounted 1000 lb bomb, two wing-mounted 100 lb bombs.

The SB2U Vindicator was ordered from Vought in October 1934 as the US Navy's first monoplane scout/bomber.

The XSB2U-1 prototype was first flown on 4 January 1936. The SB2U-2 flew on 11 August 1938 and the SB2U-3 flew on 10 January 1941. The V-156F versions were exported to France in the early days of World War II and after surrender deliveries switched to the RAF where it served as the V-156B-1 Chesapeake. US Marine pilots used Vindicators to help turn back the Japanese attempt to capture Midway Island in 1942.

Vought F4U Corsair

Manufacturer: Vought-Sikorsky Division, United Aircraft Corporation, Stratford, Connecticut; Chance Vought Division, United Aircraft Corporation (later Chance Vought Aircraft Incorporated), Dallas, Texas; Brewster Aeronautical Corporation, Long Island City, New York; Goodyear Aircraft Corporation, Akron, Ohio.
Type: carrier-borne fighter.
Crew: pilot only.
Specification: F4U-5N.
Power Plant: 2300 hp R-2800-32W.
Dimensions: span, 41 ft; length, 33 ft 6 in; height, 14 ft 9 in; wing area, 314 sq ft.
Weights: empty, 9683 lb; gross, 14,106 lb.
Performance: maximum speed, 470 mph at 26,200 ft; cruising speed, 227 mph; climb, 3780 ft per min; service ceiling, 41,400 ft; range, 1120 miles.
Armament: four 20 mm guns; two 1000 lb bomb load.

Of all the fighters built during the war the F4U was in production the longest. Its claims to fame were many, not least that it was credited with an 11:1 ratio of kills to losses in combat against Japanese aircraft and was the last piston-engined fighter in production for any of the US services. By far the finest carrier-borne fighter of the war its greatest attribute was its excellent overall performance. To achieve this Vought simply designed the small-

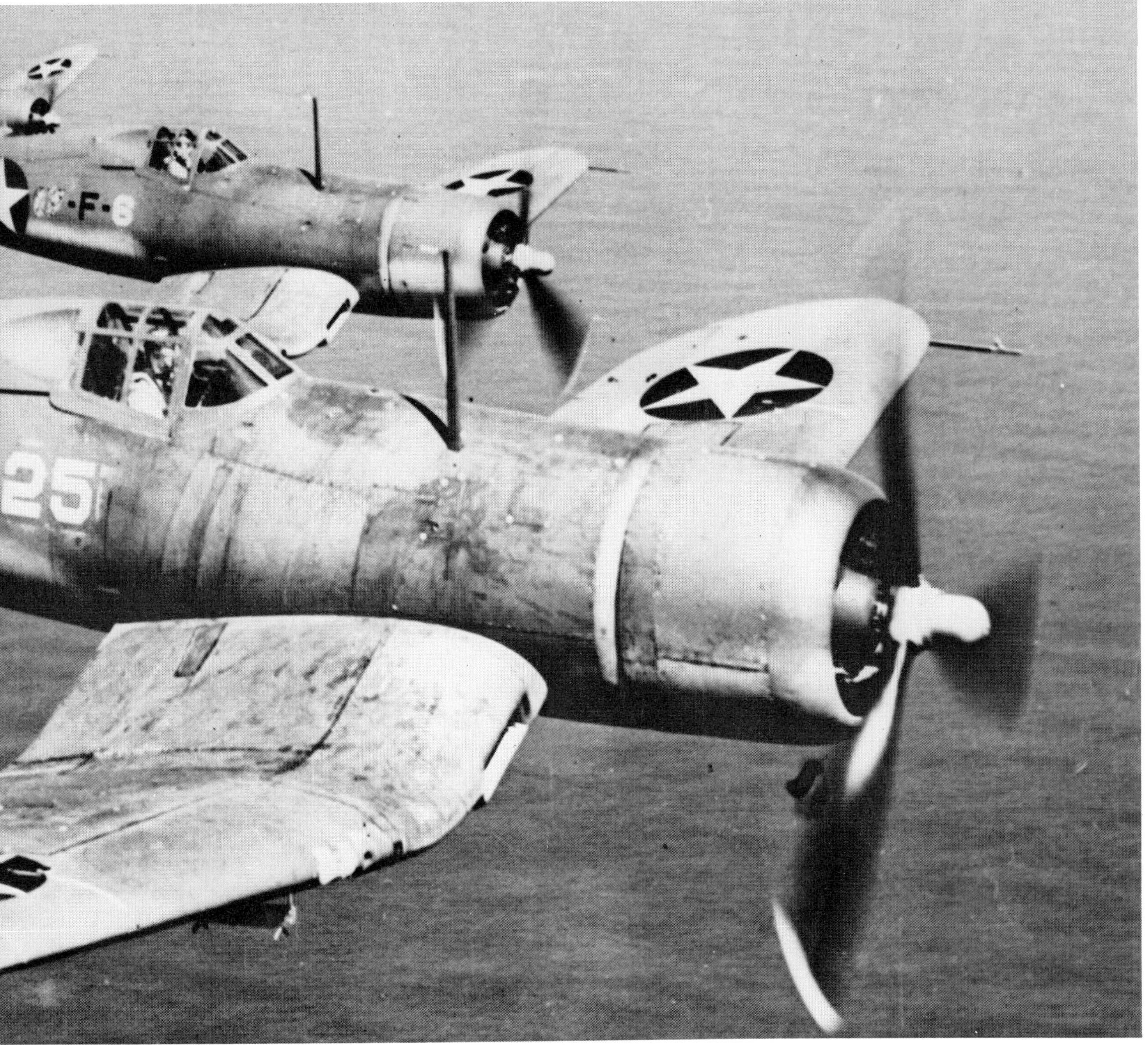
25

Left: **AU-1 Corsairs with increased armor and underwing loading capability went into production for issue to US Marine Corps squadrons operating in Korea.**
Below: **Interior of a Vought F4U Corsair.**

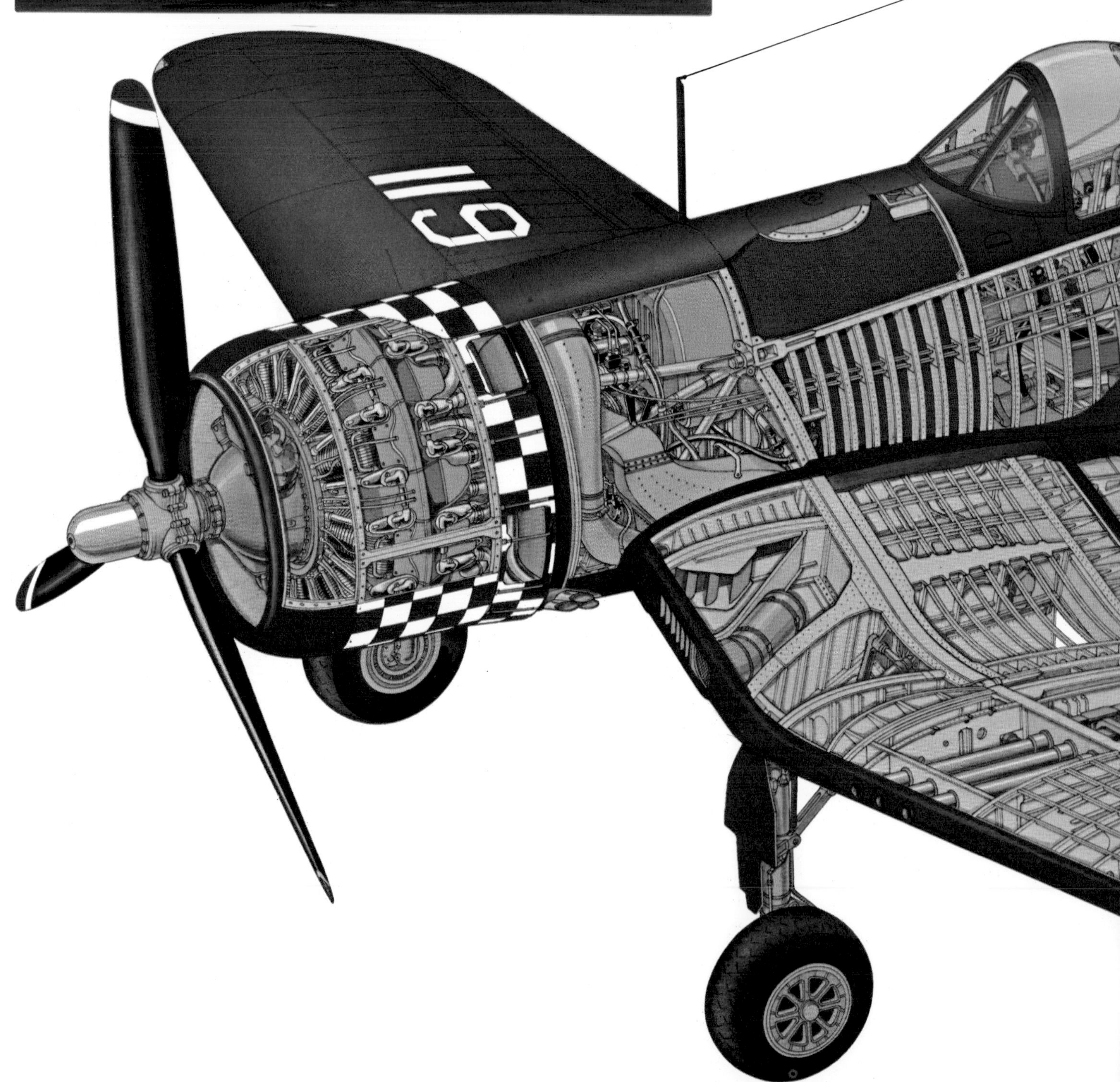

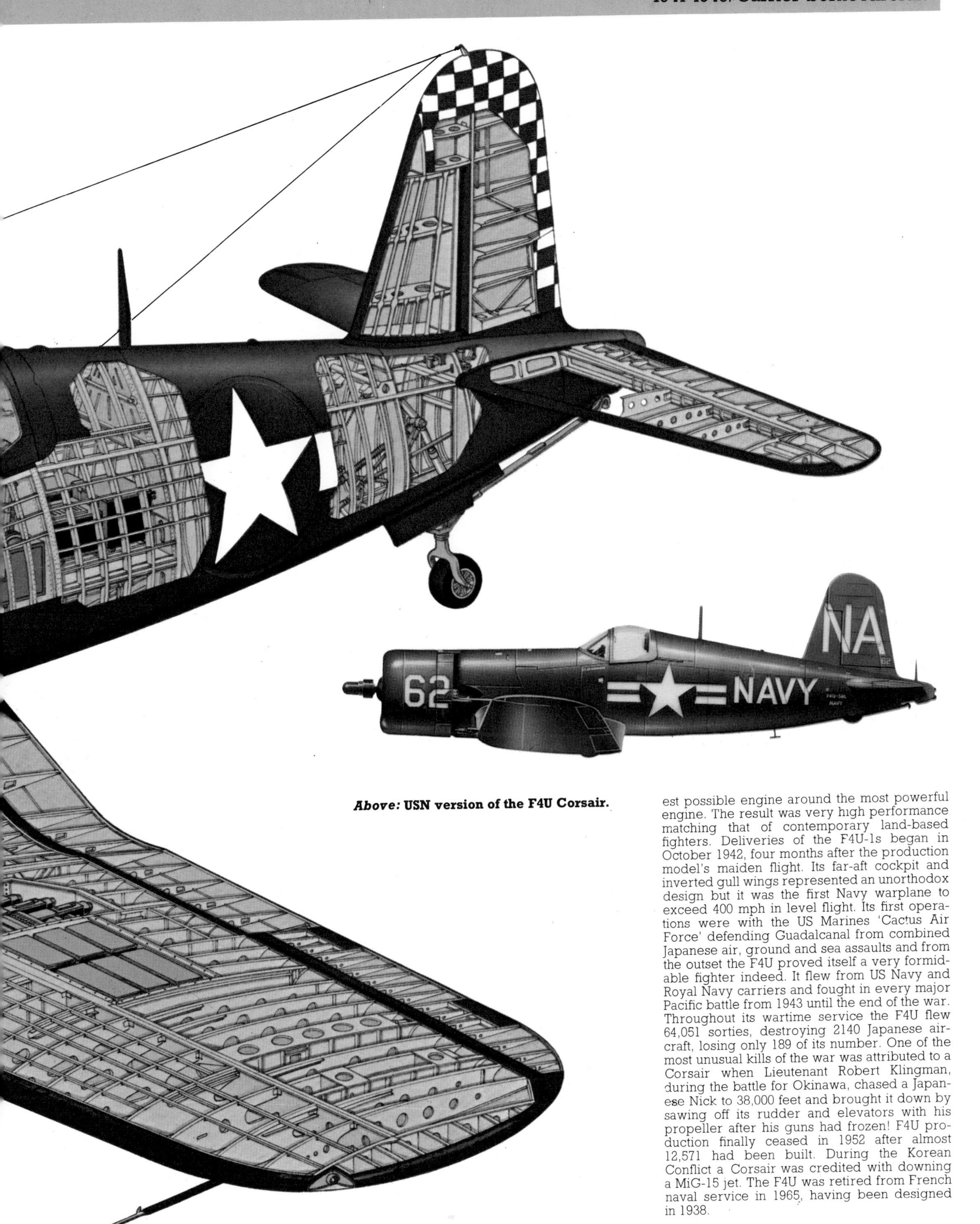

***Above:* USN version of the F4U Corsair.**

est possible engine around the most powerful engine. The result was very high performance matching that of contemporary land-based fighters. Deliveries of the F4U-1s began in October 1942, four months after the production model's maiden flight. Its far-aft cockpit and inverted gull wings represented an unorthodox design but it was the first Navy warplane to exceed 400 mph in level flight. Its first operations were with the US Marines 'Cactus Air Force' defending Guadalcanal from combined Japanese air, ground and sea assaults and from the outset the F4U proved itself a very formidable fighter indeed. It flew from US Navy and Royal Navy carriers and fought in every major Pacific battle from 1943 until the end of the war. Throughout its wartime service the F4U flew 64,051 sorties, destroying 2140 Japanese aircraft, losing only 189 of its number. One of the most unusual kills of the war was attributed to a Corsair when Lieutenant Robert Klingman, during the battle for Okinawa, chased a Japanese Nick to 38,000 feet and brought it down by sawing off its rudder and elevators with his propeller after his guns had frozen! F4U production finally ceased in 1952 after almost 12,571 had been built. During the Korean Conflict a Corsair was credited with downing a MiG-15 jet. The F4U was retired from French naval service in 1965, having been designed in 1938.

Consolidated PBY Catalina

Manufacturer: Consolidated Aircraft Corporation, San Diego, California; Canadian Vickers Limited, Montreal; Boeing Aircraft of Canada, Limited, Vancouver; and Naval Aircraft Factory, Philadelphia, Pennsylvania.
Type: patrol bomber flying-boat and amphibian.
Crew: seven to nine.
Specification: PBY-5A.
Power Plant: two 1200 hp R-1830-92.
Dimensions: span, 104 ft; length, 63ft 10 in; height, 20 ft 2 in; wing area, 1400 sq ft.
Weights: empty, 20,910 lb; gross, 35,420 lb.
Performance: maximum speed, 175 mph at 7000 ft; cruising speed, 113 mph; climb, 620 ft per min; service ceiling, 13,000 ft; range, 2350 miles.
Armament: three 0.3 in and two 0.5 in guns and four 1000 lb bombs.

The PBY Catalina was first ordered by the US Navy on 28 October 1933. Its prototype XP3Y-1 was first flown on 28 March 1935. The most successful flying-boat to see service with the US Forces in World War II and had the biggest total production of flying boats of all time.

Over 2000 Cats were built, the US Navy receiving 1196, and were used in all theaters of war by US, RAF and Soviet Air Forces. The Cat had an endurance of 24 hours and a range of over 2000 miles. In May 1941 a Catalina located and shadowed the *Bismarck* to deny it free passage to France.

Top: **A PBY Catalina of the Royal Norwegian Air Force.**
Above: **A PBY-Catalina at Watton-Griston, England.**

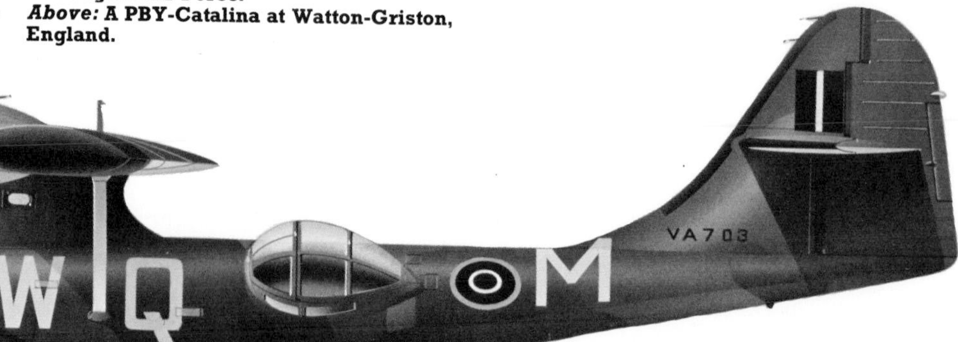

Above: **Consolidated Catalina.**

***Above:* A Consolidated PB2Y Coronado with turrets deleted for transportation role.**

Consolidated PB2Y Coronado

Manufacturer: Consolidated Aircraft Corporation, San Diego, California.
Type: patrol bomber flying-boat.
Crew: ten.
Specification: PB2Y-3.
Power Plant: four 1200 hp R-1830-88.
Dimensions: span, 115 ft; length, 79 ft 3 in; height, 27 ft 6 in; wing area, 1780 sq ft.
Weights: empty, 40,935 lb; gross, 68,000 lb.
Performance: maximum speed, 213 mph at 20,000 ft; cruising speed, 141 mph at 1500 ft; initial climb, 440 ft per min; service ceiling, 20,100 ft; range, 1490 miles.
Armament: eight 0.5 in guns; up to four 1000 lb bombs externally and eight 1000 lb bombs internally.

A prototype four-engine flying boat design was ordered in July 1936 and was first flown on 17 December 1937.

Curtiss SO3C Seamew

Manufacturer: Curtiss-Wright Corporation, Curtiss Airplane Division, Buffalo, New York.
Type: scouting and observation seaplane (or landplane).
Crew: two (pilot and observer in tandem).
Specification: SO3C-2C.
Power Plant: one 600 hp V-770-8.
Dimensions: span, 38 ft; length, 35 ft 8 in; height, 14 ft 2 in; wing area, 293 sq ft.
Weights: empty, 4800 lb; gross, 7000 lb.
Performance: maximum speed, 172 mph at 8100 ft; cruising speed, 125 mph; initial climb, 720 ft per min; service ceiling, 15,800 ft; range, 1150 miles.
Armament: one 0.3 in gun, and one 0.5 in gun; two 100 lb bombs or 325 lb depth-charges under wings; 100 lb or 500 lb bomb, or 325 lb weapon under fuselage.

The prototype was tested on its first flight on 6 October 1939. The SO3C Seamew was built to replace the Curtiss SOC Seagull biplanes and thus was given the name Seagull. However, the British name, Seamew, was adopted after it went into service.

Grumman JF Duck

Manufacturer: Grumman Aircraft Engineering Corporation, Bethpage, Long Island, New York; and Columbia Aircraft Corporation, Valley Stream, Long Island, New York.
Type: utility amphibian.
Crew: two to three (pilot, observer and, optional, radio operator).
Specification: J2F-5.
Power Plant: one 850 hp R-1820-50.
Dimensions: span, 39 ft; length, 34 ft; height, 15 ft 1 in; wing area, 409 sq ft.
Weights: empty, 4300 lb; gross, 6711 lb.
Performance: maximum speed, 188 mph; cruising speed, 150 mph; initial climb, 1500 ft per min; service ceiling, 27,000 ft; range, 780 miles.
Armament: none.

Grumman sought to improve on the design of amphibious floats and replace the series of Loening amphibians serving with the US Navy. The Duck featured an innovation – that of retractable main wheels into the sides of the central float.

***Below:* J2F Ducks in formation.**

It was first flown as the XJF-1 on 4 May 1933 and deliveries of the completed aircraft began late in 1934. The J2F-1 appeared in 1937 and served throughout World War II.

On 20 December 1934, JF-2 No. 0266, powered by an R-1820 Wright Cyclone and piloted by Lieutenant Cmdr E F Stone of the US Coast Guard, set a new unofficial world's speed record for its class of 191.796 mph.

Grumman JRF Goose

Manufacturer: Grumman Aircraft Engineering Corporation, Bethpage, Long Island, New York.
Type: utility transport amphibian.
Crew: two to three and four to seven passengers.
Specification: JRF-5.
Power Plant: two 450 hp R-985-AN-6.
Dimensions: span, 49 ft; length, 38 ft 6 in; height, 16 ft 2 in; wing area, 375 sq ft.
Weights: empty, 5425 lb; gross, 8000 lb.
Performance: maximum speed, 201 mph at 5000 ft; cruising speed, 191 mph at 5000 ft; initial climb, 1100 ft per min; service ceiling, 21,300 ft; maximum range, 640 miles.
Armament: none.

The Goose was the first in a long line of amphibious flying boats produced by Grumman, which appeared in 1937 and the following year was ordered by the US Navy. The JRF-1 was delivered late in 1939 and the JRF-5 in 1941.

US Navy and Marine Corps used the Goose for transport, target towing and aerial photography work. Seen here is a JRF-5.

Martin PBM Mariner.

Martin PBM Mariner

Manufacturer: Glenn L. Martin Company, Baltimore, Maryland.
Type: patrol flying boat.
Crew: nine.
Specification: PBM-3C.
Power Plant: two 1700 hp R-2600-12.
Dimensions: span, 118 ft; length, 80 ft; height, 27 ft 6 in; wing area, 1408 sq ft.
Weights: empty, 32,378 lb; gross, 58,000 lb.
Performance: maximum speed, 198 mph at 13,000 ft; initial climb, 410 ft per min; service ceiling, 16,900 ft; normal range, 2137 miles.
Armament: two flexible 0.5 in guns each in nose and dorsal turrets, single 0.50 in guns at waist and tail positions; up to 2000 lb bombs or depth charges.

The Mariner was designed in 1937 to succeed the Martin P2M and P3M series.

Its test flight occurred on 18 February 1939 and the PBM-1 entered service with the US Navy during 1941. The final version, PBM-5A amphibian ceased production in April 1949.

Right: **This Martin PBM-3 in silver and yellow finish was used for training.**
Below: **A PBM-5A Mariner amphibian.**

Curtiss C-46 Commando

Manufacturers: The Curtiss-Wright Corporation, Airplane Division, Buffalo, St. Louis and Louisville; Higgins Aircraft Incorporated, New Orleans.
Type: troop and freight transport.
Crew: four and provision for 50 troops or 33 stretchers with four attendants or 10,000 lb cargo.
Specification: C-46A.
Power Plant: two 2000 hp R-2800-51.
Dimensions: span, 108 ft 1 in; length, 76 ft 4 in; height, 21 ft 9 in; wing area, 1360 sq ft.
Weights: empty, 32,400 lb; gross, 56,000 lb.
Performance: maximum speed, 269 mph at 15,000 ft; cruising speed, 183 mph; initial climb, 1300 ft per min; service ceiling, 27,600 ft; range, 1200 miles.
Armament: none; provision for small arms fire through windows.

The design originated in 1937 as a 36-seat commercial transport but by the end of World War II the C-46 had been widely used in the Pacific Theater as a troop and freight transporter. It was the largest and heaviest twin-engined transport aircraft to see operational service with the USAAF. It was successfully introduced into ATC and TCC in 1942 providing much needed airlift capability. The C-46A was fitted with a large cargo loading door in the rear fuselage, a cargo floor and folding seats along the cabin walls for 40 fully equipped troops. Altogether, 1491 C-46s were built. The C-46 operated primarily in the Pacific because of its greater load-carrying ability and better performance at high altitude over the C-47. Its most famous theater of operations was the supply of war material to China from India over the 'Hump.' The C-46D had a revised nose and double loading doors. Further variants similar in appearance to the 'D' followed and many remained in service after the end of the war. They were used for a time on glider towing techniques. During the Korean War C-46s served with Combat Cargo Command. The C-46E became obsolete in 1953 but the A, D and F variants continued in service with Air Force Reserve squadrons until 1960.

Douglas C-32 Series

Manufacturer: Douglas Aircraft Company Incorporated, Santa Monica, California.
Type: cargo and personnel transport.
Crew: two and accommodation for 16.
Specification: C-39.
Power Plant: two 975 hp R-1820-55.
Dimensions: span, 85 ft; length, 61 ft 6 in; height, 18 ft 8 in; wing area, 939 sq ft.
Weights: empty, 14,729 lb; gross, 21,000 lb.
Performance: maximum speed, 210 mph at 5000 ft; cruising speed, 155 mph; initial climb, 4 min to 5000 ft; service ceiling, 20,600 ft; endurance, 5–9 hours at cruise.
Armament: none.

The Douglas C-32s design was derived from the Douglas DC-2 commercial transport. The first prototype DC-2 was first flown in April 1934. The C-33 entered service in 1936 and the C-39 in 1939.

Douglas C-47 Skytrain, R4D Skytrain, Skytrooper

Manufacturer: Douglas Aircraft Company, Long Beach, California and Tulsa, Oklahoma; built under license in Japan and the USSR (R4D-5, 8) Santa Monica, California.
Type: (C-47, R4D-5, R4D-8) Utility transport and (C-47) glider tug; (AC-47) air to ground weapon platform.
Crew: (C-47) two with capacity for 27 troops or 18–24 stretchers or 10,000 lb of cargo; (R4D-5) three and up to 27 passengers or 10,000 lb of cargo; (R4D-8) three and up to 36 troops, 30 passengers or 27 stretchers.
Power Plant: two 1200 hp R-1830-90D.
Dimensions: span, 95 ft; length, 64 ft 5.5 in; height, 16 ft 11 in; wing area, 987 sq ft.
Weights: empty, about 16,970 lb; loaded, about 25,200 lb; overload limit 33,000 lb.
Performance: max speed, 230 mph; initial climb, 1200 ft per min; service ceiling 23,000 ft; max range, 2125 miles.
Armament: (AC-47) usually three 7.62 mm miniguns; many other types of armament in other versions, but none usually fitted.

The Douglas C-47 was and is the greatest transport of all time. It is known affectionately by crews as the 'Gooney Bird.'

This is the most widely-known and probably the most widely-used aircraft in the history of the US Air Forces. It served in every combat theater in World War II and was produced in greater numbers than any other Army transport. Affectionately called, 'Gooney Bird' by its crew and passengers alike, the C-47 was one of four weapons nominated by General Eisenhower instrumental in helping win World War II. Developed from the DC-3 the C-47 had a stronger cabin floor, strengthened rear fuselage with large loading doors, more powerful engines and provision for carrying large cargo and supply units externally. It was first delivered in October 1938 but the first orders for large numbers were placed in 1940 when most of the design work for the military version had been completed. The airline interior was replaced with utility bucket-type seating along the cabin walls which led to those who flew in it nicknaming the C-47, 'old bucket seats.' By 1941 the C-47 was deployed far and wide with the Army Air Force. It was among the first aircraft delivered to Britain via the north Atlantic in 1942 and that same year it began operating in the CBI Theater over the 'Hump.' In the summer of 1942 the C-47 became the primary equipment of ATC. It also joined TCC to become famous as a paratroop transport and was used in this role during the Sicily invasion in July 1943. C-47s were used far and wide after this dropping paratroops during the invasion of Burma and towing gliders to targets on D-Day, Arnhem and on other operations. In just over two days C-47s carried

The Douglas C-47 is still in service with small companies.

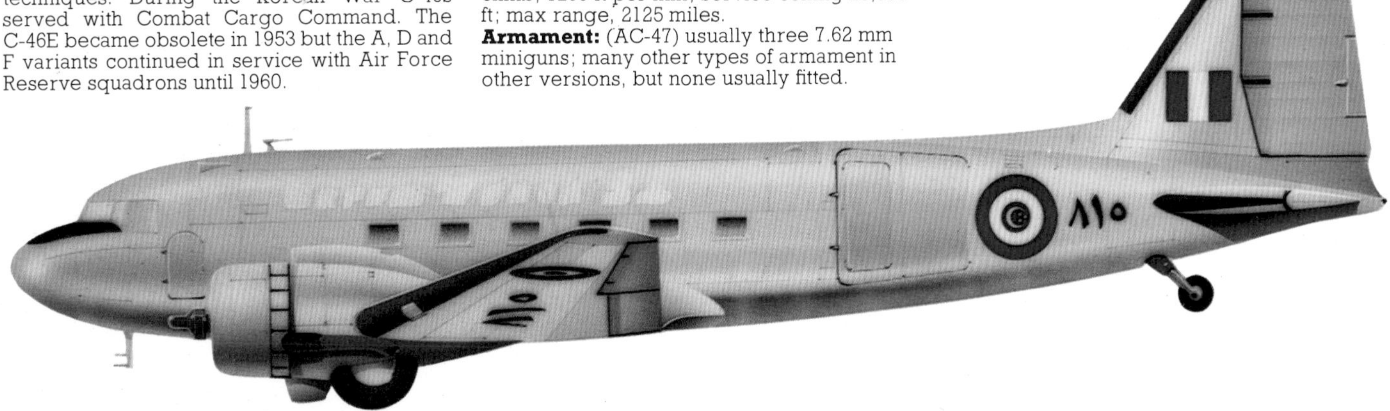

Above: **An R4D-8 showing the modified tail unit after conversion by the US Navy from R4D configuration.**
Left: **A C-47 Glider, one of the least-known versions of the Douglas transport.**

more than 60,000 paratroops and their equipment into action in Normandy. Those supplied to Britain were named Dakotas, but known as 'Daks' in RAF parlance and many remained in the UK at the war's end. Many still serve with air forces and small airlines even today.

Douglas R5D Skymaster

Manufacturer: Douglas Aircraft Company, Santa Monica, California.
Type: personnel, supply and staff transport.
Crew: four and carry up to 30 passengers.
Specification: R5D-1.
Power Plant: four 1350 hp R-2000-7.
Dimensions: span, 117 ft 6 in; length, 93 ft 11 in; height, 27 ft 6.25 in; wing area, 1462 sq ft.
Weights: empty, 37,040 lb; gross, 65,000 lb.
Performance: maximum speed, 281 mph at 15,200 ft; cruising speed, 210 mph; initial climb, 1010 ft per min; service ceiling, 22,700 ft; range, 2290 miles.
Armament: none.

The Skymaster was developed from the Douglas DC-4 transport for US Navy/Marine service in World War II.

It was operated primarily by the Naval Air Transport Service, 1941–48. The last Navy Skymaster (C-54Q) retired in 1974.

Left: **The C-47 floatplane version.**
Below: **A C-54P of the US Naval Test Pilot School.**

Above and right: **C-54s were widely used in the Korean War, operating the Pacific Airlift.**

Douglas C-54 Skymaster

Manufacturer: Douglas Aircraft Company, Long Beach, California.
Type: troop and cargo transport.
Crew: six and accommodation for 50 troops.
Specification: C-54A.
Power Plant: four 1290 hp R-2000-7.
Dimensions: span, 117 ft 6 in; length, 93 ft 10 in; height, 27 ft 6 in; wing area, 1460 sq ft.
Weights: empty, 37,000 lb; gross, 62,000 lb.
Performance: maximum speed, 275 mph; climb, 14.8 min to 10,000 ft; service ceiling, 22,000 ft; range, 3900 miles.
Armament: none.

On the outbreak of war there was no four-engined transport immediately available for service use. In early 1942 the USAAF took over the DC-4A production line changing the designation to C-54. The DC-4E had first flown on 21 June 1938.

The C-54 had a total production of 1122.

Below: **The Model 18 Lodestar first entered service in 1940 and was used for transport, hospital and glider towing.**

Lockheed C-56 Lodestar

Manufacturer: Lockheed Aircraft Corporation, Burbank, California.
Type: personnel, troop and freight transport.
Crew: two and accommodation for 17.
Specification: C-56.
Power Plant: two 1200 hp R-1820-71.
Dimensions: span, 65 ft 6 in; length, 49 ft 10 in; height, 11 ft 1 in; wing area, 550 sq ft.
Weights: empty, 11,650 lb; gross, 17,500 lb.
Performance: maximum speed, 253 mph; climb, 7.1 min to 10,000 ft; service ceiling, 23,300 ft; range, 1600 miles.
Armament: none.

The Lodestar was designed as a 17 passenger development of the Lockheed Model 14. USAAF interest in May 1941 led to a contract for four C-56s and C-57s.

Sikorsky R-4

Manufacturer: Sikorsky Aircraft Division, United Aircraft Corporation, Bridgeport, Connecticut.
Type: general purpose helicopter.
Crew: two.
Specification: YR-4B.
Power Plant: one 180 hp R-550-1.
Dimensions: rotor diameter, 38 ft; length, 48 ft 1 in; height, 12 ft 5 in; disc area, 1134 sq ft.
Weights: empty, 2020 lb; gross, 2535 lb.
Performance: maximum speed, 75 mph; climb, 45 min to 8000 ft; service ceiling, 8000 ft; range, 130 miles.
Armament: none.

In 1941 a development contract for an experimental helicopter, designated XR-4, was awarded to the Vought-Sikorsky Division of United Aircraft, following Igor Sikorsky's successful demonstration of helicopter flights starting in 1939. The XR-4 first flew on 13 January 1942.

The Sikorsky R-4 was the first non-experimental helicopter produced for the US armed forces.

Sikorsky R-5

Manufacturer: Sikorsky Aircraft Division of United Aircraft Corporation, Bridgeport, Connecticut.
Type: rescue and general purpose helicopter.
Crew: two in tandem; two external stretcher carriers.
Specification: R-5B.
Power Plant: one 450 hp R-985-AN-5.
Dimensions: rotor diameter, 48 ft; length, 57 ft 1 in; height, 13 ft; disc area, 1810 sq ft.
Weights: empty, 3780 lb; gross, 4825 lb.
Performance: maximum speed, 106 mph; climb, 15 min to 10,000 ft; service ceiling, 14,400 ft; range, 360 miles.
Armament: none.

This helicopter was a further development of the R-4 but larger and capable of performing military observation duties.

The prototype first flew on 18 August 1943 and it was the first helicopter to enter service with the Air Rescue Service.

A Beech YC-43, of London's US Embassy.

Beech C-43 Traveler

Manufacturer: Beech Aircraft Corporation, Wichita, Kansas.
Type: utility transport and communications.
Crew: pilot, three passengers.
Specification: UC-43.
Power Plant: one 450 hp R-985-AN-1.
Dimensions: span, 32 ft; length, 26 ft 2 in; height, 10 ft 3 in; wing area, 296 sq ft.
Weights: empty, 3085 lb; gross, 4700 lb.
Performance: maximum speed, 198 mph; initial climb, 1500 ft per min; service ceiling, 20,000 ft; range, 500 miles.
Armament: none.

The C-43 Traveler was the Beech Corporation's first aircraft after its foundation in 1932. Much used by private and commercial owners before the Army Air Corps took an interest in 1939 when it needed a small communications aircraft. Shortly after the US entry into World War II the Beech 17, as it was known, was comandeered for military use. An earlier YC-43 served at the US Air Attache in London and in 1944 30 were supplied to Britain under Lend-Lease.

Beech C-45, AT-7, AT-11, F-2

Manufacturer: Beech Aircraft Corporation, Wichita, Kansas.
Type: C-45, light transport and communications; AT-7/AT-11, navigation and bombardier trainer; F-2, photographic reconnaissance.
Crew: six seats.
Specification: C-45.
Power Plant: one 450 hp R-985-AN-1, -3.
Dimensions: span, 47 ft 8 in; length, 34 ft 3 in; height, 9 ft 8 in; wing area, 349 sq ft.
Weights: empty, 5890 lb; gross, 7850 lb.
Performance: maximum speed, 215 mph; Time to 10,000 ft, 8.6 min; service ceiling, 20,000 ft; range, 700 miles.
Armament: none.
Specification: AT-7.
Power Plant: one 450 hp R-985-AN-1, -3.
Dimensions: span, 47 ft 8 in; length, 34 ft 3 in; height, 10 ft; wing area, 349 sq ft.
Weights: empty, 5935 lb; gross, 7850 lb.
Performance: maximum speed, 224 mph; Time to 10,000 ft, 9.6 min; service ceiling, 18,400 ft; range, 585 miles.
Armament: none.
Specification: AT-11.
Power Plant: one 450 hp R-985-AN-1, -3.
Dimensions: span, 47 ft 8 in; length, 34 ft 2 in; height, 9 ft 8 in; wing area, 349 sq ft.
Weights: empty, 6175 lb; gross, 8727 lb.
Performance: maximum speed, 215 mph; Time to 10,000 ft, 10.1 min; service ceiling, 20,000 ft; range, 850 miles.
Armament: two 0.30 in guns, ten 100 lb bombs.
Specification: F-2.
Power Plant: one 450 hp R-985-19.
Dimensions: span, 47 ft 8 in; length, 34 ft 3 in; height, 9 ft 4 in; wing area, 349 sq ft.
Weights: empty, 5208 lb; gross, 7200 lb.
Performance: maximum speed, 225 mph; Time to 10,000 ft, 6.9 min; service ceiling, 26,200 ft; range, 930 miles.
Armament: none.

Contracts were awarded to Beech in 1940 for variants of the Model B-18S commercial light transport. More than 4000 examples were built in the ensuing five years. In the later stages of World War II UC-45Fs were used as 'directors' for radio-controlled targets, under the designation, CQ-3.

Left: **Beech AT-7 multi-engine transition and navigation trainer of the United States Army Air Corps.**
Right: **The RC-45 Beech was used for extensive transportation duties by the USAF in Korea, 1950–52.**

Above: **The Beech C-45 was used by the Italian AF.**

Above: **A Cessna AT-8 in 1940.**

Above: **The Beech AT-11 of the US Army Air Corps.**

Bell Airacomet.

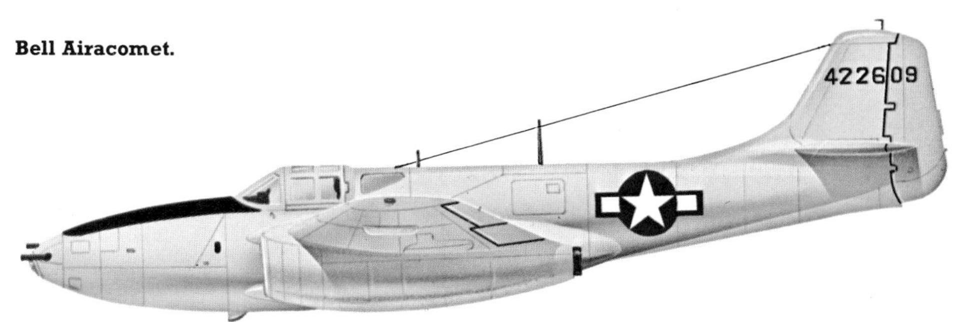

Bell P-59 Airacomet

Manufacturer: Bell Aircraft Corporation, Buffalo, New York.
Type: jet fighter familiarization trainer.
crew: pilot only.
Specification: P-59B.
Power Plant: two 2000 lb J-31-GE-5 turbojets.
Dimensions: span, 45 ft 6 in; length, 38 ft 10 in; height, 12 ft 4 in; wing area, 385 sq ft.
Weights: empty, 8165 lb; gross, 13,700 lb.
Performance: maximum speed, 413 mph at 30,000 ft; cruising speed, 375 mph; initial climb, 3.2 min to 10,000 ft; service ceiling, 46,200 ft; range, 525 miles.
Armament: one 37 mm and three 0.50 in guns in nose.

On 5 September 1941 USAAF requested Bell Aircraft Corporation to undertake development of a jet fighter design to take advantage of early British design work on gas turbine power plants. To preserve secrecy the Airacomet project was designated XP-59A. Bell were, at that time, working on the XP-59, a twin boom, radial engine design for the USAAF. The XP-59 was later cancelled. XP-59A construction commenced in the spring of 1942 as a mid-wing monoplane with a slender fuselage incorporating two turbojets and main undercarriage units further out on the wings. It initially flew on 10 October and three XP-59A Airacomets and a service trials batch of thirteen YP-59A Airacomets were ordered.

Production models of the first Airacomets were primarily as trainers despite being of single seat design. The first 20 production aircraft were designated P-59A and only 30 P-59Bs had been delivered when the project was cancelled at the end of October 1943. Successful development of the P-80 had made further work on the P-59 unnecessary. Some were allocated to the 4th Air Force for trials and test work. A few were eventually modified as drone directors with an open-front cockpit in front of the pilot.

Boeing Kaydet Series

Manufacturer: Stearman Aircraft Division, Boeing Company, Wichita, Kansas.
Type: primary trainer.
Crew: student and instructor in tandem.
Specification: N2S-5.
Power Plant: one 220 hp R-680-17.
Dimensions: span, 32 ft 2 in; length, 25 ft 0.25 in; height, 9 ft 2 in; wing area, 297 sq ft.
Weights: Empty, 1936 lb; gross, 2717 lb.
Performance: maximum speed, 124 mph at sea level; cruising speed, 106 mph at sea level; initial climb, 840 ft per min; service ceiling, 11,200 ft; range, 505 miles.

When the Stearman Aircraft Company, a Boeing subsidiary dating from 1934 became the Wichita Division of Boeing in 1939, the famous series of primary trainers, collectively called 'Kaydet' during World War II, had been in production since 1934. The first, the Model 70, was developed from the original Stearman C Models of 1926–1930. In 1934 the US Navy bought 61 Model 73s as NS-1 (Trainer, Stearman) with Wright J-5 engines. The Army bought 26 Lycoming-powered Model 75s as PT-13 in 1937. All subsequent trainer versions for the US Navy and Army were built as Model 75s.

FD972
U.S.NAVY
125453

***Left:* Boeing-Stearman A-73N3 trainers fly in formation with the markings of Peru, Britain, China, US Navy and the USAAF.**

Small numbers of a modified version fitted with Pratt and Whitney 'Wasp Jr' engines and armament were sold to several Latin American air forces just before the outbreak of World War II as Model 76s. Counting equivalant spares, 10,346 Model 70–76 Kaydets were built from 1933 to 1945.

At the end of the war approximately 4000 Kaydets were converted to crop dusting/spraying planes, most of them with the 450 hp Pratt & Whitney 'Wasp Jr' engines for better performance at high gross weights. More than twenty years later, nearly 1600 Model 75s were still in service with agricultural aircraft fleets.

Cessna AT-8, AT-17, UC-78 Bobcat

Manufacturer: Cessna Aircraft Company, Wichita, Kansas.
Type: light personnel transport.
Crew: pilot and four passengers.
Specification: UC-78.
Power Plant: two 245 hp R-755-9.
Dimensions: span, 41 ft 11 in; length, 32 ft 9 in; height, 9 ft 11 in; wing area, 295 sq ft.
Weights: empty, 3500 lb; gross, 5700 lb.
Performance: maximum speed, 195 mph at sea level; cruising speed, 175 mph at sea level; initial climb, 1325 ft per min; service ceiling, 22,000 ft; range, 750 miles.
Armament: none.

The Bobcat was first ordered by the US Army in 1940 for evaluation as advanced transition trainers for multi-engined pilot training but was not developed further.

Fairchild AT-13, AT-14, AT-21 Gunner

Manufacturer: The Fairchild Engine & Airplane Corporation, Hagerstown, Maryland Burlington, North Carolina; McDonnell Aircraft Corporation, St. Louis, Missouri; Bellanca Aircraft Corporation, New Castle, Delaware.
Type: gunnery trainer.
Crew: pilot, co-pilot/instructor and three student gunners.
Specification: AT-21.
Power Plant: two 520 hp V-770-11 piston vee in-line.
Dimensions: span, 52 ft 8 in; length, 37 ft; height, 13 ft 1 in; wing area, 375 sq ft.
Weights: empty, 8700 lb; gross, 12,500 lb.
Performance: cruising speed, 195 mph at 12,000 ft; initial climb, 10.3 min to 10,000 ft; service ceiling, 22,400 ft; range, 870 miles at cruise speed.
Armament: three 0.30 in machine guns.

The Gunner was designed to meet the requirement for air-to-air gunnery training.

The first prototype, XAT-13, was primarily designed as a bomber crew trainer. The XAT-14A became a bombardier trainer after the nose gun and turret were removed. Gunnery trainers of same basic type went into production in 1942. AT-21s were eventually replaced by training versions of operational models and relegated to target-tug duties.

North American 0-47

Manufacturer: North American Aviation, Inglewood, California.
Type: observation.
Crew: pilot and observer in tandem.
Specification: 0-47A.
Power Plant: one 975 hp R-1820-49.
Dimensions: span, 46 ft 4 in; length, 33 ft 7 in; height, 12 ft 2 in; wing area, 350 sq ft.
Weights: empty, 5980 lb; gross, 7636 lb.
Performance: maximum speed, 221 mph at 4000 ft; operational speed, 200 mph; climb, 6.8 min to 10,000 ft; service ceiling, 23,200 ft; endurance, 2.1 hr.
Armament: one fixed 0.3 in Browning (200 rounds) in wing; one flexible 0.3 in Browning (600 rounds) in rear cockpit.

The design for the North American 0-47 was instigated by General Aviation in 1934. It served as a standard observation aircraft from 1937 until Pearl Harbor. During World War II it served as a trainer and in utility duties.

***Right:* A row of six Cessna AT-17 trainers. *Below:* A Cessna UC-78 Bobcat light personnel transport.**

North American Texan.

North American AT-6 Series (Texan)

Manufacturer: North American Aviation Incorporated, Inglewood, California and Dallas, Texas.
Type: basic combat trainer (BC-1); advanced trainer (AT-6A).
Crew: pupil and instructor in tandem enclosed cockpit.
Specification: BC-1.
Power Plant: one 600 hp R-1340-47.
Dimensions: span, 43 ft; length, 27 ft 9 in; height, 14 ft; wing area, 225 sq ft.
Weights: empty, 4050 lb; gross, 5200 lb.
Performance: maximum speed, 227 mph; climb, 7.5 min to 10,000 ft; service ceiling, 24,100 ft; range, 665 miles.
Armament: one fixed forward firing and one flexible rear-mounted 0.30 in machine gun.
Specification: AT-6A.
Dimensions: span, 42 ft; length, 29 ft; height, 11 ft 9 in; wing area, 254 sq ft.
Weights: empty, 3900 lb; gross, 5155 lb.
Performance: maximum speed, 210 mph; climb, 7.4 min to 10,000 ft; service ceiling, 24,200 ft; range, 629 miles.

The North American company won the March 1937 Air Corps design competition to produce a new basic combat trainer and developed the AT-6 from their original NA-16 design of 1935. In 1940 the designation changed from BC-1A to AT-6A.

Well in excess of 2000 AT-6s remained in service with the USAAF after World War II. In 1941 a second production line at Dallas, Texas, was established to cope with demand not only from the Army Air Corps but also from abroad, including the RAF, where it served as the famous Harvard. T6Fs and later LT-6Gs flew in Korea on 'Mosquito' spotter missions close to enemy lines with trained Army observers in the second seat.

Piper L-18s of the Italian Co-Belligerent AF, *circa* 1945.

Piper L-4, L-18, L-21 Grasshopper

Manufacturer: Piper Aircraft Corporation, Lock Haven, Pennsylvania.
Type: liaison.
Crew: two (pilot and observer in tandem).
Specification: L-4.
Power Plant: 65 hp O-170-3.
Dimensions: span, 35 ft 3 in; length, 22 ft; height, 6 ft 8 in; wing area, 179 sq ft.
Weights: empty, 730 lb; gross, 1220 lb.
Performance: maximum speed, 85 mph; climb, 14 min to 5000 ft; service ceiling, 9300 ft; range, 190 miles.
Armament: none.
Specification: L-18A.
Power Plant: 90 hp C90-8F.
Dimensions: span, 35 ft 3 in; length, 22 ft 4.5 in; height, 6 ft 7 in; wing area, 179 sq ft.
Weights: empty, 800 lb; gross, 1500 lb.
Performance: maximum speed, 110 mph; cruising speed, 100 mph; climb, 624 ft per min; service ceiling, 13,500 ft.
Armament: none.
Specification: L-21A.
Power Plant: 125 hp O-290-D.
Dimensions: span, 35 ft 3 in; length, 22 ft 7 in; height, 6 ft 6 in; wing area, 179 sq ft.
Weights: empty, 950 lb; gross, 1580 lb.
Performance: maximum speed, 123 mph; cruising speed, 115 mph; climb, 1000 ft per min; service ceiling, 21,650 ft; range, 770 miles.
Armament: none.

The Grasshopper was derived from the commercial Piper Cub and selected by the US Army in 1941 for evaluation for artillery spotting, gun-laying and front line liaison roles.

Some 900 Grasshoppers were ordered by the Army in mid-1942 and were delivered as L-4Bs. Combat initiation, 1943, from the deck of an aircraft carrier during the 'Torch' operation in North Africa.

It was produced in greater numbers than any other aircraft of its type and operated in every campaign and on every front during World War II.

L-5 'Puddle jumpers' were used in the Pacific and in Burma in World War II.

Stinson L-5 Sentinel

Manufacturer: Stinson Aircraft Division of Consolidated Vultee Aircraft Corporation, Wayne, Michigan.
Type: light liaison.
Crew: two (pilot and observer in tandem in enclosed cabin).
Specification: L-5.
Power Plant: one 185 hp O-435-1 piston flat-four.
Dimensions: span, 34 ft; length, 24 ft 1 in; height, 7 ft 11 in; wing area, 155 sq ft.
Weights: empty, 1550 lb; gross, 2020 lb.
Performance: maximum speed, 130 mph; climb, 6.4 min to 5000 ft; service ceiling, 15,800 ft; range, 420 miles.
Armament: none.

Light aircraft in service with the US Army towards the end of 1941 were so successful that contracts were negotiated for a number of different types. The Sentinel was introduced as a derivative of the Stinson 105 Voyager. It was procured by the US Army in 1942 and was the second most-used Army liaison aircraft. It served as a most useful ambulance aircraft, particularly in the Pacific, during World War II and in the Korean conflict.

Vought OS2U Kingfisher

Manufacturer: Vought-Sikorsky Division, United Aircraft Corporation, and Naval Aircraft Factory, Philadelphia, Pennsylvania.
Type: observation-scout.
Crew: two (pilot and observer/gunner).
Specification: OS2U-3.
Power Plant: one 450 hp R-985-AN-2 or -8.
Dimensions: span, 35 ft 11 in; length, 33 ft 10 in; height, 15 ft 1 in; wing area, 262 sq ft.
Weights: empty, 4123 lb; gross, 6000 lb.
Performance: maximum speed, 164 mph at 5500 ft; cruising speed, 119 mph at 5000 ft; climb to 5000 ft in 12.1 min; service ceiling, 13,000 ft; range, 805 miles.
Armament: two 0.3 in machine guns.

The prototype for this famous aircraft, the XOS2U-1, was first flown on 1 March 1938. Catapulted from battleships, cruisers and destroyers, the Kingfisher performed many pilot rescues in the Pacific in World War II. The Kingfisher was built in three versions, the -1, -2 and -3. It was the first aircraft construction to employ spot welding of primary structure and the first to use the non-buckling fuselage structure. It was Vought's first production aircraft with full-span flaps and spoiler lateral control. Vought Corporation (then Chance Vought Aircraft) built 1519 Kingfishers. The Naval Aircraft Factory built another 300 as OS2N-1s.

***Above:* A CG-4A Haig comes in to land at Warton, England.**
Left:* Prewar formation of Kingfisher OS2U-1 scouts from the USS *Mississippi.

Waco CG-4, CG-15 Hadrian

Manufacturer: Waco Aircraft Company, Troy, Ohio.
Type: cargo and troop glider; accommodation for 15 troops (including two serving as pilots).
Specification: CG-4A.
Power Plant: none.
Dimensions: span, 83 ft 8 in; length, 48 ft 4 in; height, 12 ft 7 in; wing area, 852 sq ft.
Performance: maximum speed, 120 mph; stalling speed, 44 mph.
Armament: none.

Army development of troop-carrying gliders began in 1941. Trials of the XCG-4 were made in 1942 and led to large-scale production which eventually involved 16 different assembly lines delivering 12,393 models.

The Waco Hadrian entered operation in the Allied invasion of Sicily in July 1943 and also participated in March 1944 in Wingate's Second Chindit operation in Burma with great success. Thereafter, Wacos participated in every major airborne operation, including the D-Day operation of 6 June 1944, the Anvil project landings in southern France in August 1944, Market Garden the Arnhem landing, and the crossing of the Rhine. Wacos continued in service until 1955 when declared obsolete.

***Left:* Fantail and stern of USS *Alabama* shows a OS2U Kingfisher being launched from a catapult.**

***Above:* Vought Kingfisher.**

Part Two

1946-

-1960

The Douglas D-558-11S research aircraft. Four B-29s were pressed into service by the US Navy in April 1947 for use as test-beds in anti-submarine projects and as mother ships for the Douglas D-558-II research aircraft (shown here).

The Convair F-102 has a pointed tail-fin and engine inlets forward of the cockpit.

General Dynamics F-102 Delta Dagger

Manufacturer: Convair Division of General Dynamics Corporation, San Diego, California.
Type: single-seat all-weather interceptor; TF, trainer; QF, manned remotely piloted vehicle; PQM, drone target.
Crew: normally pilot only.
Specification: F-102A.
Power Plant: one 17,200 lb J57-23.
Dimensions: span, 38 ft 1.5 in; length, 68 ft 5 in; height, 21 ft 2.5 in.
Weights: empty, 19,050 lb; gross, 31,500 lb.
Performance: maximum speed, 825 mph (Mach 1.25); initial climb, 13,000 ft per min; service ceiling, 54,000 ft; range, 1350 miles.
Armament: air-to-air guided missiles carried internally; typical full load three Hughes A1M-4E Falcon beam-riders with semi-active homing and three A1M-4F with infra-red homing.

Development of the F-102 dates back to 1945 when Air Force planners saw the need for bombers that could attack at supersonic speeds to launch mass destruction bombs from the stratosphere. General Dynamics/Convair, (then Consolidated Vultee) was designated to carry out exploratory design studies. The result was the world's first delta-wing aircraft, the XF-92A, which made its first flight at Muroc (now Edwards) AFB, California on 18 September 1948. In 1951 the USAF asked American airframe manufacturers to submit designs for a faster than sound interceptor. General Dynamics/Convair's delta-wing design was the most radical among proposals submitted by the companies but was supported by data of superior performance provided by the XF-92A and the F-102 program was launched. The flight of the prototype, YF-102, took place on 24 October 1953. The F-102 entered service in 1956 and was the first USAF operational fighter to be armed with guided missiles and unguided rockets. Some 875 single-seat F-102s were built between 1953 and 1958. The production F-102As were updated to include external drop-tanks and flight refuelling equipment. The USAF also acquired 63 side-by-side two-seat TF-102As for training, and two versions were converted to target drones, the manned QF-102A and the unmanned PQM-102A for the F-15A program.

Left: **F-106 Delta Darts of Air Defense Command.**
Bottom center: **F-106s pass Mt Rushmore.**

General Dynamics F-106 Delta Dart

Manufacturer: Convair Division of General Dynamics Corporation, San Diego, California.
Type: F-106A, all-weather interceptor; F-106B, operational trainer.
Crew: F-106A, pilot only; F-106B, pilot and instructor or radar operator.
Specification: F-106A.
Power Plant: one 24,500 lb J75-17.
Dimensions: span, 38 ft 3.5 in; length, 70 ft 8.75 in; height, 20 ft 3.25 in.
Weights: empty, 23,646 lb; gross, 38,250 lb.
Performance: maximum speed, 1525 mph (Mach 2.31); initial climb, about 30,000 ft per min; service ceiling, 57,000 ft; range with drop-tanks, 1700 miles; combat radius, about 600 miles.
Armament: one internal 20 mm M-61 multi-barrel cannon; internal weapon bay for air-to-air missiles with typical load comprising one AIR-2A and one AIR-2G Genie rockets and two each of AIM-4E, -4F or -4G Falcons.

The Delta Dart was first flown on 26 December 1956 and was delivered to the Air Force from July 1959 to July 1960. It proved to be the mainstay of the USAF's manned defensive fighter force. Some 277 F-106A single-seat interceptors were built. The F-106B, a tandem two-seat dual-purpose combat trainer, was ordered in parallel production. The F-106s MA-1 electronic guidance and fire-control system, which operates in conjunction with NORAD's SAGE defense system, has been updated periodically. Other modifications have included MEISR, which enhances the reliability of the on-board radar and the introduction of the new drop-tanks which can be refuelled in flight. Further improvements permit operation in global roles as well as for continental US defense until 1980.

Lockheed F-80, T-33 Shooting Star, T-1A Sea Star, C1-30 Silver Star

Manufacturer: Lockheed-California Corporation, Burbank. Built under license by Canadair, Montreal and Kawasaki, Japan.
Type: F-80, fighter, fighter-bomber; T-33, advance trainer; RF-80, RT-33, reconnaissance, then dual-control trainer.
Crew: one.
Specification: F-80C.
Power Plant: one 4600 lb J33-A-23.
Dimensions: span, 39 ft 11 in; length, 34 ft 6 in; height, 11 ft 4 in; wing area, 238 sq ft.
Weights: empty, 8240 lb; gross, 16,856 lb.
Performance: maximum speed, 580 mph at 7000 ft; cruising speed, 439 mph; initial climb, 6870 ft per min; service ceiling, 42,750 ft; range, 1380 miles.
Armament: sixty .5 in, two 1000 lb or ten 5 in RP.
Specification: T-33.
Power Plant: one 5200 lb J33-35.
Dimensions: span (without tip tanks), 38 ft 10.5 in; length, 37 ft 9 in; height, 11 ft 8 in.
Weights: empty, 8084 lb; gross, 14,442 lb.
Performance: maximum speed, about 590 mph; service ceiling, 47,500 ft; maximum range, about 1345 miles.
Armament: provision for two 0.5 in M-3 machine guns and 2000 lb bomb load.

Work on the F-80 began in June 1943 when Lockheed were officially invited to design an airframe around the British de Havilland H-1 turbojet. The XP-80 prototype was first flown on 8 January 1944 with a General Electric J33 engine. During 1948 the US Navy acquired F-80Cs as jet advanced trainers. The F-80 and its variants were the first jets used by the USAAF and the first used by the USAF in Korea.

Bottom: **A Lockheed T-33A on a Japanese airfield during the Korean War.**
Below: **The F-80 Shooting Star was designed and built in 143 days.**

A F-94C Starfire with additional white-tipped wing pods containing 2.75-inch missiles.

Lockheed F-94 Starfire

Manufacturer: Lockheed Aircraft Corporation, Burbank, California.
Type: all-weather fighter.
Crew: two (pilot and radar operator in tandem).
Specification: F-94C.
Power Plant: one 6350 lb (8750 lb with a/b) J48-P-5 or P-5A turbojet.
Dimensions: span, 42 ft 5 in; length, 44 ft 6 in; height, 14 ft 11 in; wing area, 338 sq ft.
Weights: empty, 12,700 lb; gross, 24,200 lb.
Performance: maximum speed, 585 mph at 30,000 ft; combat speed, 522 mph at 49,700 ft; initial climb, 7980 ft per min; service ceiling, 51,400 ft; ferry range, 1200 miles.
Armament: twenty-four 2.75 in folding-fin air rockets in nose and 12 each in two wing pods.

The Starfire was developed in 1949 as a two-seat, radar-equipped successor to the T-33. The prototype YF-94 was first flown on 1 July 1949 and it was the first all-weather jet interceptor to serve with ADC.

Lockheed F-104 Starfighter

Manufacturer: Lockheed Aircraft Corporation, Burbank.
Type: (A, C) day interceptor; (G) multi-role fighter; (CF) strike-reconnaissance; (TF) dual trainer; (QF) drone RPV; (F-104S) all-weather interceptor; (RF and RTF) reconnaissance.
Crew: all except TF (2); pilot only.
Power Plant: one General Electric J79 single-shaft turbojet with afterburner; (A) 14,800 lb J79-3B; (C, D, F, J) 15,800 lb J79-7A; (G, RF/RFT, CF) 15,800 lb J79-11A; (S) 17,900 lb J79-19 or J1Q.
Dimensions: span (without tip tanks), 21 ft 11 in; length 54 ft 9 in; height, 13 ft 6 in.
Weights: empty 14,082 lb; maximum loaded, 28,779 lb.
Performance: maximum speed, 1450 mph (Mach 2.2); initial climb, 50,000 ft per min; service ceiling, 58,000 ft (zoom ceiling over 90,000 ft); range with maximum weapons, about 300 miles; range with four drop tanks (high altitude, subsonic) 1380 miles.
Armament: (most versions) external stores, (basic) 4000 lb, provision for centerline and wing-mounted, small missiles. one 20 mm M61 Vulcan multi-barrel cannon.

Design work commenced in November 1952 after talks with fighter pilots in Korea in 1951. The XF-104's first flight took place on 7 February 1954.

It was the first operational interceptor capable of sustained Mach 2+ speeds and it was the first aircraft to hold World Airspeed and Altitude records simultaneously.

Right: **F-104s of the Italian Air Force.**

Left: **A Lockheed F-104A of ADC.**
Below: **Two views of the F-104C Starfighter, or the 'missile with a man in it.'**

McDonnell F-101 Voodoo.

North American's F-82 Twin Mustang.

McDonnell F-101 Voodoo

Manufacturer: McDonnell Aircraft Company (Division of McDonnell Douglas Corporation), St. Louis, Missouri.
Type: (A, C) day fighter-bomber; (B) all-weather interceptor; (RF) all-weather reconnaissance.
Crew: (F-101A, C; RF-101A, C); pilot only; (F-101B) pilot and radar observer.
Specification: F-101B.
Power Plant: two J57 two-shaft turbojets with afterburner; 14,990 lb.
Dimensions: span, 39 ft 8 in; length, 67 ft 4.75 in; height, 18 ft; wing area, 368 sq ft.
Weights: empty, 28,000 lb; maximum loaded, 46,700 lb.
Performance: maximum speed, 1220 mph (Mach 1.85); initial climb, 17,000 ft per min; service ceiling, 52,000 ft; range on internal fuel, 1550 miles; (others), 1700 miles.
Armament: (F-101A, C) four 20 mm M-39 cannon, three Falcon air-to-air missiles and 12 rockets; (F-101B) two AIR-2A Genie nuclear rockets, and three Falcon air-to-air missiles or bombs; (RF101A, C) none; most models: provision for tactical nuclear payload on centerline and underwing pylons for two 2000 lb bombs, four 680 lb mines or other stores.

Advanced design of the XF-88, an experimental, long-range, supersonic penetration fighter for the USAF began in 1946. A shortage of funds led to cancellation of the project in 1950. It was revived in 1951 to meet a USAF requirement for a long-range escort fighter for SAC B-36s.

First flight trials began on 20 October 1948. The aircraft was first flown 29 September 1954, and service deliveries began in May 1957.

On 12 December 1957 an F-101C set an FAI World Speed Record of 1207.6 mph. At its time of introduction, it was the heaviest single-seat fighter to serve with the USAF.

The RF-101 established new transcontinental US speed records in November 1957, flying west-east at 781.74 mph, east-west at 677.73 mph, and round trip at 721.85 mph for the 4891.8 mile round trip distance.

RF-101 Voodoos extended reconnaissance performance into the supersonic field. They carried three different camera systems and could take photographs from 45,000 feet over an area 217 miles long by 8 miles wide. During the 1962 Cuban crisis, RF-101s made repeated low-level forays over Cuba to bring back evidence of the Soviet missile build-up, and carried out key reconnaissance missions in Vietnam.

Left: **At the time of its introduction the Voodoo was the heaviest fighter to see service with the USAF.**

North American F-82 Twin Mustang

Manufacturer: North American Aviation Incorporated, Inglewood, California.
Type: long-range escort and night fighter.
Crew: two pilots in individual enclosed cockpits.
Specification: F-82G.
Power Plant: two 1600 hp V-1710-143/145.
Dimensions: span, 51 ft 3 in; length, 42 ft 5 in; height, 13 ft 10 in; wing area, 408 sq ft.
Weights: empty, 15,997 lb; gross, 25,591 lb.
Performance: maximum speed, 461 mph at 21,000 ft; cruising speed, 286 mph; initial climb, 3770 ft per min; service ceiling, 38,900 ft; range, 2240 miles.
Armament: six 0.5 in guns; four 1000 lb bombs carried externally.

Having designed the best fighter of the war in the Mustang, North American went ahead in 1944 with the Twin Mustang. The requirement for a very long-range fighter, with twin engines, two pilots and a large fuel load capable of escorting the B-29s on long-range missions in the Pacific was met simply by putting two P-51 air-frames together. But the war ended before the F-82 went into production and only a few hundred were built. However, during the Korean conflict the F-82 operated as a night fighter and the first three North Korean aircraft shot down were credited to pilots flying this remarkable aircraft. Today the only flyable F-82 in the world is operated by the Confederate Air Force at Rebel Field, Texas.

North American F-86 Sabre

Manufacturer: North American Aviation Incorporated, Inglewood, California and Columbus, Ohio. Built under license by Societa per Azioni Fiat, Turin, Italy and Canadair Limited, Montreal, Canada.
Type: fighter-bomber/all weather interceptor.
Crew: pilot only.
Specification: F-86D.
Power Plant: one 5700/7630 lb J47-GE-17.
Dimensions: span, 37 ft 1 in; length, 40 ft 4 in; height, 15 ft; wing area, 288 sq ft.
Weights: empty, 12,470 lb; gross, 17,100 lb.
Performance: maximum speed, 707 mph at sea level, cruising speed, 525 mph; initial climb, 17,800 ft per min; service ceiling, 54,600 ft; range, 836 miles.
Armament: 24 2.75 in FFAR.

Although design work on what was to prove the USAF's first swept-wing fighter began during the closing stages of World War II, it was not until the results of German research into swept-wings became available that the XP-86 adopted the then radical feature. The XJF-1 first flew on 27 November 1946.

In the spring of 1948 the XP-86 became the first US fighter to exceed the speed of sound, during a shallow dive. In 1949 the Sabre established a new air speed record of 671 mph. The F-86 was followed in production in December 1950 by a new interceptor model, the F-86E with slatted wing and powered 'flying tail.' This and the F-86F, with extended leading edge and small fence, were highly successful during the Korean conflict, establishing a marked

The Sabre was the only UN fighter capable of meeting Soviet MiGs in equal combat.

North American F-86H in flight.

F86K Sabres of the Royal Netherlands Air Force, May 1963.

An F-86 Sabre in the livery of the Royal Norwegian Air Force.

superiority over the MiG-15 despite inferior climb and altitude performance. The highly complex F-86D interceptor introduced the new concept of gunless collision course interception directed by autopilot and radar. The K was equipped with guns for conventional interception and mass produced by an Italian and West German consortium. USAF Sabres were completed by the powerful H model but various US Navy versions continued to be built. Some 430 Canadair CL-13 series were supplied to the RAF by Mutual Aid Funds. RAAF CA-27 versions were equipped with Avon engines and 30 mm guns. Total production, including 300 assembled in Japan, amounted to 9502, exceeding the total of any other Western military fixed-wing aircraft since 1945.

Below: **Two F-86Ks of the Royal Norwegian Air Force. This version was intended for service with NATO Air Forces and was equipped with four 20mm cannon instead of rocket armament.**

Left: **An F-86K of the Royal Netherlands Air Force.**
Right: **A North American FJ-2 Fury (a USN development of the F-86) in US Marines livery.**
Below: **The interior and a sideview of the North American F-86 Sabre.**

An F-100 Super Sabre pulls in for refuelling.

North American (Rockwell) F-100 Super Sabre

Manufacturer: North American Aviation Incorporated, Inglewood, California and (C & D), Columbus, Ohio.
Type: (A) supersonic interceptor; (C, D) fighter-bomber; (DF) missile or RPV director; (F) trainer.
Crew: all models except F; pilot only; (F-100F) pilot and instructor.
Specification: F-100D.
Power Plant: one 11,700 lb (17,000 lb with a/b) J57-P-21A turbojet.
Dimensions: span, 38 ft 9 in; length, 50 ft; height, 15 ft; wing area, 385 sq ft.
Weights: empty, 21,000 lb; gross, 34,832 lb.
Performance: maximum speed, 864 mph at 35,000 ft; cruising speed, 565 mph at 36,000 ft; initial climb, 16,000 ft per min.
Armament: four fixed forward firing 20 mm M-39E cannon in front fuselage; underwing pylons for six 1000 lb bombs, two Sidewinder or Bullpup AAMs; FFAR pods etc.

The Super Sabre evolved from the F-86 Sabre design but incorporated a 45° swept-angle wing (F-86, 35°), a slab tailplane and an oval lip intake for the J57 turbojet. The YF-100 flew on 25 May 1953 and F-100A on 29 October 1953 but in November 1954 the F-100A was grounded after initial rapid development until the wings and fin were lengthened. The much sturdier C fighter-bomber followed, to be supplanted by the D and later, the tandem-seat F.

The Super Sabre was the world's first operational fighter capable of level supersonic

Top: **Initially the F-100 was known as the Sabre 45 because of its 45-degree wing.**
Left: **The Super Sabre was the USAF's first Century series fighter and the first aircraft capable of level supersonic flight.**
Below: **F-100Ds of the USAF Thunderbirds Demonstration Team over the Hoover Dam.**

USAF
USAF
USAF
USAF

Left: **F-100D Thunderbirds over the Grand Canyon.**
Below: **North American F-100D Super Sabre.**

performance, establishing a new world air-speed record of just over 755 mph (F-100A) on its maiden flight on 29 October 1953. Although total production of the Super Sabre only reached 2294, the 'Hun' was still in service during the Vietnam war, providing an outstanding low-level attack and high cover aircraft. It also pioneered global deployment of tactical aircraft by means of the probe/drogue refuelling system. Some 'Huns' were still in service use with the French Air Force as late as 1977.

Northrop F-89 Scorpion

Manufacturer: Northrop Aircraft Incorporated, Hawthorne, California.
Type: all-weather interceptor fighter.
Crew: pilot and radar operator in tandem.
Specification: F-89D.
Power Plant: two 5440 lb (7200 lb with a/b) J35-A-35.
Dimensions: span, 59 ft 8 in; length, 53 ft 10 in; height, 17 ft 7 in; wing area, 562 sq ft (650 sq ft including tip pods).
Weights: empty, 25,194 lb; gross, 42,241 lb.
Performance: maximum speed, 636 mph at 10,600 ft; combat speed, 523 mph at 46,500 ft; initial climb, 8360 ft per min; service ceiling, 49,200 ft; range (ferry), 1370 miles.
Armament: fifty-two 2.75 in folding fin air rockets each in wing tip pods; provision for GAR-1 Falcon missiles in place of FFAR.

The design for the Scorpion was proposed by Northrop in December 1945 and accepted by the USAF in early 1946.

The XF-89 first flew on 16 August 1948. The first service delivery was in July 1950 (F89A).

The first USAF multi-seat jet fighter capable of all-weather operation.

Republic F-84 Thunderjet Thunderstreak

Manufacturer: Republic Aviation, Corporation, Long Island, New York and General Motors Corporation, Kansas City.
Type: (F-84) fighter, fighter-bomber; (RF-84) reconnaissance.
Crew: pilot only.
Specification: F-84G.
Power Plant: one 5600 lb J35-A-29.
Dimensions: span, 36 ft 5 in; length, 38 ft 1 in; height, 12 ft 7 in; wing area, 260 sq ft.
Weights: empty, 11,095 lb; gross, 23,525 lb.
Performance: maximum speed, 622 mph at sea level; cruising speed, 483 mph; climb, 9.4 min at 35,000 ft; service ceiling, 40,500 ft; range, 2000 miles.
Armament: six 0.50 in; 32 5 in RP; two 1000 lb bomb load.

Three straight-wing prototypes were ordered in early 1945 and the first, XP-84, flew on 28 February 1946. The second flew in August 1946 and established a US national speed record of 611 mph in September that year. Development of a swept-wing design based

Above and below: **The Republic F-84F Thunderstreak. More than 1300 F versions were used by NATO countries.**

Below: **The Republic F-84 Thunderjet.**

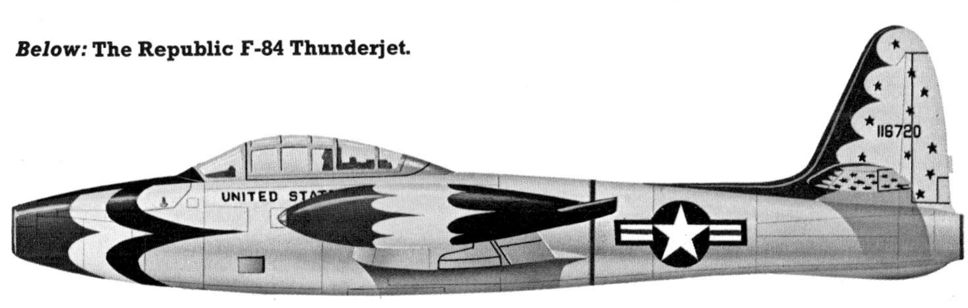

Below: **An F-89D Scorpion maintains close interest in a missile.**

on the F-84 began in late 1949. By using the standard F-84 fuselage and 60 percent of its tooling the YF-96A prototype was born and first flown on 3 June 1950. In September the designation became F-84F Thunderstreak.

It was the last of the subsonic straight wing fighter-bombers to see operational service with the USAF. In addition to providing very valuable service in the Korean Conflict it was also involved in the development of flight-refuelling techniques for fighters and was the first single-seat fighter-bomber capable of carrying a tactical nuclear weapon. On 22 September 1950 an EF-84E, with probe equipment, became the first jet to fly the Atlantic non-stop.

Right: A Republic F-84E of the Royal Norwegian AF.
Below: A Republic RF-84F of the Italian AF.
Bottom: A KB-29P refuels an F-84 Thunderjet by means of the flying boom developed by Boeing.

Boeing B-47 Stratojet

Manufacturer: Boeing Airplane Company, Seattle, Washington, and Wichita, Kansas; Douglas Aircraft, Company, Tulsa; Lockheed Aircraft Corporation, Marietta.
Type: strategic medium bomber; photo, electronic and weather reconnaissance aircraft.
Crew: two pilots and navigator (plus three electronic engineers in RB-47H only).
Specification: B-47E-II.
Power Plant: six 6000 lb J47-GE-25 turbojets.
Dimensions: span, 116 ft; length, 109 ft 10 in; height, 27 ft 11 in; wing area, 1428 sq ft.
Weights: empty, 80,756 lb; gross, 206,700 lb.
Performance: maximum speed, 606 mph at 16,300 ft; combat speed, 557 mph at 38,550 ft; initial climb, 4660 ft per min; service ceiling, 40,500 ft; range, 4000 miles.
Armament: two 20 mm M24A1 guns in remotely-controlled tail turret, 350 rpg; up to 20,000 lb bombs internally.

Boeing development of a jet bomber began in 1943 and the design underwent constant revision, the most significant being the 35° swept-back wing that permitted great increases in speed. Although heavier than the heaviest bomber of the war, the B-29, the B-47 was classed as a medium bomber.

Two XB-47 Stratojets were built in Seattle, the first flying in December 1947. The first Wichita built B-47A flew in June 1950. Major production began with the B-47B which appeared in several forms including the RB-47 reconnaissance-bomber.

***Right:* In 1957 most B-47s were modified to use low-level 'lob bombing.'**
***Below:* A Lockheed-built B-47.**

Above: **A KB-50J refuels three F-100s. When the B-50 became obsolete, most were converted to KB-50J or KB-50K three-hose aerial tankers.**
Left: **The Boeing B-50D provided flying-boom aerial refuelling.**
Below: **Boeing B-52D.**

Boeing B-50 Superfortress

Manufacturer: Boeing Airplane Company, Renton, Washington.
Type: (B-50A-D) strategic bomber; (KB-50J, K) flight refuelling tank; (RB-50E, F, G) special-purpose reconnaissance; (TB-50H) crew trainer.
Crew: (KB-50J, K) six (two pilots, engineer, radar-navigator and two refuelling operators).
Specification: B-500.
Power Plant: four 3500 hp R-4360 or -51 piston engines.
Dimensions: span, 141 ft 3 in; length, 99 ft; height, 32 ft 8 in.
Weights: empty, 80,609 lb; gross, 173,000 lb.
Performance: 380 mph at 25,000 ft; cruising speed, 277 mph; climb, 2165 ft per min; service ceiling, 36,700 ft; range, 4900 miles.
Armament: two .5 machine guns in each of three remotely-controlled turrets plus four .5s in front upper turret and two .5s and one 20 mm cannon in tail turret; provision for maximum bomb load of 20,000 lb.

Direct development of the B-29 series. A new Superfortress variant was put into production in 1945 as the B-29D but this designation was changed to B-50 before deliveries began. The B-50 incorporated many changes in the B-29 design including Wasp Major engines, taller fin and rudder, lighter but stronger alloy wing-structure and a new undercarriage.

The B-50A was first flown on 25 June 1947 and B-50B deliveries to Strategic Air Command (SAC) begun 1949.

The B-50 was the first new bomber type to appear on SAC inventory. Although rendered tactically obsolete by the advent of jet bombers converted KB-50 three-hose aerial tankers were widely used by TAC between 1957 and 1959. The last Superfortresses to be built were 24 TB-50H crew trainers completed in 1952.

Boeing B-52 Stratofortress

Manufacturer: Boeing Airplane Company, Seattle, Washington, and Wichita, Kansas.
Type: strategic heavy bomber and ECM platform.
Crew: six (two pilots side-by-side; bombardier, radar-navigator, ECM operator and tail gunner).
Specification: B-52H.
Power Plant: (B-52H) eight 17,000 lb TF33-3.
Dimensions: span, 185 ft; length, 157 ft 7 in; height, 40 ft 8 in.
Weights: empty, 171,000–193,000 lb; loaded, 505,000 lb.
Performance: maximum speed about 630 mph at over 24,000 ft; service ceiling, 45,000–55,000 ft; range on internal fuel with maximum weapon load, 12,500 miles.
Armament: remotely controlled rear turret with four 0.5 in machine guns (B-52H, 20 mm six-barrel ASG-21 cannon); internal payload normally 27,000 lb; (B-52D) internal and external capacity for up to 70,000 lb conventional bombs; (B-52G) two GAM-77 Hound Dog ASMs externally, bombs and Quail diversionary missiles internally; (B-52H) two AGM-28B Hound Dog missiles or 12 AGM-69A SRAM missiles with rotary dispenser (optional) for eight internal SRAMs (Short Range Attack Missiles).

The designation B-52 was originally assigned to a straight-wing, long-range bomber to be powered by six turboprop engines. By October 1948 the design had undergone extensive revision and at that time the Air Force approved Boeing's request to develop an entirely new jet-propelled bomber under the same designation. The new B-52 was designed and built as Boeing Model 464. The first prototype flew on 15 April 1952. In appearance the B-52 was a direct development of the B-47.

Above: **A KC-135 makes this refuelling of a B-52 look almost effortless.**
Below: **A close-up of the flying-boom in action as a B-52 noses in for a refill.**

Eight Pratt & Whitney V57 turbojets were carried in four pods under the wings and the four-unit tandem landing gear could be turned to either side to allow the aircraft to crab into the wind on crosswind landings and still roll straight down the runway. Electrical needs on early models were handled by turbine power-packs driven by air bled from the second-stage compressors of the jet engines. Fuel was carried in fuselage tanks above the bomb bay and in nylon bladder cells installed between the main wing spars and each pair of inter-connecting ribs.

Above: **The first of the Wichita-built Boeing B-52As moves in on the flying-boom of a Boeing KC-97 for refuelling.**
Above right: **Equipped with air-to-ground Short Range Attack Missiles (SRAM), B-52s can hit several targets hundreds of miles apart on one mission.**
Right: **Fifty B-52Bs were built as dual-purpose aircraft to serve on photo-reconnaissance missions as well as on bombing missions.**
Below: **A KC-135 Stratotanker refuels a B-52 Stratofortress.**

6518

3397
3394

UNITED STATES AIR FORCE

UNITED STATES AIR FORCE
5718

Below: **General Dynamics (Convair) B-58 Hustler.**

Left: **Convair (now General Dynamics) assigned production of the enormous B-36 to their Fort Worth, Texas plant.**

Convair B-36

Manufacturer: Consolidated Vultee Aircraft Corporation, Fort Worth, Texas.
Type: heavy strategic bomber and reconnaissance aircraft.
Crew: normally 15 (including four reliefs).
Specification: B-36J.
Power Plant: six 3800 hp R-4360-53 and four 5200 lb J47-GE-19.
Dimensions: span, 230 ft; length, 162 ft 1 in; height, 46 ft 8 in; wing area, 4772 sq ft.
Weights: empty, 171,035 lb; gross, 410,000 lb.
Performance: maximum speed, 411 mph at 36,400 ft; cruising speed, 391 mph; climb, 1920 ft per min; service ceiling, 39,000 ft; range, 6800 miles.
Armament: two 20 mm M24A1 cannon each in six retractable, remotely controlled fuselage turrets, tail turret and nose mounting, with 9200 rounds; maximum bomb load, 86,000 lb (at restricted gross weight); normal bomb load up to 72,000 lb.

Development was begun in 1941 to meet the need for bombing European targets from the USA should Britain have fallen. A specification for a strategic bomber capable of carrying a 10,000 lb bomb load for 5000 miles at 35,000 feet without refuelling at a maximum speed of 240–300 mph was issued in April 1941. Of four designs submitted by the Aircraft Industry, the USAAF selected the Consolidated Model, which had its test flight on 28 August 1947.

Convair B-58 Hustler

Manufacturer: Convair Division of General Motors, Fort Worth, Texas.
Type: supersonic medium bomber.
Crew: (pilot, navigator-bombardier and defensive system operator in tandem cockpits).
Specification: B-58A.
Power Plant: four 15,600 lb J79-GE-3B.
Dimensions: span, 56 ft 10 in; length, 96 ft 9 in; height, 31 ft 5 in; wing area, 7542 sq ft.
Weight: gross, over 160,000 lb.
Performance: maximum speed, 1385 mph at 40,000 ft; service ceiling, 60,000 ft.
Armament: one General Electric T-171E3 Vulcan 20 mm multi-barrel cannon in radar aimed tail mounting; mission pod under fuselage to carry nuclear or conventional bombs.

The first flight (without external weapons pod) was 11 November 1956. It entered service in March 1960. It was the winner of an Air Force competition in 1949 to determine the feasibility of a manned supersonic bomber.

It was the first supersonic bomber to equip the USAF. On 15 October 1959 a B-58A it flew 1680 miles with one refuelling, maintaining a speed of Mach 2 plus for over an hour. The last production model was flown in October 1962.

Below: **The delta-wing B-58 Hustler was equipped with a dropable pod which carried a portion of the aircraft's fuel supply in addition to its nuclear payload.**
Bottom: **A worm's eye view of the enormous B-58 Hustler, the free world's first Mach 2+ strategic bomber and the first to equip the USAF.**

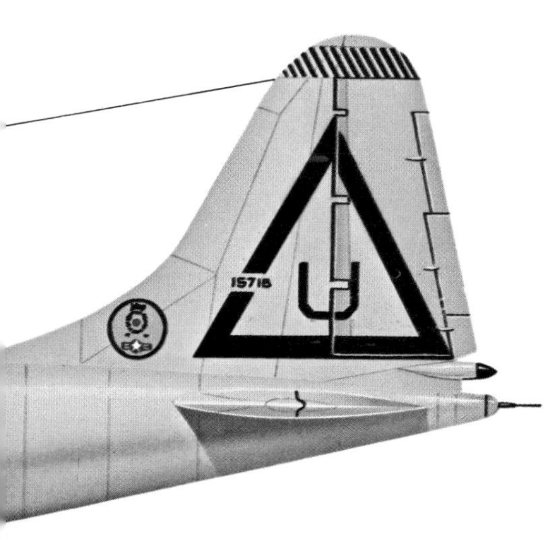

Above: **A sideview of the Convair B-36.**

Douglas A-26, B-26 Invader

Manufacturer: Douglas Aircraft Company, El Segundo, Long Beach and Tulsa.
Type: light bomber and reconnaissance.
Crew: three (pilot, navigator/bombardier, gunner).
Specification: A-26C.
Power Plant: two 2000 hp R-2800-27 or -79 piston radials.
Dimensions: span, 70 ft; length, 51 ft 3 in; height, 18 ft 3 in; wing area, 540 sq ft.
Weights: empty, 22,850 lb; gross, 35,000 lb.
Performance: maximum speed, 373 mph; cruising speed, 284 mph; climb, 8 min to 10,000 ft; service ceiling, 22,100 ft; range, 1400 miles.
Armament: six 0.5 in in nose, top, ventral turrets; 4000 lb bomb load.

Developed as a follow-up to the A-20, the A-26 was designed in January 1941 and first flown in July 1942. It was ordered for trials by the US Army for use as an attack bomber and, in another configuration, as a night fighter. Later production models actually carried twice the bomb load required by the original specifications. Although designed to a USAAF requirement in 1940 development and production was so rapid that the A-26 entered service in the European Theater before the end of 1944. It proved a powerful offensive weapon in Europe and in the Pacific. A total of 2446 A-26s were built by the time Japan capitulated in August 1945. The Invader continued in USAF service and in 1958 was redesignated the B-26. It was employed with great success in the Korean conflict as a night intruder and saw service in Vietnam in night interdiction missions.

Martin B-57 Canberra, B-57A to B-57G Night Intruder, RB-57A, D and F

Manufacturer: Original US prime contractor, Glen Martin Company, Baltimore, MD (RB 57D) General Dynamics, Fort Worth, Texas.
Type: tactical attack and strategic reconnaissance (RB-57D), trainer (B-57C), target tug (B-57E).
Crew: pilot and navigator.
Specification: B-57G.
Power Plant: two 7220 lb J65-5 single-shaft turbojets.
Dimensions: span, 64 ft; length, 67 ft; height, 15 ft 7 in.
Weights: empty, about 28,000 lb; maximum loaded, 55,000 lb.
Performance: maximum speed, 582 mph at 40,000 ft; initial climb, 3500 ft per min; service ceiling, 48,000 ft; maximum range with combat load (high altitude); 2100 miles.
Armament: provision for four 20 mm or eight 0.5 in guns fixed in outer wings (very rarely, other guns in nose); internal bomb load, 6000 lb on rotary bomb bay plus eight rockets, two 500 lb bombs or other stores on under-wing pylons (while retaining tip tanks).

Failure of the highly advanced XB-51 tri-jet attack bomber in October 1949 prompted an American interest in the English Electric Canberra, first flown in May that year. Less advanced than the XB-51 it nevertheless proved to have precisely all the qualities the USAF were looking for. On 21 February 1951 the first Canberra to carry American markings (British built B.Mk 2) was flown to Baltimore where Martin began production of license-built B-57As.

The prototype B-57A had its first flight on 20 July 1953.

The Canberra was the first aircraft of non-US design adopted for operational service with the USAF since 1918. General Dynamic's RB-57Ds, with extended wing area, made reconnaissance sorties adjacent to and over Soviet territory. The B-57s also saw service in Vietnam in night-attack roles.

***Below:* Martin's B-57 development of the successful British Canberra.**

Below: Martin B-57.

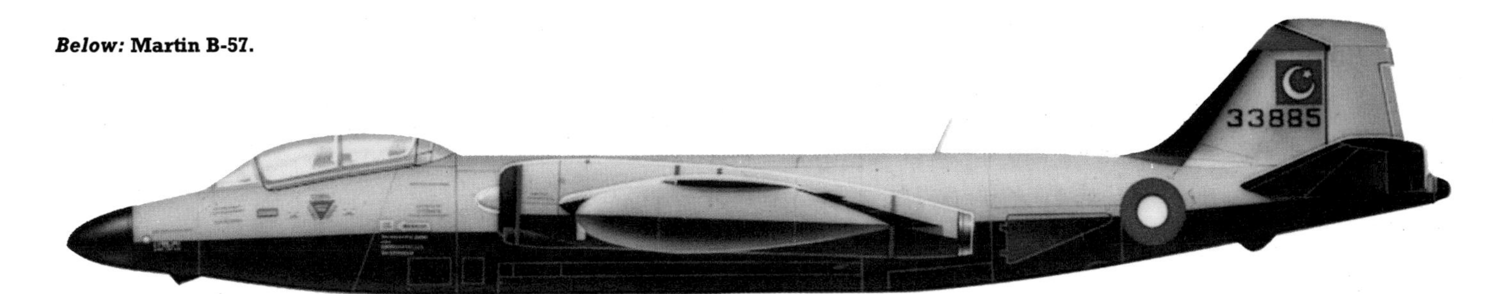

North American B-45 Tornado

Manufacturer: North American Aviation Incorporated, Inglewood, California.
Type: light tactical bomber.
Crew: two pilots in tandem, bombardier and tail gunner.
Specification: B-45C.
Power Plant: four 5200 lb J47-GE-13/15.
Dimensions: span (without tip tanks), 89 ft; length, 75 ft 4 in; height, 25 ft 2 in; wing area, 1175 sq ft.
Weights: empty, 48,903 lb; gross, 112,952 lb.
Performance: maximum speed, 579 mph at sea level; cruising speed, 456 mph; initial climb, 5800 ft per min; service ceiling, 43,200 ft; range, 1910 miles.
Armament: two 0.5 in Browning M-7 guns in tail turret; up to 22,000 lb of bombs.

Towards the end of World War II official specifications called for a four-jet bomber which sought to apply jet propulsion techniques to piston-engined bomber techniques. The first of three prototypes first flew in March 1947 by which time orders for 96 B-45As had been placed. Deliveries of the C began in 1949, of which only ten were built. These were followed by 33 of the RB-45C model which added photo-reconnaissance capability to the tactical bombing duties of the former type. Deliveries were made in June 1950–October 1951. The B-45 served in Korea and Europe.

The RB-45C Tornado four-jet bomber.

North American XB-70A Valkyrie

Manufacturer: North American Aviation Incorporated, Inglewood, California.
Type: strategic bomber.
Specification: XB-70A.
Power Plant: six J93-GE-3.
Dimensions: span, 115 ft; length, 170 ft.
Weight: gross, approximately 550,000 lb.
Performance: Mach 3 (maximum).
Armament: none.

Development of the first Mach 3 strategic bomber for the USAF was started in July 1955. The Valkyrie was intended to supersede the Boeing B-52 but a change in policy led to cancellation of the project in favor of intercontinental missiles. Two XB-70As were completed for use as research aircraft and their ability to cruise at three times the speed of sound (2000 mph) at 70,000 feet provided valuable information for America's supersonic airliner projects.

Above: **The Valkyrie was the fastest of the true 'tail first' aircraft to cruise at three times the speed of sound.**
Left: **A Douglas A-26B in flight. Deliveries of this type first began in November 1944.**
Below: **Douglas A-26B.**

An AD6 Skyraider in flight.

Douglas A-1 Skyraider

Manufacturer: Douglas Aircraft Company, El Segundo, California.
Type: initially, torpedo/dive bomber.
Crew: pilot only.
Specification: A-1J.
Power Plant: one 3020 hp R-3350-26W or 3050 hp R-3350-26WB.
Dimensions: span, 50 ft 9 in; length, 38 ft 10 in; height, 15 ft 8.25 in.
Weights: empty, 12,313 lb; maximum loaded, 25,000 lb.
Performance: maximum speed, 318 mph; initial climb, 2300 ft per min; service ceiling, 32,000 ft; range, from 900 miles with maximum ordnance to 3000 miles with maximum external fuel.
Armament: (attack) normally four 20 mm cannon. Ordnance/fuel load, 8000 lb.

The A-1 was ordered by the US Navy on 6 July 1944 to meet the requirement for a carrier-borne torpedo/dive bomber. The XBT2D-1 was first flown on 18 March 1945 and service delivery of the AD-1 began in the month of November in 1946.

The Skyraider was the first single-seat torpedo-carrier/dive bomber to serve with the US Navy. Its versatility during both the Korean and Vietnam wars led to serious considerations in 1966 of reopening production, which had ceased in February 1957.

Douglas F3D Skynight

Manufacturer: Douglas Aircraft Company, El Segundo, California.
Type: all-weather carrier-fighter.
Crew: pilot and radar observer.
Specification: F3D-2.
Power Plant: two 3400 lb J34-WE-36/36As.
Dimensions: span, 50 ft; length, 45 ft 6 in; height, 16 ft; wing area, 400 sq ft.
Weights: empty, 18,160 lb; gross, 26,850 lb.
Performance: maximum speed, 600 mph at 20,000 ft; cruising speed, 350 mph; initial climb, 4500 ft per min; range, 1200 miles.
Armament: four 20 mm cannon.

The US Navy contracted with Douglas on 3 April 1946 to build three prototypes of a new all-weather fighter.

The Skynight prototype was first flown on 23 March 1948.

The F3D was the first of its class to use jet engines. The tunnel from the cockpit to the floor was so constructed to facilitate bale out at high speed. It was responsible in Korea for destroying more enemy aircraft than any other aircraft flown by the US Navy or Marines and was the first jet aircraft to destroy another at night (MiG-15 on 22 November 1952). The F3D-2Q was the first tactical jet aircraft in an electronic warfare role, playing an important part during both the Cuban missile crisis and Vietnam war.

Below: **An F3D Skynight in suitably all-over black finish.**

Above: **The F4D-1 Skyray of the US Marines.**

Douglas F4D Skyray

Manufacturer: Douglas Aircraft Company, El Segundo, California.
Type: carrier-borne interceptor.
Crew: pilot only.
Specification: F4D-1.
Power Plant: one 9700 lb J57-P-2 or 10,500 lb J57-P-8B.
Dimensions: span, 33 ft 6 in; length, 45 ft 8.25 in; height, 13 ft; wing area, 557 sq ft.
Weights: empty, 16,024 lb; gross, 25,000 lb.
Performance: maximum speed, 695 mph at 36,000 ft; initial climb, 18,000 ft per min; service ceiling, 55,000 ft; range, 1200 miles.
Armament: four 20 mm cannon; up to 4000 lb of bombs, rockets, or other stores.

The Skyray was built to fulfill the US Navy's proposal, in 1947, for a short-range, carrier-borne, delta-wing interceptor.

Two prototypes were ordered on 16 December 1948 and the XF4D-1 was first flown on 23 January 1951. The first models were delivered to the Navy on 16 April 1956 after test problems. Production ceased in December 1958 and the Skyray was phased out by 1964.

Grumman F7F Tigercat

Manufacturer: Grumman Aircraft Engineering Corporation, Bethpage, Long Island, New York.
Type: carrier-borne fighter-bomber.
Crew: pilot only.
Specification: F7F-3.
Power Plant: two 2100 hp R-2800-34Ws.
Dimensions: span, 51 ft 6 in; length, 45 ft 4 in; height, 16 ft 7 in; wing area, 455 sq ft.
Weights: empty, 16,270 lb; gross, 25,720 lb.
Performance: maximum speed, 435 mph at 22,200 ft; cruising speed, 222 mph; initial climb, 4530 ft per min; service ceiling, 40,700 ft; range, 1200 miles.
Armament: four 20 mm guns and four 0.5 in guns; up to 1000 lb under each wing; one torpedo under fuselage.

Grumman capitalized on its long-standing experience of fighters for the US Navy by moving into the multi-engine fighters for carrier deck operation. As early as June 1938 the Navy had ordered a prototype twin-engined fighter from the Grumman stable. The XF5F-1 (Grumman G-45) provided a useful basis for development and when in June 1941 the Navy ordered a

Left: **The F7F-3 single-seat Tigercat.**

Grumman F7F-3N Tigercat night-fighter.

larger twin-engined fighter, the company was able to meet it with added experience. The first of two XF7F-1s flew in December 1943 by which time the US Marine Corps squadrons required 500 of the twin-engined fighter. Deliveries commenced in April 1944 but operational problems and a change in requirements led to far-reaching delays. The 34 single-seat versions were delivered and then production switched to two-seat night fighter versions. Orders for various models of the Tigercat, as the type had been named by the Navy, led to the aircraft remaining in production until late 1946. The F7F served with a few Marine squadrons after the war, having been too late in developing to enter the conflict. However the jet-age soon replaced the need for this and other piston engined aircraft.

Grumman F8F Bearcat

Manufacturer: Grumman Aircraft Engineering Corporation, Bethpage, Long Island, New York.
Type: carrier-borne interceptor fighter.
Crew: pilot only.
Specification: F8F-1.
Power Plant: one 2100 hp R-2800-34W.
Dimensions: span, 35 ft 10 in; length, 28 ft 3 in; height, 13 ft 10 in; wing area, 244 sq ft.
Weights: empty, 7070 lb; gross, 12,947 lb.
Performance: maximum speed, 421 mph at 19,700 ft; cruising speed, 163 mph; initial climb, 4570 ft per min; service ceiling, 38,700 ft; range, 1105 miles.
Armament: four 0.5 caliber machine guns; (F8F-1B) four 20 mm cannon.

The Bearcat was originally intended as a higher performance Hellcat derivative.

The prototype XF8F-1 was first flown on 31 August 1944. First production aircraft were delivered to the US Navy during February 1945. The VF-19 commenced training with the F8F-1 on 21 May 1945.

Although primarily designed to counter the Japanese Kamikaze attacks, US Navy combat service never materialized. However the Bearcat forged a link between the great World War II fighters and those of the jet age. On 20 November 1946 the Bearcat established a climb record of 10,000 feet in 94 seconds after a take-off run of only 115 feet. On 16 August 1969 a modified Bearcat, Conquest II, took the piston-engine World Air Speed Record at 483.041 mph.

Above right: **A Grumman F8F Bearcat of the Confederate Air Force, Texas.**
Right: **Grumman F8F Bearcat.**

Grumman F9F-2/5 Panther

Manufacturer: Grumman Aircraft Engineering Corporation, Bethpage, Long Island, New York.
Type: carrier-borne fighter.
Crew: pilot only.
Specification: F9F-5.
Power Plant: one 6250 lb J48-P-6A.
Dimensions: span, 38 ft; length, 38 ft 10 in; height, 12 ft 3 in; wing area, 250 sq ft.
Weights: empty, 10,147 lb; gross, 18,721 lb.
Performance: maximum speed, 579 mph at 5000 ft; cruising speed, 481 mph; initial climb, 5090 ft per min; service ceiling, 42,800 ft; range, 1300 miles.
Armament: four 20 mm cannon.

The first of two prototype XF9F-2s flew on 24 November 1947. Production models were dubbed Panther to perpetuate the Cat family and were powered by a license-built Rolls-Royce Nene, the Pratt and Whitney J42. Operational deliveries began in May 1949. An F9F-2 was the first Navy plane to down a MiG-15 on 9 November 1950. Panthers flew more than 78,000 sorties. Following their replacement by swept-wing versions (the Cougar) straight-wing Panthers were modified for special assignments, including the F9F-5KD which was used as a target drone or drone controller.

Top: **A Panther lands on USS *Lake Champlain.***
Below: **Grumman F9F-2/-5 Panther.**

Grumman F9F-6/8 Cougar

Manufacturer: Grumman Aircraft Engineering Corporation, Bethpage, Long Island, New York.
Type: operational trainer.
Crew: pupil and instructor in tandem.
Specification: F9F-8T.
Power Plant: one 7200 lb J48-P-8A.
Dimensions: span, 34 ft 6 in; length, 44 ft 5 in; height, 12 ft 3 in.
Weight: gross, 20,600 lb.
Performance: maximum speed, 705 mph at sea level; initial climb, 8.5 min to 40,000 ft; service ceiling, 50,000 ft; range, 600 miles.
Armament: two 20 mm guns.

The Cougar was a swept-wing fighter version of the F9F Panther which prolonged production of the basic family for seven years.

The prototype XF9F-6 first flew on 20 September 1951.

This plane was the first swept-wing aircraft used by the US Navy's Blue Angels aerobatics team (1955–1958).

Left: **The Grumman F9F-6 Cougar was the first version developed from the straight-wing F9F Panther. The Cougar was the first swept-wing aircraft to equip the Blue Angels aerobatic team and replaced the earlier Grumman Panther in many squadrons.**

Grumman F-11 Tiger

Manufacturer: Grumman Aircraft Engineering Corporation, Bethpage, Long Island, New York.
Type: carrier-borne fighter.
Crew: pilot only.
Specification: F-11F-1.
Power Plant: one 7450 lb J65-W-18.
Dimensions: span, 31 ft 7.5 in; length, 46 ft 2.5 in; height, 13 ft 2.75 in; wing area, 250 sq ft.
Weights: empty, 13,428 lb; gross, 22,160 lb.
Performance: maximum speed, 750 mph at sea level; cruising speed, 577 mph at 38,000 ft; initial climb, 5130 ft per min; service ceiling, 41,900 ft; range, 1270 miles.
Armament: four 20 mm cannon, four Sidewinder 1A of 1C air-to-air missiles.

The F-11A Tiger underwent its first flight on 30 July 1954. It had originally been designated F9F-9 (as a Cougar variant) but it was then redesignated as F-11. The Tiger was the first aircraft to use 'Coke bottle' fuselage or area rule' concept from its early stages. It was also the first carrier-borne, single-seat fighter with supersonic capability. Deliveries of the Tiger commenced in March 1957 and production continued until December 1958. Two first-line squadrons in the Atlantic Fleet and three in the Pacific were equipped with Tigers. However in 1959 the Tiger was phased out and assigned to training. Two Tigers were modified, F11-1F, with a 15,000 lb thrust J79-GE-3A engine and in 1956 one set unofficial world speed and altitude records of 1220 mph at 40,000 feet and reached an altitude of 70,000 feet.

Left: **Grumman F9F-8 Cougar.**
Below: **Grumman F-11A Tigers in the livery of the famous 'Blue Angels' Navy aerobatic team.**

Above: **An F8U-1 (F8A) Crusader on a test flight.**
Left: **An F8U reposes on the deck of the USS *Shangri-La* in April 1961.**

LTV (Vought) F-8 Crusader

Manufacturer: LTV Aerospace Corporation (originally Chance-Vought Corporation).
Type: carrier-borne day fighter.
Crew: pilot only.
Specification: F-8E.
Power Plant: one 10,700 lb J57-P-20A.
Dimensions: span, 35 ft 2 in; length, 54 ft 6 in; height, 15 ft 9 in.
Weights: gross, 34,000 lb.
Performance: maximum speed, 1120 mph at 40,000 ft; cruising speed, 560 mph at 40,000 ft; climb, 6.5 min to 57,000 ft; service ceiling, 58,000 ft; range, 1100 miles.
Armament: four 20 mm cannon, four Sidewinders 12 Mk 81 bombs, or two Bullpups or 8 Zuni rockets.

The Crusader was the declared winner, in May 1953, of a US Navy day fighter competition entered by eight companies.

The prototype XF80-1 was first tested on 25 March 1955 and after trials on F-8A the model was accepted by the US Navy in 1956.

It was the first US carrier-borne supersonic aircraft. On 16 July 1957 Major John Glenn established the first supersonic crossing of the USA (Los Angeles to New York in 3 hours 23 minutes). RF-8A photo-reconnaissance versions played a major role in revealing Russian missile sites were being built on Cuba. Crusaders, called 'The Last of the Gunfighters' by many pilots, also proved effective early in the Lebanese crisis. In seven known instances F-8s have taken off with wings still folded for carrier-deck storage. On the first known occasion a Navy pilot reached 5000 feet before realizing his wings were still folded! He circled and landed safely.

The Crusader was phased out after 1965 but one two-seat trainer, designated F8U-1T, was built and called the 'Twosader.' It was used for about 10 years by the Naval Test Pilot School, and then turned over to NASA in October 1975.

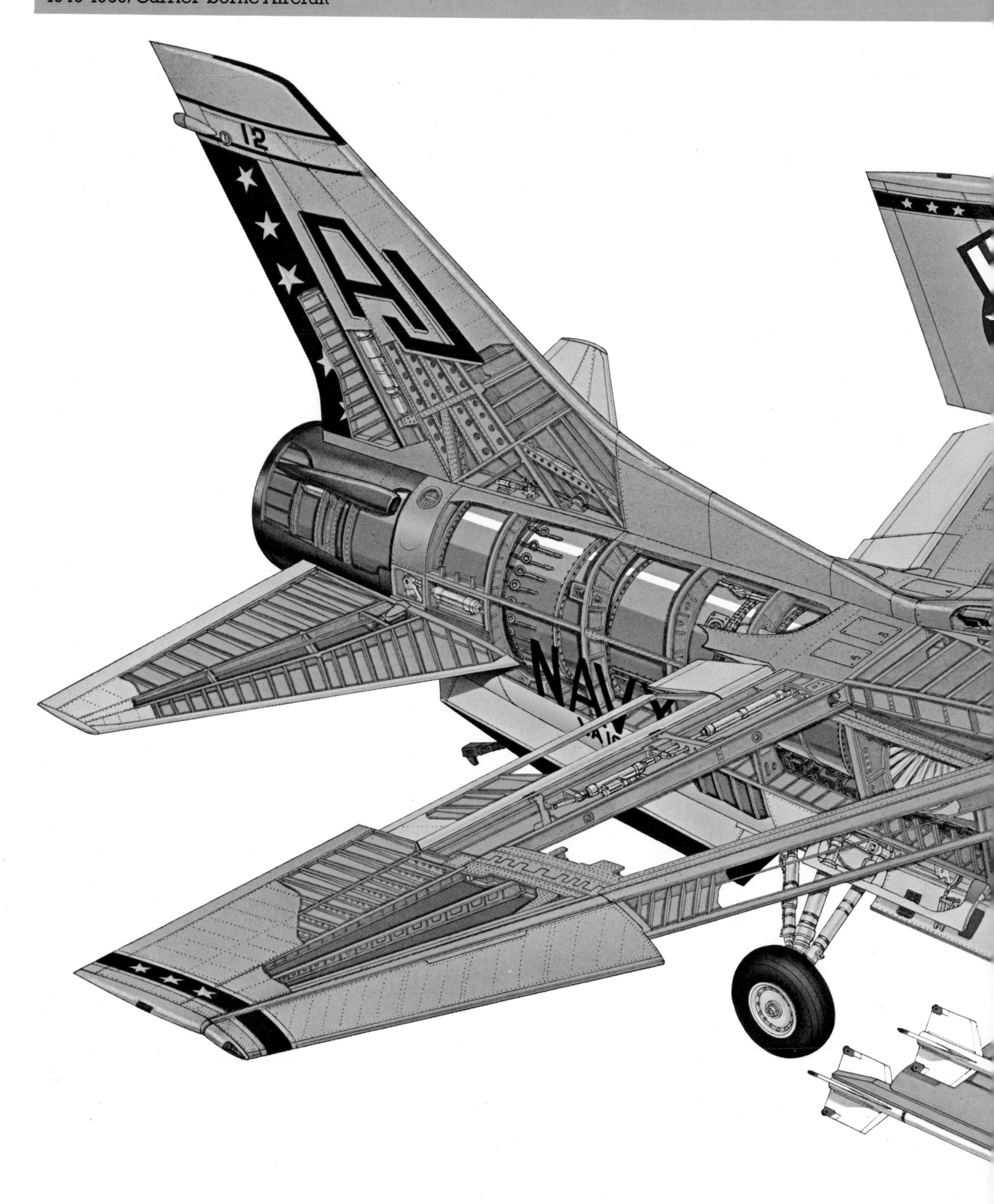
12
AJ
NAVY

Right: **Crusaders carried internally mounted 20mm cannon and early models had built-in rocket pods containing 32 rockets. The major aerial weapon (carried here) was the Sidewinder missile carried on fuselage mounts.**
Below: **Interior view of the Vought F-8H Crusader.**

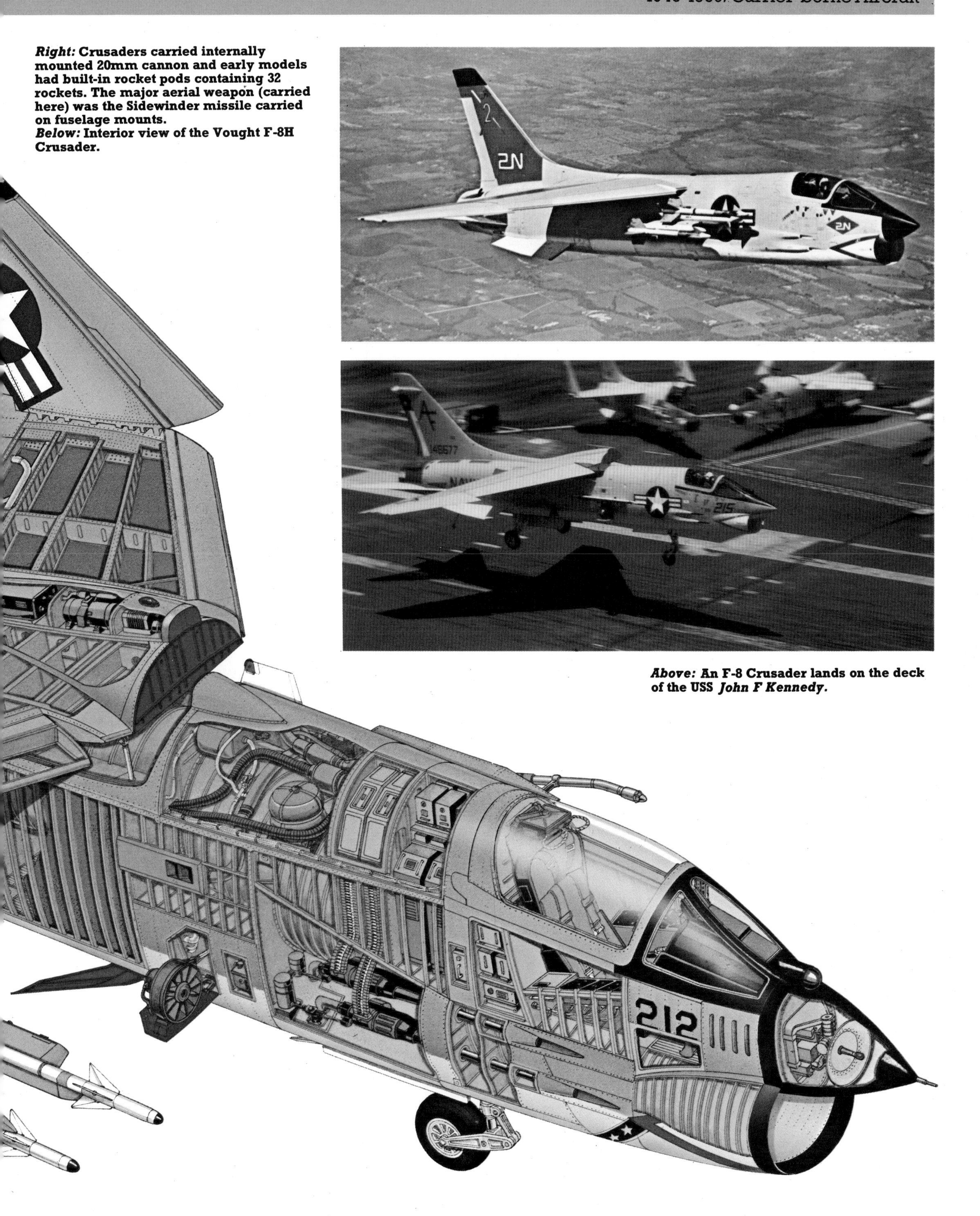

Above: **An F-8 Crusader lands on the deck of the USS *John F Kennedy*.**

McDonnell FD/FH Phantom

Manufacturer: McDonnell Aircraft Corporation, St Louis, Missouri.
Type: carrier-borne fighter.
Crew: pilot only.
Specification: FD1/FH-1.
Power Plant: two 1600 lb J30-WE-20.
Dimensions: span, 40 ft 9 in; length, 38 ft 9 in; height, 14 ft 2 in; wing area, 276 sq ft.
Weights: empty, 6683 lb; gross, 12,035 lb.
Performance: maximum speed, 479 mph at sea level; cruising speed, 248 mph; initial climb, 4230 ft per min; service ceiling, 41,100 ft; range, 980 miles.
Armament: four 0.50 in guns.

In 1943 the US Navy asked McDonnell to undertake the design of a new carrier-borne fighter to take advantage of the new found jet propulsion concept. The first prototype XFD-1 was tested on 26 January 1945.

The Phantom was the first McDonnell aircraft for the US Navy and the first jet fighter to serve with the US Marine Corps.

McDonnell F-2H Banshee

Manufacturer: McDonnell Aircraft Division (now McDonnell-Douglas Corporation), St Louis, Missouri.
Type: carrier-borne fighter.
Crew: pilot only.
Specification: F2H-2.
Power Plant: two 3250 lb J34-WE-34.
Dimensions: span, 44 ft 10 in; length, 40 ft 2 in; height, 14 ft 6 in; wing area, 294 sq ft.
Weights: empty, 11,146 lb; gross, 22,312 lb.
Performance: maximum speed, 532 mph at 10,000 ft; cruising speed, 501 mph; initial climb, 3910 ft per min; service ceiling, 44,800 ft; range, 1475 miles.
Armament: four 20 mm cannon; provision for two 500 lb bombs.

In 1945 the US Navy authorized McDonnell to proceed with a larger development of the FD-1. The first prototype first flew on 11 January 1947 and service deliveries began in March 1949.

Right: **Gleaming new F2H-2 Banshees.**
Below: **The F2H-1 Banshee was first introduced in 1947.**

McDonnell F3H Demon

Manufacturer: McDonnell Aircraft Corporation, St Louis, Missouri.
Type: carrier-borne fighter.
Crew: pilot only.
Specification: F3H-2.
Power Plant: one 9700 lb J71-A-2E.
Dimensions: span, 35 ft 4 in; length, 58 ft 11 in; height, 14 ft 7 in; wing area, 519 sq ft.
Weights: empty, 22,133 lb; gross, 33,900 lb.
Performance: maximum speed, 647 mph at 30,000 ft; initial climb, 12,795 ft per min; service ceiling, 42,650 ft; maximum range, 1370 miles.
Armament: four 20 mm cannon; provision for external ordnance.

The Demon was designed to bridge the performance gap between US Navy land-based and carrier-borne aircraft. On 30 September 1949 the US Navy ordered two prototypes.

The first one, XF3H-1, was flown on 7 August 1951; however, its operational career was com promised by the costly failure of the Westinghouse J40 engine program. Production ended in November 1959 but the Demon remained in front-line service until 1965.

It was an essential link in the development of the highly successful F-4 Phantom.

Above: **North American's T-28A Trojan.**

Martin AM Mauler

Manufacturer: Glenn L Martin Company, Baltimore, Maryland.
Type: carrier-borne attack aircraft.
Crew: pilot only.
Specification: AM-1.
Power Plant: one 2975 hp R-3350-4.
Dimensions: span, 50 ft; length, 41 ft 2 in; height, 16 ft 10 in; wing area, 496 sq ft.
Weights: empty, 14,500 lb; gross, 23,386 lb.
Performance: maximum speed, 367 mph at 11,600 ft; cruising speed, 189 mph; initial climb, 2780 ft per min; service ceiling, 30,500 ft; range, 1800 miles.
Armament: four 20 mm machine guns; approximately 4500 lb of assorted ordnance on 15 external points; (maximum demonstrated ordnance load, 10,689 lb).

In 1944 the US Navy sought a carrier-borne aircraft that combined SB (Scout and dive) and TB (torpedo) bombing characteristics. Martin went ahead in May 1944 with the XBTM-1 in competition with the Douglas XBT2D-1 and two others.

The XBTM-1 got its first outing on 26 August 1944. The first Maulers were delivered to the Navy on 1 March 1948 but production ceased in October 1949 and the following year all Maulers were assigned to US Navy Reserve units to permit all front-line squadrons to equip with the Douglas AD Skyraider.

Below: **An F3H Demon of the US Navy armed with four Sparrow missiles.**

North American AJ Savage

Manufacturer: North American Aviation Incorporated.
Type: AJ-1, carrier-borne nuclear strike; AJ-2P, reconnaissance; AJ-2, flight-refuelling tanker.
Crew: two.
Specification: AJ-1.
Power Plant: two 2400 hp R-2800-44W engines plus a 4600 thrust turbojet in tail.
Dimensions: span, 75 ft 2 in; length, 63 ft.
Weight: gross, 52,862 lb.
Performance: maximum speed, 471 mph.
Armament: none.

The Savage was ordered in June 1946 as a high-performance aircraft with nuclear capability. The XAJ-1 was first flown on 3 July 1948 and production models were delivered in September 1949.

Vought F7U Cutlass

Manufacturer: Chance Vought Division of United Aircraft Corporation (later Chance Vought Aircraft Incorporated), Dallas, Texas.
Type: carrier-borne fighter.
Crew: pilot only.
Specification: F7U-3.
Power Plant: two 4600 lb J46-WE-8A.
Dimensions: span, 38 ft 8 in; length, 44 ft 3 in; height, 14 ft 7.5 in; wing area, 496 sq ft.
Weights: empty, 18,210 lb; gross, 31,642 lb.
Performance: maximum speed, 680 mph at 10,000 ft; initial climb, 13,000 ft per min; service ceiling, 40,000 ft; range, 660 miles.
Armament: four 20 mm cannon; provision for four Sparrow I AAMs.

The Cutlass was initiated after Arado tailless designs were discovered among German aeronautical research data.

The XF7U-1 was first flown on 29 September 1948. An improved F7U-3 was tried out on 20 December 1951 and production ceased with this model in December 1955.

Below: **The F7U-3 Cutlass.**

***Above and below:* The Grumman UF-1 Albatross enjoyed more than 30 years of successful air-sea rescue operations work. *Center bottom:* The AF-2 Guardian, another in the long line of successful Grumman 'Iron Works' aircraft.**

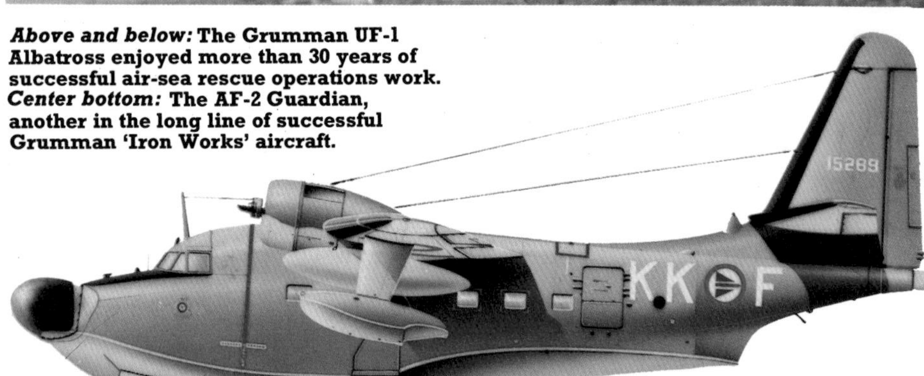

Grumman UF-1 Albatross

Manufacturer: Grumman Aircraft Engineering Corporation, Bethpage, Long Island, New York.
Type: general purpose amphibian.
Crew: four-six; provision for up to ten stretchers.
Specification: UF-2.
Power Plant: two 1425 hp R-1820-76As or Bs.
Dimensions: span, 96 ft 8 in; length, 61 ft 3 in; height, 25 ft 10 in; wing area, 1035 sq ft.
Weights: empty, 22,883 lb; gross, 35,700 lb.
Performance: maximum speed, 236 mph; cruising speed, 150 mph; initial climb, 1450 ft per min; service ceiling, 21,500 ft; range, 2850 miles.
Armament: none.

First flown on 1 October 1947, the SA-16 Albatross (redesignated HU-16), entered military service in July 1949. More than 450 of these amphibians were delivered to the USAF, the US Navy, the US Coast Guard and the flying services of many foreign governments. During almost 30 years of operation, the Albatross played an important role in air-sea rescue work. During the Korean War the Albatross is credited with saving the lives of more than 900 men. The Albatross also flew many other missions, such as, ASW, ambulance, cargo and personnel transport, escort, search and patrol. The Albatross was withdrawn from service with the US Navy in late September 1976.

Grumman AF Guardian

Manufacturer: Grumman Aircraft Engineering Corporation, Bethpage, Long Island, New York.
Type: anti-submarine search or strike aircraft.
Crew: AF-2S, two; AF-2W, four.
Specification: AF-2S.
Power Plant: one 2400 hp R-2800-48W.
Dimensions: span, 60 ft 8 in; length, 43 ft 4 in; height, 16 ft 2 in; wing area, 560 sq ft.
Weights: empty, 14,580 lb; gross, 25,500 lb.
Performance: maximum speed, 317 mph at 16,000 ft; initial climb, 1850 ft per min; service ceiling, 32,500 ft; range, 1500 miles.
Armament: one 2000 lb torpedo or two 2000 lb bombs or two 1600 lb depth charges in weapons-bay.

Originally designed late during World War II to be the successor to the TBF/TBM Avenger, the Grumman Design 70 (XTB3F-1) first took to the air in December 1946. The US Navy directed Grumman to revise the design to accomplish anti-submarine missions and accordingly, a production contract was placed for the first specialized 'hunter-killer' carrier-borne ASW aircraft, the AF-2W and the AF-2S. The first production Guardian, AF-2S, was flown on 17 November 1959 and squadron deliveries began in October 1950. Production ceased in April 1953 after some 387 Guardians had been built. In 1953 they were transferred from front-line to reserve Navy squadrons. They were replaced by S2F-1 Tracker, a hunter-killer aircraft.

Left: **Steam rises from the catapult of the ASW support carrier USS *Intrepid* as an S-2E Tracker is prepared for launching.** ***Below:*** **Grumman S-2 Tracker.**

Grumman S-2 Tracker, C-1A Trader, E-1B Tracer

Manufacturer: Grumman Aircraft Engineering Corporation, Bethpage, Long Island, New York; built under license in Canada.
Type: S-2, carrier-borne SASW; C-1, COD transport; E-1, AEW.
Crew: four (two pilots, two radar operators).
Specification: S-2E.
Power Plant: two 1525 hp R-1820-82WA.
Dimensions: span, 72 ft 7 in; length, 43 ft 6 in; height, 16 ft 7 in.
Weights: empty, 18,750 lb; gross, 29,150 lb.
Performance: maximum speed, 267 mph; initial climb, 1390 ft; service ceiling, 21,000 ft; range, 1300 miles.
Armament: maximum weapon load, 4810 lb; central weapon bay for one depth-bomb or two electric acoustic-homing torpedoes or rockets; up to 32 sono-buoys in nacelles.

The original design won the ASW competition in June 1950. The prototype XS2F-1 was first flown on 4 December 1952 and the S-2A on 30 April 1953. The S-2 Tracker was delivered to front-line squadrons in February 1954 and served in the Navy until it was retired from service on 28 August 1976. It was the first aircraft design to combine ASW equipment and operate from an aircraft carrier. In 1954 the S2F-1 was the first aircraft to be launched by steam catapult from the deck of an American carrier, the USS *Hancock*.

Below: **An E-1 Tracer aboard the USS *Wasp*.**

140964
NAVY

The P-2H (P2V-7) Lockheed Neptune in flight reveals its submarine detection apparatus and pod-mounted jet engines for additional power for high-speed attacks or short runway operation.

Lockheed P2V Neptune

Manufacturer: Lockheed-California Company, Burbank.
Type: maritime patrol and ASW.
Crew: nine/ten.
Specification: P2V-7.
Power Plant: two 3500 hp R-3350-32W; two 3400 lb J34-WE-34.
Dimensions: span, 103 ft 10 in; length, 91 ft 4 in; height, 29 ft 4 in; wing area, 1000 sq ft.
Weights: empty, 47,456 lb; gross, 75,500 lb.
Performance: maximum speed, 345 mph at 10,000 ft; cruising speed, 207 mph at 8500 ft; service ceiling, 22,000 ft; range, 2200 miles.
Armament: none.

The P2V was the result of Lockheed's Model 26 private venture formally initiated on 6 December 1941. US Navy placed a contract for two prototypes on 4 April 1944. The XP2V was first flown on 17 May 1945. The P2V-1 deliveries began in March 1947. Further contracts kept production going until April 1962. The final production version, P2V-7H, was first flown on 26 April 1954. This was the only version equipped with underwing jet pods.

In September 1946 a specially modified P2V-1 named 'Truculent Turtle' established a world distance record of 11,236 miles. From 1947 to 1962, it was the mainstay of US Navy land-based patrol squadrons.

Top: **P2V Neptune *Truculant Turtle*.**

Martin P5M Marlin

Manufacturer: Glenn L Martin Company, Baltimore, Maryland.
Type: patrol flying-boat.
Crew: 11.
Specification: P5M-2.
Power Plant: two 3450 hp R-3350-32WAs.
Dimensions: span, 118 ft 2 in; length, 100 ft 7 in; height, 32 ft 8.5 in; wing area, 1406 sq ft.
Weights: empty, 50,485 lb; gross, 85,000 lb.
Performance: maximum speed, 251 mph at sea level; cruising speed, 150 mph at 1000 ft; initial climb, 1200 ft per min; service ceiling, 24,000 ft; range, 2050 miles.
Armament: four torpedoes, four 2000 lb bombs or mines, or combinations of smaller stores weighing up to 8000 lb total internally in nacelles; up to eight 1000 lb bombs or mines externally.

The Marlin was the development of the wartime PBM Mariner. Design work began in 1946 using a Mariner wing and upper hull.

The prototype was first flown on 30 May 1948 and the first production model on 22 June 1951. Service deliveries to the US Navy began in April 1952. Production ceased in late 1960.

The Marlin was the US Navy's last operational flying boat and remained in front-line service from 1952 until 1966.

Above: **The four Pratt and Whitney turbojets burst into action as the P6M takes off. Carrier-borne aircraft eventually render P6Ms obsolete.**

Martin P6M-1 Seamaster

Manufacturer: Glenn L Martin Company, Baltimore, Maryland.
Type: long-range minelaying and reconnaissance flying boat.
Crew: four.
Power Plant: four 17,500 lb J57-P-2.
Dimensions: span, 100 ft; length, 134 ft; height, 31 ft; wing area, 1900 sq ft.
Weights: loaded, about 150,000 lb; disposable load, 30,000 lb.
Performance: (estimated) maximum speed, 633 mph at 40,000 ft; cruising altitude, 40,000 ft; combat radius, 1500 to 1750 miles.
Armament: two 20 mm cannon in radar-directed barbette. Provision for bombs and mines on rotary door in hull.

The first of two XP6M-1 Seamaster prototypes was flown on 14 July 1955 and a production order for 24 P6M-1s was placed on behalf of the US Navy in August 1956. The Seamaster is probably the most advanced flying-boat ever built. Its combat radius of 1500 miles plus could be extended by in-flight refuelling and other advanced features included a pressurized flight deck and ejection seats for all the crew. However, carrier-borne aircraft then coming into service rendered obsolete aircraft which operated independently from the surface of the sea.

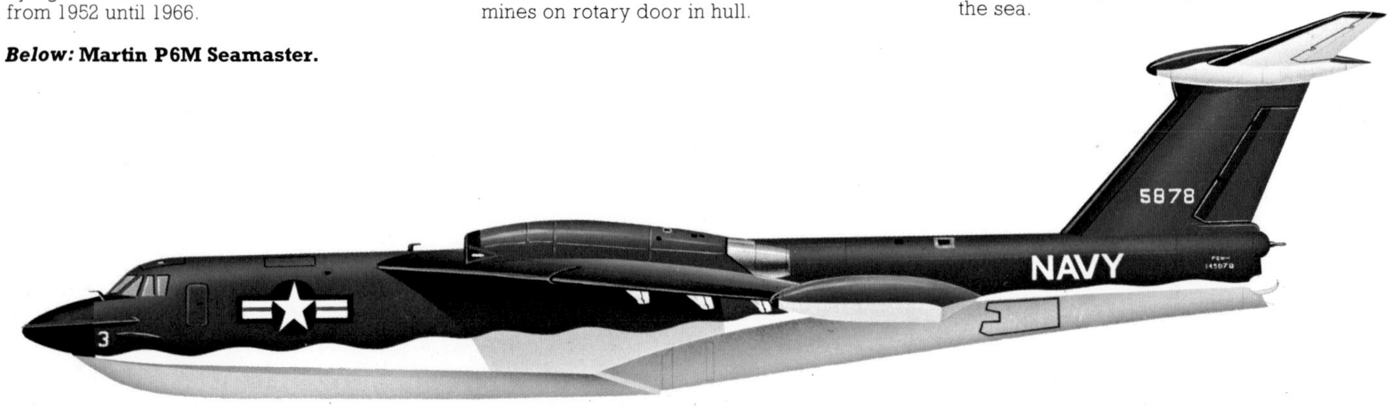

Below: **Martin P6M Seamaster.**

***Above:* An L-15 Scout liaison aircraft is loaded into a C-97 Stratofreighter.**
***Left:* A C-97A Stratofreighter takes off.**

Boeing C-97 Stratofreighter

Manufacturer: Boeing Airplane Company, Renton, Washington.
Type: flight refuelling tanker and transport.
Crew: KC-97G, five (two pilots, flight engineer, navigator- radio operator, boom operator); provision for 96 combat troops or 69 stretchers with attendants.
Specification: C-97.
Power Plant: four 3500 hp R-4360-59B.
Dimensions: span, 141 ft 3 in; length, 117 ft 5 in; height, 38 ft 3 in.
Weights: empty, 85,000 lb; gross, 175,000 lb.
Performance: maximum speed, 370 mph; service ceiling, 30,000 ft; range at 300 mph without using transfer fuel 4300 miles.
Armament: normally none.

The Stratofreighter was designed in 1942 as a heavy cargo transport for military purposes, with the same aerodynamic and structural relationship to the B-29 that the Model 307 Stratoliner bore to the B-17. The XC-97 was first flown on 15 November 1944 and the first production model C-97A was flown on 28 January 1949. The final models were delivered in July 1956.

Above: **A KC-135 refuels E4B 50125 during one of its transcontinental flights.**
Right: **An officer and a team of controllers on an EC-135 airborne command post.**

Boeing C-135 Family

Manufacturer: Boeing Airplane Company Transport Division, Renton, Washington.
Type: tanker and transport.
Crew: two or three pilots, radio-navigator, boom operator.
Specification: KC-135A.
Power Plant: four 13,750 lb thrust (water injection rating) J57-59W.
Dimensions: span, 130 ft 10 in; length, 136 ft 3 in; height, 38 ft 4 in.
Weights: empty, 109,000 lb; loaded, 297,000 lb.
Performance: maximum speed, 600 mph; cruising speed, 552 mph; service ceiling, 40,000 ft; typical range, 4000 miles.
Armament: none.

The KC-135 was a logical outgrowth of the basic 707 design and was given the company designation 717. As a follow-up to the successful KC-97 series tanker-transports, the new jet was ordered into limited production in July 1954. The first prototype was flown on 15 July 1954. Before completion of the first KC-135A, a new, highly streamlined aerial refueling flying boom had been installed and tested on the versatile 367–80. The KC-135 was similar in design and overall size to the 707 prototype but had only a single large cargo door, instead of two. Fuel tanks, located in the lower lobe of the two-deck body and in the wings, allowed an unobstructed upper deck for cargo and personnel. Several hundred KC-135As were delivered to SAC and were followed, in 1961 by an order from MATS for C-135A and B types to re-equip its logistic transport fleet. Numerous KC/C-135s were extensively modified after delivery into special-purpose aircraft for electronic and weather reconnaissance, airborne command communications duty, airborne telemetry, command posts and other roles.

***Above:* A Samaritan of the Military ATS.**

Convair C-131 Samaritan

Manufacturer: Convair Division of General Dynamics Corporation, San Diego, California.
Type: (C-131) personnel transport and casualty evacuation; (T-29) navigator-bombardier trainer.
Crew: two.
Specification: C-131B.
Accommodation: four crew plus 48.
Power Plant: 2500 hp R-2800-99W.
Dimensions: span, 105 ft 4 in; length, 79 ft 2 in; height, 28 ft 2 in; wing area, 920 sq ft.
Weights: empty, 29,248 lb; gross, 47,000 lb.
Performance: maximum speed, 293 mph; cruising speed, 254 mph; initial climb, 1410 ft per min; service ceiling, 24,500 ft; range, 450 miles.

The Samaritan was purchased by the USAF for training and transportation and was first flown on 22 September 1949.

Douglas C-124 Globemaster II

Manufacturer: Douglas Aircraft Company, Long Beach, California.
Type: heavy cargo transport.
Crew: eight; provision for 68,500 lb of cargo or 200 passengers or 127 stretchers.
Specification: C-124C.
Power Plant: four 3800 hp R-4360-63A.
Dimensions: span, 174 ft 2 in; length, 130 ft; height, 48 ft 4 in; wing area, 2506 sq ft.
Weights: empty, 101,165 lb; gross, 194,500 lb.
Performance: maximum speed, 271 mph at sea level; cruising speed, 230 mph at 10,000 ft; initial climb, 625 ft per min; service ceiling, 18,400 ft; range, 4030 miles with 26,375 lb cargo.
Armament: none.

USAF transport aircraft were heavily engaged throughout the 11 months during the Berlin Airlift but only one, the Fairchild C-82, was designed especially as a military transport. Experience dictated the need for a purpose-built heavy transport aircraft. Among the first to be built was the C-124, based on the C-74 Globemaster, one of those aircraft which had taken part in the Berlin Airlift. C-124 development began in 1947 using the same wing, power plant and tail unit as the C-74 but with a new deep fuselage with clam shell nose loading doors and a built-in ramp, at the same time retaining the elevator hoist amidships which had been a feature of the C-74.

***Left and below:* The Globemaster carrier has a large but light fuselage.**

***Right:* Douglas C-133 Cargomaster.**

Douglas C-133 Cargomaster

Manufacturer: Douglas Aircraft Company, Long Beach, California.
Type: strategic heavy freighter.
Crew: ten (three pilots, two navigators, three systems engineers and two loadmasters); capacity for 13,000 cu ft freight volume or 200 personnel.
Specification: C-133.
Power Plant: 7500 hp T34-9W.
Dimensions: span, 179 ft 8 in; length, 157 ft 6.5 in; height, 48 ft 3 in.
Weights: empty, 120,263 lb; maximum loaded, 286,000 lb.
Performance: maximum speed, 359 mph; initial climb, 1280 ft per min; service ceiling at gross weight, 29,950 ft; range with 44,000 lb payload, 4300 miles.
Armament: none.

The Cargomaster was built in 1952 to meet an operational requirement for a heavy turboprop strategic freighter.

The prototype was first flown on 23 April 1956. Service deliveries began 29 August 1957 and the Cargomaster remained in service for over 20 years so that it is due to be retired from service in 1980.

Late production models permitted the shipment of all operational IRBMs and ICBMs, including the Titan, in one unit instead of disassembled, to Europe and throughout the USA.

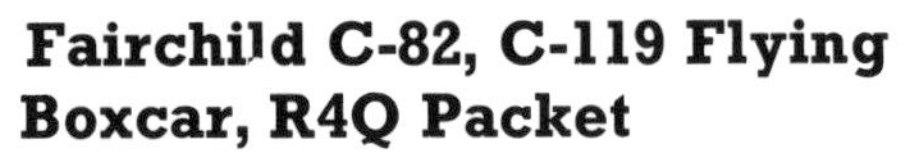

Fairchild C-82, C-119 Flying Boxcar, R4Q Packet

Manufacturer: Fairchild Engine and Airplane Corporation, Aircraft Division, Hagerstown, Maryland.
Type: troop and supply transport.
Specification: C-82A.
Power Plant: two 2100 hp R-2800-85.
Dimensions: span, 106 ft 5.5 in; length, 77 ft 1 in; height, 26 ft 6 in; wing area, 1400 sq ft.
Weights: empty, 32,500 lb; gross, 54,000 lb.
Performance: maximum speed, 281 mph at 18,000 ft; initial climb, 950 ft per min; service ceiling, 21,200 ft; range, 3785 miles.
Armament: none.
Specification: C-119C.
Power Plant: two 3500 R-4360-20.
Dimensions: span, 109 ft 3 in; length, 86 ft 6 in; height, 26 ft 6 in; wing area, 1447 sq ft.
Weights: empty, 39,800 lb; gross, 74,000 lb.
Performance: maximum speed, 281 mph at 18,000 ft; initial climb, 1010 ft per min; service ceiling, 23,900 ft; range, 1770 miles.

The C-82 was built to meet a USAAF requirement in 1941 for a specialized service freighter. The first prototype XC-82 was flown on 10 September 1944. Service deliveries began at the end of 1945. The R4Q was adopted by the Marine Corps in 1950 to replace R4Ds and other smaller types. Deliveries of the R4Q-1 began in early 1950 and they served primarily in the Korean conflict.

Fairchild C-119C Flying Boxcars (above center and below) and the R4Q-1 Packet (right).

Fairchild (Chase) C-123 Provider

Manufacturer: The Fairchild Engine and Airplane Corporation, Aircraft Division, Hagerstown, Maryland.
Type: troop and supply transport.
Crew: two pilots, 61 troops or 50 stretchers; provision for six sitting wounded and six attendants.
Specification: C-123B.
Power Plant: two 2300 hp R-2800-99W.
Dimensions: span, 110 ft; length, 75 ft 9 in; height, 34 ft 1 in; wing area, 1223 sq ft.
Weights: empty, 29,900 lb; gross, 71,000 lb.
Performance: maximum speed, 245 mph; cruising speed, 205 mph; initial climb, 1150 ft per min; service ceiling, 29,000 ft; range, 1470 miles.
Armament: none.

The Provider was developed from a cargo glider produced by Chase in 1949.
The all-metal XG-20 (first prototype) first flew 14 October 1949. Chase built the C-123Bs first flown in 1953 but the contract was later given to Fairchild. The first Fairchild-built C-123B was tried out on 1 September 1954 and the C-123Bs were eventually delivered to the USAF in July 1955.

Below: **Fairchild Providers entered service with Troop Carrier Command in 1955.**

Lockheed C-130 Hercules

Manufacturer: Lockheed Aircraft Corporation, later Lockheed-Georgia Company, Marietta, Georgia.
Type: C-130B, personnel and supplies transport; KC-130F, flight refuelling tanker and transport; C-130H, multi-role transport.
Crew: C-130B, four/five with capacity for 92 troops or 64 paratroops or 70–74 stretchers; KC-130F, seven; C-130H, four with capacity for a maximum of 92 fully-equipped troops, 64 paratroops, or 74 stretchers and two medics.
Specification: C-130H.
Power Plant: four 4050 hp T56-A-7A.
Dimensions: span, 132 ft 7 in; length, 97 ft 9 in; height, 38 ft 3 in; wing area, 1745 sq ft.
Weights: empty, 72,892 lb; gross, 175,000 lb.
Performance: maximum speed, 384 mph; maximum cruise, 368 mph; range (with maximum payload and 5 percent plus 30 min reserves), 2450 miles; initial climb, 1900 ft per min; maximum range, 4770 miles.
Armament: normally none; AC-130H, one 105 mm howitzer, one 40 mm cannon; two 20 mm cannon or T-171 'Gatlings'; two 7.62 mm 'Gatling' miniguns; optional grenade dispenser, rockets, missiles, bombs and various night or day sensors and target designators.

Left: **Vietnamese workers prepare a hardstand for the growing number of C-130s in their country.**

The development of the Hercules coincided with a top USAF policy decision to equip its transport fleet with turboprop transports.

The YC-130 was first flown on 23 August 1954 and the production C-130A on 7 April 1955. Service delivery began in December 1956.

The USAF's Jack of all trades and one of the American aircraft industry's greatest exports, selling to over 39 countries. Herky birds have been in production for more than 23 years with no end to production envisaged at this time. The RAF is currently increasing its cargo-carrying capacity among its fleet of almost 50 C-130s by 'stretching' them an extra 15 feet. This is the equivalent of adding at least six new C-130s. The C-130s will more than meet the needs of most countries well into the 1980s.

Right: **A C-130D at the South Pole.**

Above: **A KC-130F Hercules tanker of the US Marines with two Phantoms in tow.**
Left: **A camouflaged C-130H Hercules.**

Above: **Lockheed C-130 Hercules.**

Lockheed C-69, C-121 Constellation, EC-121 Warning Star

Manufacturer: Lockheed-California Company, Burbank.
Type: C-69, C-121, personnel and cargo transport; C-121D, airborne early warning; EC-121, electronic reconnaissance and specialist duties; WV-2, long-range airborne early warning patrol.
Crew: twenty-seven; C-121, capacity for 72 troops; C-69, capacity for 60 troops.
Specification: C-121G.
Power Plant: four 3250 hp R-3350-91.
Dimensions: span, 123 ft; length, 116 ft 2 in; height, 24 ft 8 in; wing area, 1650 sq ft.
Weights: empty, 72,815 lb; gross, 145,000 lb.
Performance: maximum speed, 368 mph at 20,000 ft; cruising speed, 259 mph at 10,000 ft; initial climb, 1100 ft per min; service ceiling, 22,300 ft; range, 2100 miles.
Armament: none.

The Constellation was requisitioned from commercial production lines at the time of Pearl Harbor and designated C-69. It was first flown on 9 January 1943 and the US Navy transport versions were acquired in 1945. The C-121C was first flown in 1952 and final deliveries of the EC-121T took place in 1973.

Top right: **Lockheed VC-121 Constellation.** ***Right:*** **A WV-1 Radar Sentry version of the USN's Constellation.**

Lockheed U-2

Manufacturer: Lockheed-California Company, Burbank.
Type: high-altitude photo reconnaissance, multi-sensor reconnaissance and special reconnaissance; (CT) dual trainer; (EPX) electronics patrol experiment; (WU) weather research; (HASP) high-altitude sampling program.
Crew: pilot only.
Specification: U-2.
Power Plant: one 17,000 lb J75-13.
Dimensions: span, 80 ft; length, 49 ft 7 in; height, 13 ft.
Weights: empty, 11,700 lb; loaded, maximum over 21,000 lb.
Performance: maximum speed, 528 mph; service ceiling, 85,000 ft; maximum range, 4000 miles.
Armament: none.

Work commenced in 1954 amid great secrecy on an espionage reconnaissance aircraft.

The U-2 was first flown on 1 August 1955 and service deliveries began early in 1956. Final deliveries took place July 1958.

A U-2 was shot down and crashed near Sverdlovsk, USSR on 1 May 1960 while on an unarmed reconnaissance flight from Turkey via Russia to Norway. The pilot, Gary Powers, survived and was tried in Moscow in 1960.

Right and below: **Two versions of the U-2.**

Bell 47, AB 47, KH-4, H-13 Sioux

Manufacturer: Bell Helicopter Company (now Bell Helicopter Textron), Fort Worth, Texas; license-built by Kawasaki, Japan; Agusta, Italy; Westland, UK.
Type: three-seat utility and training helicopter.
Crew: pilot; provision for two passengers.
Specification: OH-135.
Power Plant: 270 hp TVO-435.
Dimensions: diameter of two-blade main rotor, 37 ft 1.5 in; length overall (rotors turning), 43 ft 4.75 in; height overall, 9 ft 3.5 in.
Weights: empty, 1819 lb; maximum loaded, 2950 lb.
Performance: maximum speed, 105 mph; cruising speed, 86 mph; range at low level, no reserve, 210 miles.
Armament: many equipped with fixed forward-firing gun (LMG, GPMG or Minigun), rocket pods or early anti-tank wire-guided missiles.

The prototype was first flown on 8 December 1945. The Bell 47 Model has been in service use since 1946, distinguishing itself all over the world. It has served in various roles including casualty evacuation, training, reconnaissance and observation. Today it is mostly used by military forces for liaison and training.

Right: **This Westland-built Sioux served with the British Army.**

Piasecki (Vertol) H-21 Workhorse

Manufacturer: Piasecki Helicopter Corporation, Morton, Pennsylvania.
Type: troop and cargo transport helicopter.
Crew: two pilots, provision for 14 troops or 12 stretchers.
Specification: H-21.
Power Plant: one 1425 hp R-1820-103.
Dimensions: rotor diameter, 44 ft 6 in; overall length, 86 ft 4 in; height, 15 ft 5 in.
Weights: empty, 8000 lb; gross, 13,300 lb.
Performance: maximum speed, 131 mph at sea level; cruising speed, 98 mph at sea level; initial climb, 1080 ft per min; service ceiling, 9450 ft.
Armament: none.

In 1949 the USAF ordered an evaluation and service trials batch of 18 YH-21s and subsequently pressed H-21As into service with MATS Air Rescue Service, principally in the Arctic.

The YH-21 was first tested on 11 April 1952. The 'Flying Banana,' as it was called, was the first tandem-rotor helicopter to serve with the USAF.

Sikorsky H-19 Chickasaw

Manufacturer: Sikorsky Aircraft Division of United Aircraft Corporation, Stratford and Bridgeport, Connecticut.
Type: utility helicopter.
Crew: two; provision for ten troops or six stretchers.
Specification: H-19B.
Power Plant: one 800 hp R-1300-3.
Dimensions: rotor diameter, 53 ft; fuselage length, 42 ft 3 in; height, 13 ft 4 in; disc area, 2206 sq ft.
Weights: empty, 5250 lb; gross, 7900 lb.
Performance: maximum speed, 112 mph at sea level; cruising speed, 91 mph; initial climb, 1020 ft per min; range, 360 miles.
Armament: none.

The H-19 was Sikorsky's larger utility helicopter, designed in 1948. The USAF awarded a contract to produce five for evaluation.

On 10 November 1949 YH-19 was first flown. Production models of the H-19A were delivered to the USAF in 1951. Starting in 1952 the US Army took delivery of H-19Cs and H-19Ds, adopting the name Chickasaw.

Below and bottom: **Sikorsky Chickasaws.**

Above: **A Kaman HH-43 carries out an emergency fire drill.**

Kaman H-43 Huskie Series

Manufacturer: Kaman Aerospace Corporation, Bloomfield, Connecticut.
Type: H-43B, local crash rescue helicopter; SH-2D, ship-board multi-role helicopter.
Crew: H-43, pilot, observer and fire-fighting crew or up to ten passengers or four stretchers and attendant.
Specification: H-43B.
Power Plant: one 860 hp T53-L-1A.
Dimensions: span, 51 ft 6 in; length, 25 ft; height, 15 ft 6.5 in.
Weights: empty, 4469 lb; gross, 8800 lb with slung load.
Performance: maximum speed, 120 mph; cruising speed, 97 mph; initial climb, 2000 ft per min; service ceiling, 25,700 ft; range, 235 miles; endurance, 3.2 hours.
Armament: none.

The Kaman K-600 won a US Navy design competition in 1950 which led to orders for the Marines (HOK-1) and the US Navy (HUK-1). The USAF decided to purchase 18 H-43s for airborne fire-fighting and crash rescue. The prototype was first tested on 19 September 1958 and service delivery began in November 1958. The Huskie series have been in operation for over twenty years. Final deliveries of later models took place in 1972 but some were reconverted and retained in service.

Sikorsky H-37 Mojave

Manufacturer: Sikorsky Aircraft Division of United Aircraft Corporation, Stratford and Bridgeport, Connecticut.
Type: troop and supply transport helicopter.
Crew: two; provision for 23 troops or 24 stretchers.
Specification: H-37.
Power Plant: two 2100 hp R-2800.
Dimensions: rotor diameter, 72 ft; fuselage length, 64 ft 3 in; height, 22 ft.
Weights: empty, 20,831 lb; gross, 31,000 lb.
Performance: maximum speed, 130 mph at sea level; cruising speed, 115 mph; initial climb, 910 ft per min; service ceiling, 8700 ft; range, 145 miles.
Armament: none.

The H-37 Mojave was developed to meet a joint US Navy-Marines requirement for an assault transport helicopter.

The H-37 prototype's first flight took place on 18 December 1953. In 1954 the US Army tested a YH-37 and subsequently ordered production of H-37As. Deliveries began in 1956.

At the time of its introduction, it was the largest helicopter operational with the US forces, with a cargo capacity capable of accommodating two jeeps.

Sikorsky HO4S, HRS

Manufacturer: Sikorsky Aircraft Division of United Aircraft Corporation, Stratford, Connecticut.
Type: transport helicopter.
Crew: pilot and provision for eight troops.
Specification: HRS-2.
Power Plant: one 550 hp R-1340.
Dimensions: rotor diameter, 53 ft; length, 42 ft 2 in; height, 13 ft 4 in; rotor disc area, 2210 sq ft.
Weights: empty, 4590 lb; gross, 7900 lb.
Performance: maximum speed, 101 mph at sea level; cruising speed, 85 mph at 1000 ft; initial climb, 700 ft per min; service ceiling, 10,500 ft; range, 370 miles.
Armament: none.

This was the US Navy version of the H-19A.

The Navy placed a contract for it on 28 April 1950. Deliveries began on 27 December 1950.

Below:* US Marine Corps UH-34s take off from the decks of USS *Palau.

Sikorsky HR2S-1

Manufacturer: Sikorsky Aircraft Division of United Aircraft Corporation, Stratford, Connecticut.
Type: transport helicopter.
Crew: two pilots; provision for 20 troops or 24 stretchers.
Specification: HR2S-1.
Power Plant: two 1900 hp R-2800-54s.
Dimensions: rotor diameter, 72 ft; length, 64 ft 3 in; height, 22 ft; rotor disc area, 4080 sq ft.
Weights: empty, 20,831 lb; gross, 31,000 lb.
Performance: maximum speed, 130 mph at sea level; cruising speed, 115 mph; initial climb, 910 ft per min; service ceiling, 8700 ft; range, 145 miles.
Armament: none.

The HR2S-1 was built to meet a Marine Corps requirement in 1950.

It was tested on 18 December 1953 and after further tests was delivered to the Marines on 26 July 1956.

Above:* Sikorsky HSS-1N hovers over the *Lake Champlain.

Sikorsky H-34/S-58 Series: US Army CH-34A and C Choctaw, SH-34J Seabat, USMC UH-34D, E, VH-34D Seahorse

Manufacturer: Sikorsky Aircraft, Division of United Aircraft (now United Technologies) Corporation, Stratford; built under license by Sud-Aviation (now Aérospatiale) France and redesigned with turbine power by Westland.
Type: multi-role helicopter including utility transport, ASW and search rescue.
Power Plant: one 1525 hp R-1820-84.
Dimensions: diameter of four-blade main rotor, 56 ft; fuselage length (ignoring rotors), 46 ft 9 in; height overall, 14 ft 3.5 in.
Weights: empty, 7750 lb; gross, 14,000 lb.
Performance: typical cruise, 98 mph; range with full payload, 280 miles.
Armament: none.

The series was a larger version of the Sikorsky H-19 Chickasaw and was developed originally to meet a US Navy requirement for an anti-submarine helicopter. The prototype was first flown on 8 March 1954 and the first models entered service with the US Army in April 1955. The US Navy received its SH-34G in August 1955 and the US Marines received the UH-34D in February 1957. By 1958 the H-34 was the principal US Army transport helicopter. French-built Sikorskys served in the Algerian war. The H-34 was built under license in the UK by Westland and was known as the Wessex.

Left: **UH-34Ds take off from the USS *Okinawa*.**
Below: **Two views of the Beechcraft T-34C Turbo Mentor.**

Beechcraft T-34 (Turbine Mentor) Series

Manufacturer: Beech Aircraft Corporation, Wichita, Kansas.
Type: primary trainer.
Crew: instructor and student.
Specification: T-34C.
Power Plant: one 680 shp (derated to 400 shp) PT6A-25.
Performance: maximum speed, 213 mph at sea level, 239 mph at 10,000 ft; range (5 percent and 20 min reserve), 787 miles at 220 mph at 17,500 ft, 915 miles at 222 mph at 25,000 ft; initial climb, 1430 ft per min.
Weights: empty equipped, 3015 lb; normal loaded, 4249 lb; maximum take-off weight of 5425 lb.
Dimensions: span, 33 ft 4.75 in; length, 28 ft 8 in; height, 9 ft 10.75 in; wing area, 179.5 sq ft.
Armament: (T-34A) none; (T-34C) external stores; capacity for 1800 lbs ordnance; typical tactical strike ordnance (single-seat configuration), four 250 lb Mk 81 bombs or two BLU-10/B fire bombs and two SUU-11 gun pods.

On 4 March 1953 the Beech 45 was declared the winner of an evaluation program begun in early 1950 to select a new primary trainer for the USAF. It went into production as the T-34A Mentor (the first YT-34 having flown in May 1950). The prototype first flew on 21 September 1974. Service delivery began in September 1976.

The Beechcraft was the first primary trainer for the USAF since 1944 and the last of its type purchased in quantity

Beech L-23, U-8 Seminole

Manufacturer: Beech Aircraft Corporation, Wichita, Kansas.
Type: army staff transport and all-weather battlefield surveillance.
Specification: L-23F.
Accommodation: 6 seats.
Power Plant: two 340 hp Lycoming IGSO-480-A1A6.
Dimensions: span, 45 ft 10.5 in; length, 33 ft 4 in; height, 14 ft 2 in; wing area, 277 sq ft.
Weights: empty, 4996 lb; gross, 7700 lb.
Performance: maximum speed, 240 mph; cruising speed, 200 mph; initial climb, 1300 ft per min; service ceiling, 27,000 ft; range, 1370 miles.
Armament: none.

The Seminole was adopted by the US Army in 1952 for communications, transport and liaison duties. Four examples of the Beech Twin Bonanza were purchased off the shelf for evaluation and designated YL-23.

The first model was delivered on 30 January 1952.

Below: **A Beechcraft L-23 (U-8) of the US Army.**

Cessna L-19, O-1 Bird Dog

Manufacturer: Cessna Aircraft Company, Wichita, Kansas.
Type: army liaison and observation monoplane.
Crew: pilot and observer/passenger in tandem.
Specification: L-19E.
Power Plant: one 213 hp C-470-11.
Dimensions: span, 36 ft; length, 25 ft 9.5 in; height, 7 ft 3.5 in; wing area, 174 sq ft.
Weights: empty, 1614 lb; gross, 2400 lb.
Performance: maximum speed, 151 mph at sea level; cruising speed, 104 mph at 5000 ft; initial climb. 1150 ft per min; service ceiling, 18,500 ft; range, 530 miles.
Armament: none.

This aircraft, Model 305A, won 1950 competition for a new two-seat liaison and observation monoplane.

Cessna delivered the L-19A from December 1950 onward.

The XL-19B powered by a 210 ehp Boeing XT51-T-1 turboprop set a light aircraft altitude record of 37,063 feet on 5 November 1952.

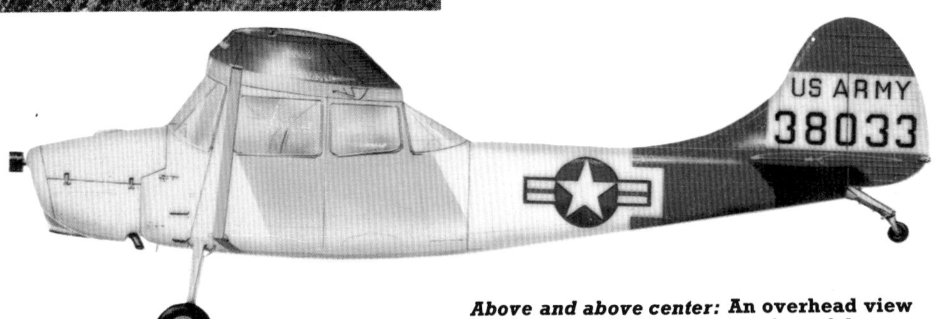

Above and above center: **An overhead view of a Cessna L-19A and a sideview of the Cessna O-1 Bird Dog.**

Cessna O-1 Bird Dog of the US Army.

The XFV-1 VTOL development aircraft was cancelled in 1955 with the advent of jet-lift principles.

***Above:* The XB-43 three-man jet bomber.**

Douglas XB-43 Mixmaster

Manufacturer: Douglas Aircraft Company.
Type: experimental jet bomber.
Crew: three.
Specification: XB-43.
Power Plant: two 3750 lb J35-GE-3.
Dimensions: span, 71 ft 2 in; length, 51 ft 5 in;
Weight: gross, 40,000 lb.
Performance: maximum speed, 507 mph.
Armament: none.

The design of the XB-43 began in 1944 based on the unconventional XB-42, with two piston engines in the fuselage driving pusher contra-props. The aircraft first flew on 17 May 1946.

It was the first American jet bomber although it did not go into production.

Lockheed XFV-1 Salmon

Manufacturer: Lockheed-California, Burbank.
Type: VTOL development aircraft.
Crew: pilot only.
Specification: XFV-1.
Power Plant: 5500 shp Allison XT40-A-6.
Dimensions: span, 27 ft 4.75 in; length, 37 ft 6 in; wing area, 246 sq ft.
Weights: empty, 11,599 lb; gross, 16,221 lb.
Performance: 580 mph (estimated).
Armament: none.

The Lockheed XFV-1 was designed for vertical and horizontal flight. For flight tests the XFV-1 was equipped with conventional landing gear. It hung suspended like a humming bird by contra-rotating propellers geared to a single turboprop engine. The research program was concluded in 1955, a year after the Rolls-Royce Flying Bed-Stead had hovered, using jet lift.

Lockheed C-140 Jetstar

Manufacturer: Lockheed California, Burbank.
Type: utility transport.
Crew: two and up to eight passengers.
Specification: C-140.
Power Plant: two J-60.
Dimensions: span, 53 ft 8 in; length, 60 ft 5.5 in; height, 20 ft 6 in.
Weight: gross, 40,100 lb.
Performance: maximum speed, 540 mph.
Armament: none.

The Jetstar was built to meet a USAF requirement for a utility transport after the Air Force had invited industry-financed prototypes in 1956. Lockheed's Model 1329 design was adopted in October 1959.

The Model 1329 was first flown on 4 September 1957.

North American T-28 Trojan

Manufacturer: North American Aviation Incorporated, Inglewood, California.
Type: (T-28A) basic trainer; (T-28R Hamilton Nomair/Pacair Nomad) desert warfare/reconnaissance; (T-28D) Mutual Aid Program/attack; (T-CH-1, Taiwan built); trainer/light attack.
Crew: (T-38A), pupil and instructor in tandem.
Specification: T-28D.
Power Plant: one 800 hp R-1300-1.
Dimensions: span, 40 ft 1 in; length, 32 ft; height, 12 ft 8 in; wing area, 268 sq ft.
Weights: empty, 6521 lb; gross, 8495 lb.
Performance: maximum speed, 380 mph; typical range, 500 miles with full weapon load, 1000 miles with maximum fuel.
Armament: normally, none; Sud Aviation Fennec (Desert Rat) used in Algeria with two .5 in machine gun pods and 2000 lb bomb load; (T-28D) 4000 lb weapon load; (YAT-28E) 7000 lb weapon load.

The prototype for the T-28 won the 1948 USAF design competition to replace the Texan.

The T-38A was test flown on 26 September 1949 and then ordered by the US Navy in 1952 as part of the US forces standardization program.

North American (Rockwell International) T-39 Sabreliner

Manufacturer: North American Aviation Incorporated, Los Angeles, California, later Rockwell International Sabreliner Division, El Segundo.
Type: utility jet trainer and transport also pilot proficiency and administration support aircraft.
Crew: two.
Specification: T-39E.
Power Plant: two 3000 lb J60-3.
Dimensions: span, 44 ft 5 in; length, 43 ft 9 in; height, 16 ft.
Weights: empty, 9257 lb; gross, 17,760 lb.
Performance: maximum speed at 21,500 ft, 563 mph (Mach 0.8); economical cruise at high altitude, Mach 0.75; service ceiling or maximum certificated altitude, 45,000 ft; maximum range with typical load and reserves, 2000 miles.
Armament: none.

North American went ahead with the NA-246 as a private venture to meet the USAF's requirement for a utility and combat readiness trainer. The Sabreliner made its maiden flight on 16 September 1958 as the newest member of the Sabre family of high-performance jets. Besides having the capability for the training of multi-engine pilots, navigators and instrument rating instructors the T-39 has the facility for passenger or cargo carrying. The aircraft may be flown from either cockpit seat. Features include 20° sweptwings, tricycle landing gear, nose gear power steering, speed brakes and aerodynamically operated wing slats. It has single point refuelling and a design which permits all servicing from ground level. Batteries installed provide a self-starting capability and an air-conditioning system provides a complete change of air every two minutes. The pressurization system generates an 8000-foot cabin pressurization at 45,000 feet. Its more powerful and much larger sister, the Sea Sabre 75, was developed for the US Coast Guard.

***Below:* A T-39 Sabreliner at altitude.**
***Bottom:* C-140 Jetstar.**

Part Three

1961 -

-1968

TA-4J Skyhawks carried out successful peripheral battlefield operations in Vietnam.

Left: **An F-111 with four auxiliary drop tanks each containing 500 gallons.**
Below: **An interior view of the F-111E, powered by two Pratt & Whitney TF 30-9 afterburning turbofans of 19,600 lb thrust.**

General Dynamics F-111

Manufacturer: General Dynamics, Fort Worth, Texas.
Type: (EF-111A) Grumman Aerospace); all-weather attack bomber; (EF) Electronic warfare; (FB) strategic bomber.
Crew: two.
Specification: F-111F.
Power Plant: two RF30 100 at 25,100 lb.
Dimensions: span, 72.5° sweep, 31 ft 11.5 in; span, 16° sweep, 63 ft; length, 73 ft 6 in; height, 17 ft 1.5 in.
Weights: empty, about 49,000 lb; gross, 99,000 lb.
Performance: maximum speed, Mach 2.2 at 35,000 ft or above, or about 1450 mph; maximum speed at low level (clean) Mach 1.2 or 800 mph; maximum speed at maximum weight, subsonic at low level; service ceiling (clean), 60,000 ft; range on internal fuel, 3165 miles.
Armament: internal weapons bay for two 750 lb bombs or 20 mm M-61 rotary cannon; eight underwing pylons for a maximum of 31,500 lb of stores.

The variable-wing concept was conceived by Dr Barnes Wallis, the famous British inventor. However, the British Government blew hot and cold and the concept was taken up by the USA. The Department of Defense called for a fighter/bomber to meet all future US military tactical needs in much the same way as the MRCA Tornado is supposed to do now. The prototype of the F-111 first flew on 21 December 1964 but contractual disagreements and production problems preceded the F-111As introduction to service in June 1967. RAF cancelled its order for 50 and the US Navy F-111B project was also scrapped. The E incorporated improved engines and intakes and the D, improved avionics. The F-111F, the most successful model, incorporated an improved engine of greatly increased thrust and less expensive avionics.

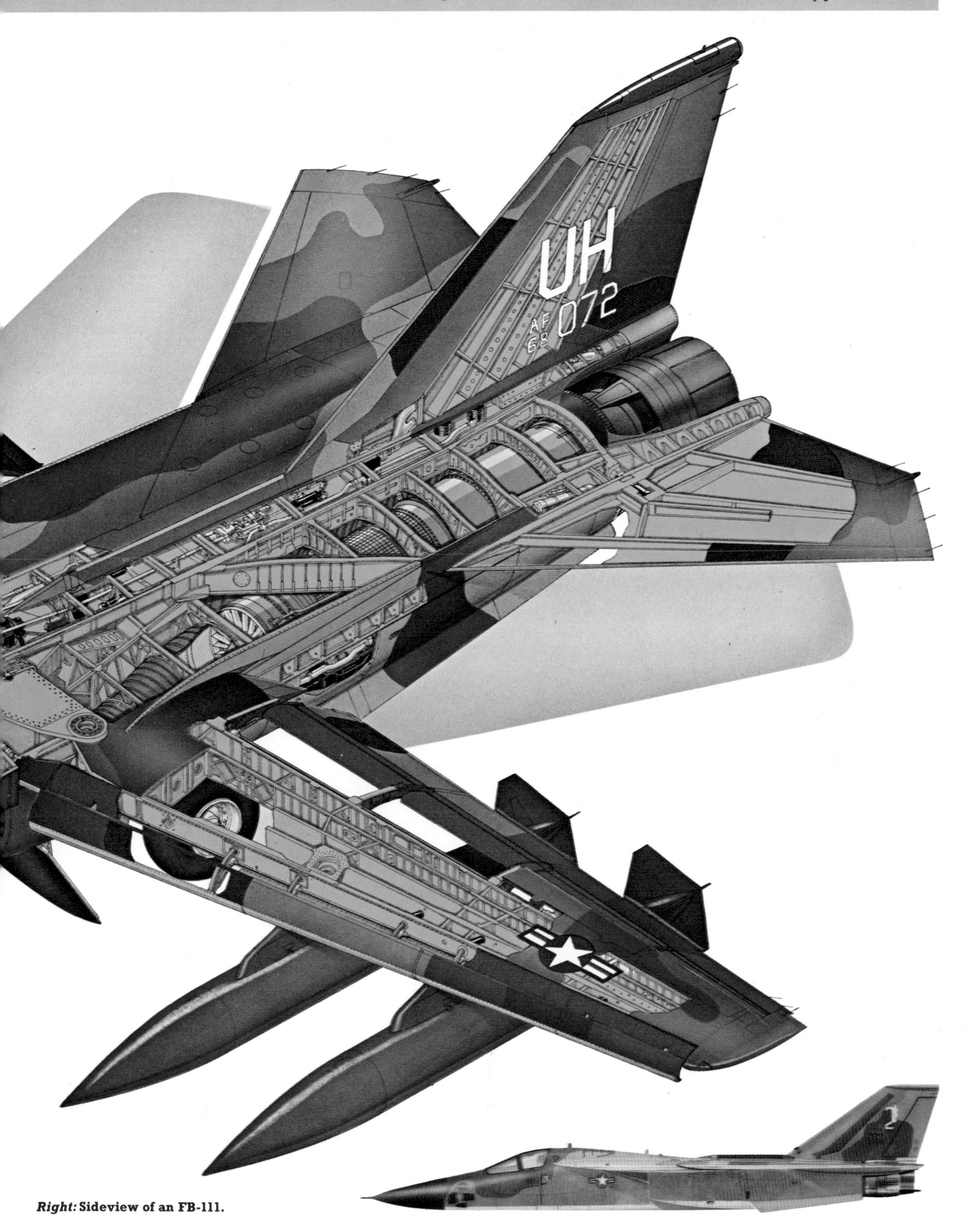

Right: **Sideview of an FB-111.**

F-111s under construction at the massive General Dynamics plant at Fort Worth, Texas.

NB
038
NB
039
NC
NB
054
NB
047
F.O.

McDonnell Douglas F-4 Phantom II

Manufacturer: McDonnell Aircraft Company (Division of McDonnell Douglas Corporation), St Louis, Missouri; built under license by Mitsubishi, Japan (F-4EJ) and substantial subcontracting by W German industry.
Type: originally carrier-borne all-weather interceptor; now all-weather multi-role fighter for land/sea operation; (RF) all-weather multisensor reconnaissance; (QF) RPV; (EF) defense-suppression aircraft.
Crew: normally pilot and radar intercept officer.
Specification: F-4E.
Power Plant: two 11,870 lb dry and 17,900 lb reheat J79-GE-17.
Performance: maximum speed without external stores, 910 mph or Mach 1.2 at 1000 ft, 1500 mph or Mach 2.27 at 40,000 ft; tactical radius (with four Sparrow III and four Sidewinder AAMs), 140 miles, (plus one 500 imp gallons auxiliary tank), 196 miles, (hi-lo-hi mission profile with four 1000-lb bombs, four AAMs, and one 500 imp gallons and two 308 imp gallon tanks), 656 miles; maximum ferry range, 2300 miles at 575 mph.
Dimensions: span, 38 ft 4.75 in; length, 62 ft 10.5 in; height, 16 ft 3.33 in; wing area, 530 sq ft.
Weights: empty, 30,425 lb; gross, 60,630 lb.
Armament: one 20 mm M-61A1 rotary cannon and (intercept) four or six AIM-7E plus four AIM-9D AAMs, or (attack) up to 16,000 lb of external stores.

The US Navy placed a letter of intent for a twin-engine strike aircraft on 18 October 1954. In early 1955 changes in specification made the F-4s primary role into that of long-range, high-altitude interceptor.

The new XF4H-1 was flown on 27 May 1958 for the first time and service delivery of the F-4A started in February 1960 (carrier trials).

Possibly the most famous aircraft to serve with the US Navy. By the first quarter of 1979 over 5000 models of the F-4 had been delivered to the US Navy.

Above: A USAF Phantom based in Iceland maintains a careful watch on a Russian Tu-20 'Bear.'

Above: **McDonnell Douglas F-4 Phantom.**

Top center: **An RF-4C Phantom II serving with the 3rd Air Force in the UK.**
Above center: **For five years the F-4J was flown by the Blue Angels.**

A McDonnell A-4K Skyhawk with refuelling boom and missile clusters.

McDonnell A-4 Skyhawk

Manufacturer: Douglas Aircraft Company, El Segundo (now a division of McDonnell Douglas, Long Beach, California).
Type: attack; TA, dual-control trainer.
Crew: pilot only.
Specification: A-4S.
Power Plant: one 7700 lb J65-16A.
Dimensions: span, 27 ft 6 in; length, 40 ft 1.5 in; height, 15 ft.
Weights: empty, 10,465 lb; gross, 24,500 lb.
Performance: maximum speed clean, 670 mph; maximum speed with 4000 lb bomb load, 645 mph; initial climb, 8440 ft per min; service ceiling, about 49,000 ft; range, about 920 miles; maximum range, 2055 miles.
Armament: two Mk 12 cannon on most models; H, N, two 30 mm French DEFA 553 cannon (optional on export models); underwing and centerline stores (most models) 8200 lb; M, N, 9155 lb.

The Skyhawk was designed as a jet-powered successor to the AD-1 Skyraider in 1952. The XA4D-1 was first flown on 22 June 1954 and the A-4A on 14 August 1954. The first production models were delivered to service in October 1956 and later models continued to be updated until June 1972 (A-4N). The Skyhawk was used on a large scale in Vietnam for close-support and interdiction missions. They also saw action with the Heyl Ha'Avir during the Arab-Israeli conflict of October 1973. The last Skyhawks (A-4M for the US Marine Corps) rolled off the assembly line in February 1979 after almost 22 years of continuous A-4 production during which 2960 had been built.

***Below:* This TA-4F demonstrates that it's more than just a trainer by launching one of its missiles.**

***Left:* Lt JG Denny Earl, both legs shattered by North Vietnamese AA fire, successfully lands his A-4 Skyhawk.**
***Below:* McDonnell Douglas A-4M Skyhawk.**

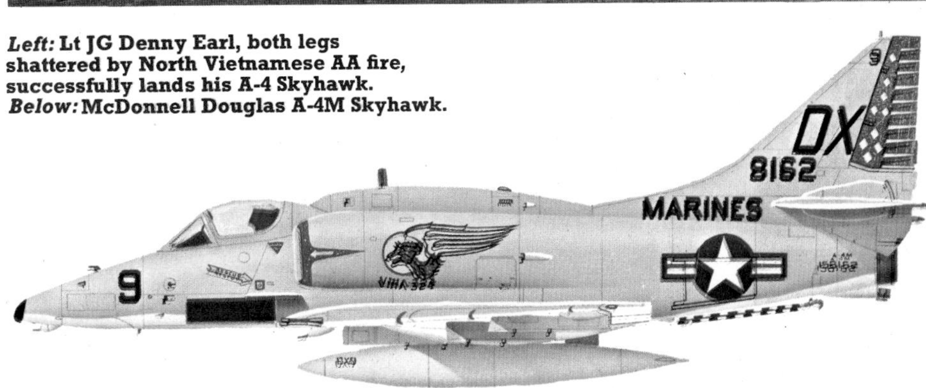

RESCUE
DANGER

A-4M Skyhawk of the US Marine Corps.

***Center top:* NF-5Bs of the Royal Netherlands AF.**
***Center below:* More than 1000 F-5 Freedom Fighters were supplied to anti-Communist nations. This photograph shows three NF-5Bs of the Dutch AF.**
***Right:* Sideview of a Northrop F-5E Tiger II.**

Northrop F-5 Freedom Fighter and Tiger II

Manufacturer: prime contractor, Northrop Aircraft Division, Hawthorne, California; manufactured/assembled under license by Spain and Canada/Netherlands.
Type: A, E, G; air-superiority fighter; B, D; dual fighter/trainer.
Crew: A, E, G; pilot only.
Specification: F-5A.
Power Plant: two 4080 lb J85-13.
Dimensions: span, 25 ft 3 in; length, 47 ft 2 in; height, 13 ft 2 in.
Weights: empty, 8085 lb; gross, 20,677 lb.
Performance: maximum speed at altitude, 925 mph Mach 1.40; initial climb, 28,700 ft per min; service ceiling, 50,500 ft; range, 1387 miles.
Specification: F-5E Tiger II.
Power Plant: two 3500 lb dry and 5000 reheat J85-GE-21.
Dimensions: span, 26 ft 8.5 in; length, 48 ft 2.5 in; height, 13 ft 4 in; wing area, 186 sq ft.
Performance: maximum speed (at 13,220 lb), 1000 mph or Mach 1.6 at 36,090 ft, 760 mph or Mach 1.0 at sea level, (with wingtip missiles), 990 mph or Mach 1.5 at 36,099 ft; combat radius (internal fuel), 173 miles (with 229 imp gallons 1 drop tank), 426 miles, initial climb (at 13,220 lb), 31,600 ft per min; combat ceiling, 53,500 ft.
Weights: empty, 15,400 lb; gross, 24,083 lb.
Armament: two 20 mm M-39 cannon with 280 rpg and two wingtip-mounted AIM-9 Sidewinder AAMs; up to 7000 lb of ordnance

Developed in the light of experience gained in Korea which revealed the need for a lightweight, uncomplicated high performance fighter. Design work began initially in 1955 with added refinements to meet a US Navy specification. By June 1956 the Navy had lost interest and the USAF only ordered the trainer version, the T-38 Talon. Undaunted, Northrop developed a demonstration fighter as a private venture. The test flight of the XT-38 took place on 10 April 1959 and in October 1962 the Department of Defense decided to buy the Freedom Fighter, as it was now called, in large numbers for delivery to third-world countries.

Freedom Fighters: NF-5B (below), N-156F (below right).

Republic F-105 Thunderchief

Manufacturer: Republic Aviation Corporation, Farmingdale, Long Island, New York (now Fairchild Republic Company).
Type: all-weather fighter-bomber; (F-105F) two-seat operational trainer; (G) two-seat ECM.
Crew: pilot only.
Specification: F-105G.
Power Plant: one 24,500 lb J75-19W.
Dimensions: span, 34 ft 11.25 in; length, 69 ft 7.5 in; height, 20 ft 2 in.
Weights: empty, 28,393 lb; gross, 54,000 lb.
Performance: maximum speed, 1480 mph Mach 2.25; initial climb, 32,000 ft per min; service ceiling, 52,000 ft; ferry range with maximum fuel, 2390 miles.
Armament: one 20 mm M-61 gun with 1029 rounds in left side of fuselage; internal bay for ordnance load of up to 8000 lb, and five external pylons for additional load of 6000 lb.

Top: **US Air Force Reserve F-105 'Thuds' gather around a KC-135 for an aerial refuelling exercise.**
Above: **F-105 Thunderchiefs are still in service with some Air National Guard and USAF Reserve Units.**

The first supersonic tactical fighter-bomber designed from scratch and the largest single-seat, single-engine combat aircraft in history. On 22 October 1955 the first Thunderchief (YF-105A) exceeded the speed of sound despite its Pratt & Whitney J57 stop-gap engine. Altogether, 75 Bs were built and 600 of the advanced D version. Production of the F-105 finished in 1965 with the tandem seat F model of which 143 were built. About 350 Ds were rebuilt during the Vietnam war and about 30 Fs were converted to ECM attackers. The 'Thud' as it is known, is recognizable by its large bomb bay and unique swept-forward engine inlets in the wing roots.

Lockheed C-141 Starlifter

Manufacturer: Lockheed-Georgia Company.
Type: strategic transport.
Crew: four; provision for 154 troops, 123 paratroops or 80 stretchers and 16 attendants; reputed to be able to carry 90 percent of all portable items on Army/USAF inventory.
Specification: C-141A.
Power Plant: four 21,000 lb TF33-7.
Dimensions: span, 159 ft 11 in; length, 145 ft; height, 39 ft 3 in.
Weights: empty, 133,773 lb; loaded, 316,600 lb.
Performance: maximum speed, 571 mph; initial climb, 3100 ft per min; service ceiling, 41,600 ft; range with maximum 70,847 lb payload 4080 miles.
Armament: none.

The Starlifter was developed for MAC and designed to lift very heavy loads out of short airstrips.

It was first flown on 17 December 1963 and was delivered to service in October 1964.

The C-141 holds world record for air-dropping, with a load of 70,195 lb. In Vietnam C-141s performed superbly, airlifting supplies and returning with casualties but its main use was for logistic supply from the USA.

Below: **The C-141A Starlifter which first flew in 1963.**

***Left:* An aeromedical C-9A Nightingale of Military Airlift Command.**

McDonnell Douglas C-9 Nightingale/Skytrain II

Manufacturer: Douglas Aircraft Company, Long Beach, California.
Type: (C-9A) aeromedical airlift transport; (VC-9C) special executive transport; (C-9B) passenger/cargo transport.
Crew: seven (pilot, co-pilot, two flight nurses, three aeromedical technicians).
Specification: C-9A.
Power Plant: two 14,500 lb JT8D-9.
Dimensions: span, 93 ft 5 in; length, 119 ft 3.5 in; height overall, 27 ft 6 in.
Weights: empty, about 65,283 lb; gross, 121,000 lb.
Performance: maximum cruise 564 mph; typical long-range cruise, 510 mph; range with full payload and reserves, about 1923 miles.
History: first flight (DC-9) 25 February 1965; service delivery (C-9A) 10 August 1968, (C-9B) 8 May 1973, (VC) 1975.

Douglas has produced, in addition to 800 civil examples, 38 military models. The C-9A is a medium, high speed jet transport purchased as an off-the-shelf item for aeromedical evacuation missions of which 21 are serving in this role with MAC of the USAF. A replacement for the C-118 and C-131 aeromedical transports; the Nightingale is also used by the USAFE and Pacific Air Forces for intratheater operations. A military version of the DC-9, the C-9A was modified to carry 30 stretcher patients, 40 ambulatory patients, or a combination of both with medical attendants. It has an intensive care treatment area with its own ventilation system for patient isolation. The flying hospital also has a special nurses' section, provisions for special medical equipment, improved lighting and uninterrupted cabin air-conditioning. The US Navy's order for Skytrain II transports rose from five to eight, and finally fourteen.

***Above:* A C-9B Skytrain II of the USMC.**
***Below:* A C-9B of the US Navy passes over the *Queen Mary*.**

***Right:* The final production OV-1D Mohawk with APS-94 radar.**

Grumman OV-1 Mohawk

Manufacturer: Grumman Aircraft Engineering Corporation, Bethpage, Long Island, New York.
Type: OV, muti-sensor tactical observation and reconnaissance; EV, electronic warfare; JOV, armed reconnaissance; RV, electronic reconnaissance.
Crew: pilot and observer side-by-side.
Specification: OV-1D.
Power Plant: two 1160 hp T53-701.
Dimensions: span, 48 ft; length, 41 ft; height, 12 ft 8 in.
Weights: empty, 12,054 lb; gross, 18,109 lb.
Performance: maximum speed, 297–310 mph; initial climb, 3618 ft per min; service ceiling, 28,800–31,000 ft; range with external fuel, 1011 miles.
Armament: normally none but in Vietnam the 1A, 1B and 1C all operated air-to-air ground weapons including grenade launchers, mini-gun pods and small guided missiles.

The YOV-1A was first flown on 14 April 1959 and service delivery began in February 1961. Production continued for nearly ten years and the final Mohawk was delivered in December 1960. The OV-1D was the most successful version and was a completely integrated battle-field surveillance system which supplied the army field commander with information on the strength, disposition and activity of enemy forces. It was equipped with photographic and electric sensors which were capable of monitoring enemy operations in daylight, darkness and bad weather.

***Above:* The P-3C Orion (Update II) current production model is used by some Western Nations in preference to the more costly MR Nimrod.**
***Left:* Lockheed P-3B Orions were purchased by the Norwegian Air Force, Australia and New Zealand.**

Lockheed P-3 Orion

Manufacturer: Lockheed-California Company, Burbank.
Type: martime reconnaissance and anti-submarine patrol bomber; (EP-3E) electronic reconnaissance.
Crew: normally, ten; (five accommodated in tactical compartment); capacity for up to 50 combat troops and 4000 lbs of equipment.
Specification: P-3C.
Power Plant: four 4910 eshp T56-A-14W.
Dimensions: span, 99 ft 8 in; length, 116 ft 10 in; height, 33 ft 8.5 in; wing area, 1300 sq ft.
Weights: empty, 61,491 lb; gross, 142,000 lb.
Performance: maximum speed at 105,000 lb, 473 mph at 15,000 ft; normal cruise, 397 mph at 25,000 ft; patrol speed, 230 mph at 1500 ft; loiter endurance (all engines) at 1500 ft, 12.3 hours, (two engines), 17 hours; maximum mission radius, 2530 miles with 3 hrs on station at 1500 ft, 1933 miles; initial climb, 2880 ft per min.
Armament: internal ordnance; 2 Mk 101 depth bombs and four Mk 43, 44 or 46 torpedoes, or 8 Mk 54 bombs; external ordnance capacity for up to 13,713 lbs.

US Navy called for design proposals in August 1957 for a new high-performance, anti-submarine patrol aircraft to replace the Neptune.

Lockheed's adapted commercial Electra turboprop won them the design contest in April 1958. The Electra aerodynamic test vehicle was first flown on 19 August 1958. It was first delivered to service in 1962 and is notable because of the comprehensive search and destruct equipment (including nuclear depth bombs) it carries.

Top: **A Lockheed Orion.**
Above: **A Lockheed Orion and Neptune pass low over a US submarine during an exercise.**

Above: **Lockheed Orion P-3C.**

Lockheed SR-71A Blackbird

Manufacturer: Lockheed-California Corporation.
Type: YF-12, research interceptor; SR-71, strategic reconnaissance.
Crew: two.
Specification: SR-71A.
Power Plant: two 32,500 lb J58(JT11D-20B).
Dimensions: span, 55 ft 7 in; length, 107 ft 5 in; height, 18 ft 6 in.
Weights: empty, 60,000 lb; gross, 170,000 lb.
Performance: maximum speed, 2000 mph (Mach 3); service ceiling, 86,000 ft; range at Mach 3 at 78,740 ft, 2982 miles.
Armament: none.

The SR-71, a highly sophisticated reconnaissance aircraft equipped with advanced sensor systems, was the first operational airplane capable of flying at sustained supersonic speeds. Flown at or above Mach 3 since it was introduced to the USAF's Strategic Air Command in 1966, the SR-71 pioneered flight above 85,000 feet at sustained speeds of more than 2000 mph. The aircraft withstood the high temperatures of Mach 3 because it was built of titanium. On 1 September 1974 an SR-71 set a new transatlantic record of 1 hour 54 minutes 56 seconds on a 3470-mile flight from New York to London. Three SR-71s, flown by three different crews, set seven new world speed and altitude records on 27 and 28 July 1976.

Right: **The SR-71 can survey over 100,000 square miles in one hour from 80,000 ft.**
Below: **An SR-71 takes on fuel from a KC-135 Stratotanker.**

Lockheed QT-2, X-26, YO-3

Manufacturer: Lockheed Missiles and Space Company, San Jose, California.
Type: quiet reconnaissance.
Crew: pilot.
Specification: QT-2.
Power Plant: one 100 hp 0-200A.
Dimensions: span, 57 ft 1 in; length, 30 ft 10 in.
Weights: empty, 1576 lb; gross, 2182 lb.
Performance: operating speed range, 50–120 kt; quietest speed, around 71 mph; endurance, 4 hours.
Armament: none.
Specification: YO-3A.
Power Plant: one 210 hp 10-360D.
Dimensions: span, 57 ft 1 in; length, 30 ft.
Weights: empty, about 2200 lb; gross, 3200 lb.
Performance: same as QT-2 except endurance; 6 hours.
Armament: none.

This aircraft was born from the experience gained in Vietnam when it was found impossible to monitor the elusive Vietcong in the open with conventional noisy piston and jet aircraft. Lockheed's MSC was assigned the task of developing the Schweizer SGS 2-32 sailplane with a heavily muffled engine and large slow rotating propeller. The operational Q-2PC (PC from the project code name, Prize Crew) was so successful it is said to be barely discernible at 400 feet and virtually impossible to detect at 800 feet.

McDonnell Douglas A-3D/ EA-3 Skywarrior

Manufacturer: Douglas Aircraft Company (later McDonnell Douglas), El Segundo, California.
Type: originally, carrier-borne strategic bomber; (A3D-2, restyled A-38B); (A3D-2P-RA-3B) reconnaissance; A3D-2Q (EA-3B) electronic countermeasures; A3D-2T (TA-3B) radar-navigator trainer; KA-3B, tanker, EKA-3B ECM/tanker.
Crew: three.
Specification: A3D-2.
Power Plant: two 12,400 lb J57-P-10.
Dimensions: span, 72 ft 6 in; length, 76 ft 4 in; height, 22 ft 9.5 in; wing area, 812 sq ft.
Weights: empty, 39,409 lb; gross, 82,000 lb.
Performance: maximum speed, 610 mph at 10,000 ft; service ceiling, 41,000 ft.
Armament: two 20 mm cannon in remotely-controlled tail-turret; provision for 15,000 lb bomb load.

Douglas was awarded a two-prototype contract on 31 March 1949 for a two-jet bomber capable of carrier operation.

The XA3D-1 was first flown on 28 October 1952 with XJ40-WE-3 engines. Fitted with the Pratt & Whitney J57-P-6 engines. A3D-1s were delivered in December 1954.

The Skywarrior was the largest and heaviest carrier-borne aircraft to serve with the US Navy.

McDonnell Douglas B-66/EB-66 Destroyer

Manufacturer: Douglas Aircraft Company, Long Beach, California.
Type: originally, tactical attack bomber; (RB-66B) reconnaissance; (RB-66C) electronic reconnaissance; (WB66D) weather reconnaissance; (EB-66E) clandestine intelligence gathering.
Crew: three.
Specification: B-66B.
Power Plant: two 10,000 lb J71-A-13.
Dimensions: span, 72 ft 6 in; length, 75 ft 2 in; height, 23 ft 7 in.
Weights: empty, 42,369 lb; maximum loaded, 83,000 lb.
Performance: maximum speed, 594 mph at 36,000 ft; range, 1500 miles.
Armament: same as A3D-2.

Although developed from the US Navy A3D to provide the USAF with a tactical light bomber with reconnaissance capability. The B-66 became an entirely different aircraft. Very few airframe and equipment pieces were derived from the A3D and this led to a difficult and costly production. The B-66B first flew in January 1954 and was the only variant in the Destroyer series designed exclusively for the bomber role. It could carry conventional or nuclear weapons and a B-66B took part in Operation Redwing, the H-bomb drop at Bikini Atoll. The EB-66Es served in Vietnam but were withdrawn from combat in 1974.

***Above:* McDonnell Douglas B-66 Destroyers.**
***Below:* McDonnell Douglas EA-3 Navy Skywarrior.**

North American (Rockwell) A-5 Vigilante

Manufacturer: North American Aviation, Incorporated, Columbus, Ohio, now Rockwell International.
Type: (A, B) carrier-borne attack; (C) carrier-borne reconnaissance.
Crew: pilot and observer/radar operator.
Specification: RA-5C.
Power Plant: two 10,800 lb J79-GE-8.
Dimensions: span, 53 ft; length, 76 ft 6 in; height, 19 ft 4.75 in; wing area, 754 sq ft.
Weights: empty, 37,498 lb; maximum gross, 79,588 lb.
Performance: maximum speed, Mach 2.1 (1385 mph at 40,000 ft); cruising speed, 1254 mph; service ceiling (C) 67,000 ft; range with external fuel, about 3200 miles.
Armament: none.

The A-5 Vigilante was designed to meet a US Navy requirement in 1955 for a high-performance attack aircraft. The prototype YA3J-1 was first flown on 31 August 1958 and the A-5A in January 1960. The final delivery date of the new aircraft was 1971.

Apart from the Douglas A-3 Skywarrior, it was the heaviest aircraft to serve aboard USN carriers. Advanced features included variable-geometry engine intakes, and between the tailpipes, a linear bomb bay from which a free-falling nuclear weapon was to be ejected rearwards. Part of the fuel load was carried in two tanks attached to this weapon, emptied en route to the target and acting as aerodynamic stabilizers during the weapon's descent. No ailerons were used in the low aspect ratio sweptback wing. Instead, it had blown flaps for low-speed control, a combination of spoilers located in the wing surface, all-moving differential tailerons, and a slab fin-rudder providing control in three axes.

Above: **An RA-5C Vigilante waits the signal to launch from the catapult of the USS *Coral Sea*.**
Top: **An RA-5C Vigilante of the USS *Enterprise*.**
Below: **Rockwell RA-5C Vigilante.**

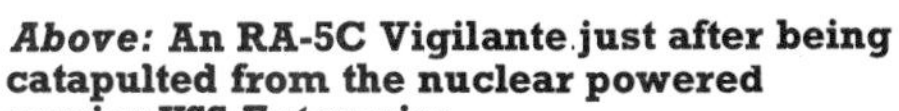
***Above:* An RA-5C Vigilante just after being catapulted from the nuclear powered carrier USS *Enterprise*.**

***Above:* Bell 205 Iroquois.**

Bell Huey Family UH-1 Iroquois Series, CH-118, CH-135

Manufacturer: Bell Helicopter Textron, Fort Worth, Texas; built under license by Agusta, Italy; Fuji, Japan; and AIDC, Taiwan.
Type: Casevac (casually evacuation), assault transport and utility helicopter.
Crew: variable.
Specification: 214.
Power Plant: originally, one T53 at 600–640 shp, later rising in stages to 825, 930, 1100 and 1400 shp.
Dimensions: diameter of twin-blade main rotor, 50 ft; overall length (rotors turning), 57 ft 3.25 in; height, 14 ft 4.75 in.
Weights: empty, about 6000 lb; gross, 16,000 lb.
Performance: maximum speed, typically 127 mph; maximum range with useful payload, typically 248 miles.
Armament: (UH-1B) experimental installations of six Nord SS-11 missiles; four Emerson Electric M-60 7.62 guns, General Electric turret-mounted grenade-launcher. Early versions were equipped with machine guns while the UH-1N versions have carried torpedoes; many models carry machine-guns, night fighting armament and anti-tank missiles.

This helicopter was Bell's Model 204 entry in a June 1955 competition to select a new utility helicopter which the US Army accepted.

The test flight of XH-40 took place on 22 October 1956.

The Huey helicopters were in service with more nations and produced in greater numbers than any other military aircraft since 1945.

***Right:* A Dornier-built UH-1D of the West German Army.**
***Below:* A UH-4D of the Luftwaffe.**

Bell Kiowa

Manufacturer: Bell Helicopter Textron, Fort Worth, Texas; built under license by Agusta, Italy; some by Commonwealth Aircraft, Australia.
Type: light multi-role helicopter.
Crew: pilot only.
Specification: 206B.
Power Plant: one 420 shp 250-C20B or 400 shp C20.
Dimensions: diameter of two-blade main rotor, 33 ft 4 in; length overall (rotors turning), 38 ft 9.5 in; height, 9 ft 6.5 in.
Weights: empty, 1464 lb; gross, 3200 lb.
Performance: economical cruise, 5000 ft, 138 mph; maximum range S/L no reserve with maximum useful load, 345 miles.
Armament: normally none however, US Army Kiowas equipped with the XM27 kit with Minigun and various other weapons.

The Bell Kiowa was named loser in the US Army Light Observation Helicopter contest of 1962 but renamed winner of the re-opened LOH competition of 1968.

296

Bell 209 Hueycobra

Manufacturer: Bell Helicopter Textron, Fort Worth, Texas.
Type: two-seat combat helicopter.
Crew: two (pilot and gunner).
Specification: AN-1G.
Power Plant: one 1100 hp T53-L-13.
Dimensions: main rotor diameter, 44 ft; overall length (rotors turning), 52 ft 11.5 in; length of fuselage, 44 ft 5 in; height, 13 ft 5.5 in.
Weights: empty, 6073 lb; gross, 9500 lb.
Performance: maximum speed, 219 mph; maximum rate of climb, 1230 ft per min; service ceiling, 11,400 ft; hovering ceiling in ground effect, 9000 ft; range at sea level with eight percent reserve, 357 miles.
Armament: typically one 7.62 mm multi-barrel Minigun, one 40 mm grenade launcher, both in remote-control turrets, or 20 mm six-barrel or 30 mm three-barrel cannon, plus four stores pylons for 76 rockets of 2.75 in caliber or Minigun pods or 20 mm gun pod, or (TOWCobra) eight TOW missiles in tandem tube launchers on two outer pylons, inners being for other stores.

The Hueycobra was a development of the UH-1 Iroquois 'family.' It was a completely rebuilt Huey with a large cabin with a tandem-seat cockpit for a crew of two. The Hueycobra was the first purpose-built gunship helicopter and was first flown on 7 September 1965. It entered service in June 1967 and was ordered in thousands instead of the expensive and complicated AH-56 Cheyenne.

Boeing-Vertol H-46 Family CH-46 Sea Knight, UH-46, CH-113, KV-107

Manufacturer: The Boeing Company, Vertol Division, Morton, Pennsylvania.
Type: combat assault helicopter; later models; transport, search/rescue, minesweeping.
Crew: provision for three and up to 17 assault troops or 15 stretchers with two attendants.
Specification: CH-46D.
Power Plant: two 1400 shp T58-GE-10.
Dimensions: rotor diameter, each 51 ft; length, 44 ft 10 in; height, 16 ft 8.5 in; disc area, total, 4086 sq ft.
Weights: empty, 13,065 lb; gross, 23,000 lb.
Performance: maximum speed, 166 mph at sea level; cruising speed, 154 mph; initial climb, 1715 ft per min; service ceiling, 14,000 ft; range, 230 miles.

Boeing-Vertol successfully competed in a 1960 competition to select a new assault helicopter for the US Marines. The Model 107M was announced the winner on 20 February 1961 and an order placed for 14 HRB-1s (later designated CH-46A Sea Knight).

Left: **CH-46D Sea Knight.**
Right: **Sikorsky CH-3 Jolly Green Giant.**
Below: **Boeing Vertol H-46.**

Hughes TH-55 Osage Models, 300 and 300C, TH-55A Osage, NH-300C

Manufacturer: Hughes Helicopters, Culver City, USA (NH 300C) BredaNardi, Ascoli, Italy, Kawasaki, Japan.
Type: light helicopter.
Crew: accommodation for two personnel.
Specification: TH-55A.
Power Plant: one 180 hp HIO 360 A1A (300C, NH 300C) 190 hp HIO 360 D1A.
Dimensions: diameter of three-blade main rotor, 25 ft 3.5 in; length overall (rotors turning), 28 ft 10.75 in; height overall, 8 ft 2.75 in.
Weights: empty, 1008 lb; gross, 1850 lb.
Performance: maximum cruise, 75 mph; range with no reserve, 204 miles.

The 269 Model was first flown in October 1956 and it passed evaluation in 1958 as a US Army command/observation helicopter being designated YHO-2HU. In 1964 it was adopted as the TH-55A Osage to become the US Army's standard training helicopter.

Sikorsky S-61 Sea King

Manufacturer: Sikorsky Aircraft, Division of United Technologies; built under license by Agusta (Italy), Mitsubishi (Japan) and Westland (UK).
Type: amphibious anti-submarine helicopter.
Crew: four (two pilots, one controller, one sonar operator).
Specification: S-61D.
Power Plant: two 1500 hp T58-GE-10.
Dimensions: rotor diameter, 62 ft; fuselage length, 54 ft 9 in.
Weights: empty, 12,087 lb; gross, 20,500 lb.
Performance: maximum speed, 172 mph at sea level; inclined climb, 2200 ft per min; hovering ceiling (out of ground effect), 8200 ft; range (with ten percent reserves), 622 miles.
Armament: highly variable.

The S-61 was another helicopter family in production from 1958–72 which had many specially equipped variants. It had been originally built to carry ASW (anti-submarine warfare) gear, homing torpedoes and depth charges. Other S-61 versions were used to carry bulky freight, pick up astronauts, fly ECM (electronic countermeasures). The final S-61R was based on the S-61A but had a tricycle undercarriage and a rear loading ramp.

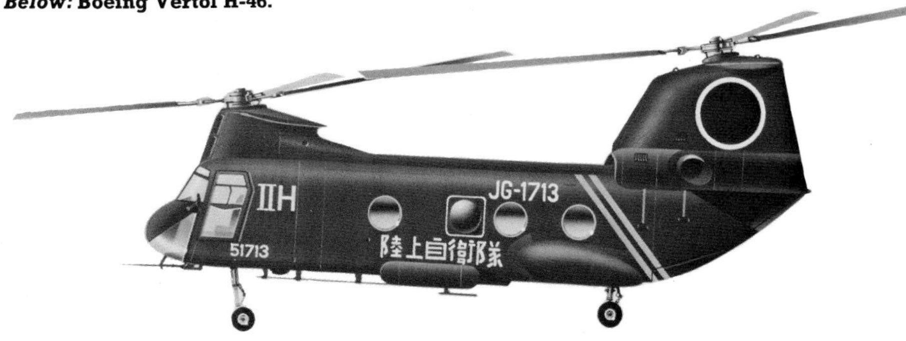

AFRES

A USAF Reserve Special Operations CH-3 disgorges its complement of troops. Note the machine-gun crew in the opening. The troops are incorrectly sporting berets which could be sucked in by the overhead engine.

Sikorsky S-64, CH-54A and B Tarhe

Manufacturer: Sikorsky Aircraft, Division of United Technologies, Stratford, USA.
Type: crane helicopter.
Crew: three pilots.
Specification: S-64A.
Power Plant: (CH-54A) two 4500 shp T73-1; (CH-54B) two 4800 shp T73-700.
Dimensions: diameter of six-blade main rotor, 72 ft; length overall (rotors turning), 88 ft 6 in; height overall, 18 ft 7 in.
Weights: empty, 19,234 lb; maximum loaded, 42,000 lb.
Performance: maximum cruise, 105 mph; hovering ceiling out of ground effect, 6900 ft; range with maximum fuel and 10 percent reserve (typical), 230 miles.

The S-64 was developed using the Sikorsky S-56 design and the piston-engined S-60. The prototype S-64 first flew on 9 May 1962 and the production model, CH-54A, was delivered late in 1964. The later model, B Tarhe, began production late in 1969.

Sikorsky S-65, CH-53A Sea Stallion, YCH-53E

Manufacturer: Sikorsky Aircraft, Division of United Technologies; built under license by VFW-Fokker, Germany.
Type: CH-53D, assault transport/casualty evacuation; YCH-53E, amphibious assault transport helicopter.
Crew: CH-53D, two pilots and a crew chief with up to 55 troops in cabin; YCH-53E, two pilots and a crew chief with up to 56 troops.
Specification: CH-53D.
Power Plant: two 3925 hp T64-GE-413.
Dimensions: rotor diameter, 72 ft 2.75 in; length, 88 ft 2.5 in; height, 17 ft 1.5 in; rotor disc area, 4070 sq ft.
Weights: empty, 22,444 lb; gross, 42,000 lb.
Performance: maximum speed, 196 mph at sea level, cruising speed, 173 mph; initial climb, 2180 ft per min; service ceiling, 21,000 ft; range, 257 miles.
Armament: none.
Specification: YCH-53E.
Power Plant: three 4380 T64-GE-415.
Dimensions: rotor diameter, 79 ft; fuselage length, 73 ft 5 in.
Weights: empty, 33,000 lb; gross, 69,750 lb.
Performance: rotor diameter, 79 ft; fuselage length, 73 ft 5 in.
Armament: none.

The Sikorsky S-65 was ordered in August 1962 for service with the US Marine Corps. The prototype CH-53A was first flown on 14 October 1964 and deliveries began in May 1966. The YCH-53E was a growth version of the CH-53D, embodying a third engine, an uprated transmission system, a seventh main rotor blade and increased rotor diameter. It was first flown on 1 March 1974.

***Right:* A Cessna U-17A utility transport.**
***Below:* An HH-53 Super Jolly Green Giant.**

Cessna U-3

Manufacturer: Cessna Aircraft Company, Wichita, Kansas.
Type: administrative liaison and cargo transport.
Crew: accomodates 5.
Specification: U-3.
Power Plant: two 240 hp Continental O-470M flat-sixes.
Dimensions: span (over tanks), 36 ft 11 in; length overall (U-3A), 27 ft 1 in; (U-3B and modern 310), 31 ft 11.5 in; height overall, 10 ft 8 in.
Weights: empty (U-3B, modern 310), 3337 lb; maximum loaded (U-3A), 4700 lb; (U-3B and modern 310), 5500 lb.
Performance: maximum cruise, 223 mph; range, depending on sub type and fuel, up to 1740 miles.
Armament: none.

The Cessna U-3 was derived from the Cessna 310 and purchased in 1957 (as L-27A utility) by the USAF. In 1962 it was redesignated U-3A, to be followed by the U-3B and the more powerful 310E.

Cessna U-17

Manufacturer: Cessna Aircraft Company, Wichita, Kansas.
Type: utility transport.
Crew: pilot and capacity for up to 5 passengers.
Specification: U-17.
Power Plant: one 300 hp IO 520D.
Dimensions: span, 35 ft 10 in; length overall, 25 ft 7.5 in; height overall, 7 ft 9 in.
Weights: empty, 1600 lb; maximum loaded, 3350 lb.
Performance: maximum cruise, 169 mph; range on standard tankage, no reserve, 660 miles.

The Cessna U-17 was developed from the Cessna Model 185 Skywagon. In 1963 U-17A-C versions were purchased by the USAF for MAP issue to favored air forces.

***Right:* A Cessna O-2B.**

Cessna O-2

Manufacturer: Cessna Aircraft Company, Whichita, Kansas; built under license by Reims-Aviation, France.
Type: (O-2A) FAC, (O-2B) psy-war, (FTB 337G) multi-role.
Crew: pilot only with capacity for up to 5 passengers.
Specification: O-2.
Power Plant: two (front and rear), 210 hp IO-360C.
Dimensions: span, 38 ft 2 in; length, 29 ft 9 in; height, 9 ft 2 in.
Weights: empty, 2848 lb; maximum loaded, 4630 lb; USAF overload, 5400 lb.
Performance: maximum cruise, 195 mph; takeoff or landing over 50 ft, 1675 ft; maximum range with maximum fuel (typical), 1325 miles.

Designed to meet a requirement for a twin-engined aircraft that could be flown by private pilots holding only single engine rating. Following the test flight of the civil Skymaster adopted by the USAF in 1966 to act as a Forward Air Control aircraft to replace the O-1A Bird Dog.

Cessna T-41

Manufacturer: Cessna Aircraft Company, Wichita, Kansas; built under license by Reims Aviation, France.
Type: basic pilot trainer/utility aircraft.
Crew: instructor and student.
Specification: T-41A.
Power Plant: one flat-six piston engine; 150 hp O-320-E2D.
Dimensions: span, 35 ft 10 in; length, 26 ft 11 in; height, 8 ft 9.5 in.
Weights: empty, 1363 lb; maximum loaded, 2300 lb.
Performance: maximum speed, 144 mph; initial climb, 645 ft per min; service ceiling, 13,100 ft; range with maximum fuel at 10,000 ft, 737 miles.

Developed from the best-selling Cessna 172/Cardinal and adopted by the USAF to give pilot candidates 30-hour initial training after it had decided to discontinue ab initio jet training in 1964.

Cessna A-37 Dragonfly

Manufacturer: Cessna Aircraft Company, Wichita, Kansas.
Type: light attack (A-37) Dual trainer (T-37).
Crew: pilots 2(A-37); pupil and instructor side-by-side (T37B).
Specification: A-37B.
Power Plant: two 2850 lb J85-17A. Electric J85-17A single-shaft turbojets.
Dimensions: span (over tip tanks), 35 ft 10.5 in; length (not including refuelling probe), 29 ft 3 in; height, 8 ft 10.5 in.
Weights: empty, 6211 lb; loaded, 14,000 lb.
Performance: maximum speed, 507 mph at 16,000 ft; initial climb at gross weight, 6990 ft per min; service ceiling, 41,765 ft; range (maximum weapons), 460 miles, (maximum fuel), 1012 miles.
Armament: one 7.62 mm GAU-2B/A six-barrel Minigun in nose; eight wing pylon stations, two inners for up to 870 lb, intermediate for 600 lb and outers for 500 lb; maximum ordnance load, 5680 lb.

The Dragonfly was developed as a jet-trainer for the USAF starting in late 1952. The Cessna Model 318 won the design competition in early 1953 and two XT-37 prototypes were ordered. T-37 production was completed in 1975. In 1960 Cessna restressed the airframe and replaced the Continental J-69 with a much more powerful General Electric J85 to create the A-37.

Deliveries of A-37A (converted from T-37s) began in May 1967.

The Model 318 was the first American jet trainer to be developed.

Above: **A Cessna T-37B of the USAF.**
Below: **A Cessna T-41A of the USAF.**

An A-37B of USAF Tactical Air Command complete with full array of stores and in-flight refuelling probe located in the nose. A-37Bs are not pressurized and are not fitted with ejector seats. Pilots are protected by layered nylon flak curtains.

14807

***Above:* A Marine Corps OV-10 Bronco.**
***Right:* An OV-10A and a parachutist.**

North American (Rockwell) OV-10 Bronco

Manufacturer: North American (Rockwell Corporation International), Columbus, Ohio.
Type: (A) multi-role counter-insurgency; (B) target rug.
Crew: pilot and observer in tandem.
Specification: OV-10A.
Power Plant: two 715 ehp T76-410/411 plus J85-4 turbojet of 2950 lb.
Dimensions: span, 40 ft; length, 41 ft 7 in; height, 15 ft 2 in.
Weights: empty, 6969 lb; maximum loaded, 14,466 lb.
Performance: maximum speed at 5000 ft, 281 mph; initial climb, 2300 ft per min; service ceiling, 30,000 ft; range with maximum weapon load, about 600 miles; ferry range at 12,000 lb gross, 1428 miles.
Armament: four 7.62 mm M60C machine guns in sponsons; 1200 lb hardpoint on centerline and four 600 lb points under sponsons; one Sidewinder missile rail under each wing; (OV-10D) as other versions plus three-barrel 20 mm cannon in remotely aimed ventral power turret.

Ordered into production for the US Marine Corps and USAF in 1966 to meet requirements for a counter-insurgency (COIN) operations aircraft.

The YOV-10A prototype was first flown on 16 July 1965. Service deliveries began (one each to USMC and USAF) on 23 February 1968. Operational debut (USMC) with VMO-2 operating out of Da Nang, Vietnam took place in July 1968. It was the first aircraft designed from the start to meet COIN requirements.

***Above:* A T2J-1 (later T-2A) Buckeye trainer of the USN.**
***Left:* An OV-10 Bronco of the USAF.**

Rockwell T-2 Buckeye

Manufacturer: Rockwell International Corporation, Columbus Aircraft Division, Columbus, Ohio.
Type: all-purpose jet trainer/light attack aircraft.
Crew: pupil and instructor in tandem.
Specification: T-2C.
Power Plant: two 2950 lb J85-4.
Dimensions: span (over tip tanks), 38 ft 1.5 in; length, 38 ft 3.5 in; height, 14 ft 9.5 in.
Weights: empty, 8115 lb; maximum loaded, 13,179 lb.
Performance: maximum speed, 522 mph; initial climb, 6200 ft per min; service ceiling, 40,400 ft; maximum range, 1047 miles.
Armament: provision for gun pods, bombs or rockets.

The Buckeye was designed to meet a US Navy requirement in 1956 for an all-purpose jet trainer suitable for *ab initio* training through to carrier qualification. North American won the contract and evolved a design using proven components like the control system similar to that used in the T-28C.

The test flight for T-2B took place on 30 August 1962 and for T-2C on 17 April 1968.

Part Four

1969

1979

The first of the high-performance F-16 Multirole Fighters built by General Dynamics is shown here with its widely hailed prototype, the YF-16. The first production model F-16 rolled out of the company's Fort Worth plant on 20 October 1976.

Fairchild Republic A-10A Thunderbolt II

Manufacturer: Fairchild Republic Company.
Type: close-support aircraft.
Crew: pilot only.
Specification: A-10A.
Power Plant: two 9065 lb TF34-GE-100.
Performance: (at 38,136 lb) maximum speed, 433 mph at sea level, 448 mph at 10,000 ft; initial climb, 5340 ft per min; service ceiling, 34,700 ft; combat radius (with 9540-lb bomb load and 1170 lb of 30 mm ammunition, including 1.93 hr loiter at 5000 ft) 288 miles at (average) 329 mph at 25,000–35,000 ft; ferry range, 2487 miles.
Weights: empty, 19,856 lb; basic operational, 22,844 lb; maximum take-off, 46,786 lb.
Dimensions: span, 57 ft 6 in; length, 53 ft 4 in; height, 14 ft 8 in; wing area, 506 sq ft.
Armament: one seven-barrel 30 mm General Electric GAU-8 Avenger rotary cannon; eleven external stations for maximum of 9540 lb ordnance (with full internal fuel and 1170 lb 30 mm ammunition).

Below: **The A-10 or 'flying can opener.'**

Piston-engined aircraft such as the single-seat Mustang and the F-82 Twin Mustang (in the Korean Conflict) and the Douglas A-1 Skyraiders (in Vietnam) proved highly successful in a predominantly jet environment. Experience gained in both Vietnam and Korea prompted the need for a modern equivalent. What was needed, it seemed, was a close-air-support aircraft capable of carrying a heavy payload, had good endurance and could withstand severe damage inflicted by ground fire. Extensive studies into such a concept between 1963 and 1969 began with pre-supposing a twin turboprop but culminating with two turbofans. Competition within the American Aerospace Industry resulted in a two-horse race between the Northrop A-9A and the Fairchild A-10. Prototype fly-off evaluation between two of each type took place between October and December 1972 with the A-10 emerging as the winner.

The first of two prototypes was flown on 10 May 1972, and first of six pre-production aircraft was flown on 15 February 1975. The first production aircraft was flown on 21 October 1975.

The A-10 is the first USAF aircraft developed specifically to deliver aerial firepower to defeat potential enemy ground threat. Its versatility and flexibility are best displayed by its large payload, wide-radius capabilities, its ability to loiter for hours within the battle area, where it can operate under 1000-foot ceilings with less than two miles visibility.

GE were winners of the contest to produce the 30 mm tank busting gun, the most powerful yet devised in aerial warfare. The muzzle horsepower is 20 times that of the 75 mm gun developed in World War II. The GAU-8/A 30 mm Gatling gun system, named Avenger, is mounted internally along the aircraft's centerline and is capable of firing at either 2100 or 4200 rounds per minute. Driven hydraulically, and fed by a drum containing 1350 rounds the GAU-8A has proven to be a cost effective weapon to defeat the full array of ground targets encountered in the close-air-support role, including heavy main battle tanks. Empty cases are fed back into the appropriately dustbin shaped drum. In tests conducted at Nellis AFB Nevada the Avenger demonstrated its tank-killing ability by defeating the Soviet T-62 tank with one and two second bursts. In addition to the armor-piercing projectile, which is capable of penetrating medium and heavy tanks, the gun fires high explosive ammunition

Below: **It is claimed that the A-10 can lose one engine, half a tail, two-thirds of the wing and parts of the fuselage and still remain airborne.**

which is extremely effective against other vehicles.

The A-10s structure is conventional with approximately 95 percent of the airframe constructed from aluminium. Single curvature skins are used on all areas aft of the cockpit permitting ease of maintenance, especially in forward operating locations. Redundant load paths are used throughout the aircraft and provide greater airframe reliability and greater damage tolerance. Numerous aircraft parts are interchangeable left and right, including the engine, main landing gear and vertical stabilizers.

Pilot survivability is achieved through a combination of high maneuverability at low airspeeds and altitudes plus the A-10s overall 'hardness.' The pilot is ensconced by a titanium armor-plated 'bathtub' which also protects the vital elements of the flight control system. Redundant primary structural elements can survive major damage; self-sealing fuel cells are protected with internal and external foam; and the primary redundant hydraulic flight control system is further enhanced by a backup 'manual reversion' system which permits the pilot to fly and land the aircraft when all hydraulics are lost.

General Dynamics F-16

Manufacturer: General Dynamics, Fort Worth, Texas, with subcontract manufacture in Europe and European assembly of aircraft for European customers.
Crew: (F-16A) pilot only.
Specification: F-16.
Type: fighter bomber (F-16A); two-seat operational trainer (F-16B).
Dimensions: span (excluding missiles), 31 ft; length, 47 ft 7.75 in; height, 16 ft 5.25 in; wing area, 300 sq ft.
Power Plant: one 25,000 lb F100-PW-100(3).
Performance: maximum speed (with two Sidewinder AAMs), 1255 mph at 36,000 ft, or Mach 1.95, 915 mph at sea level, or Mach 1.2; tactical radius (interdiction mission hi-lo-hi on internal fuel with six Mk 82 bombs), 340 miles; ferry range, 2300 plus miles; initial climb, 62,000 ft per min; service ceiling, 52,000 ft
Weights: operational empty, 14,567 lb; loaded (intercept mission with two Sidewinders), 22,785 lb; maximum take-off, 33,000 lb.
Armament: one 20 mm M61A-1 Vulcan multibarrel cannon with 515 rounds and maximum external ordnance load of 15,200 lb with reduced internal fuel or 11,000 lb with full internal fuel distributed between two wingtip, six underwing and one fuselage stations.

Top: **An F-16A in flight.**
Above: **A KC-135 aerial tanker refuels the F-16A development aircraft.**

Below: **General Dynamics F-16.**

The General Dynamics F-16 was originally built as a technology demonstration aircraft to discover to what degree it was possible to reduce the cost and size of the F-15. What began as the USAF Lightweight Fighter (LWF) program developed, after four NATO countries sought a replacement for their ageing F-104Gs, into the Air Combat Fighter (ACF) program in April 1974. In December 1974 the F-16 was determined the winner over the Northrop P-530 (YF-17).

The YF-16 first flew on 20 January 1974. The first production aircraft was flown on 8 December 1976. The first two-seater was flown on 8 August 1977. Service delivery began August 1978.

***Left:* The Westinghouse Multi-mode radar used in the F-16.**
***Below:* The cockpit layout of the F-16 showing Stores Control Panel (top left), Head Up Display HUD (top), Radar/EO Display (bottom center) and fire control/ navigation panel (far right).**
***Right and bottom (left and right):* Three views of the highly maneuverable F-16.**

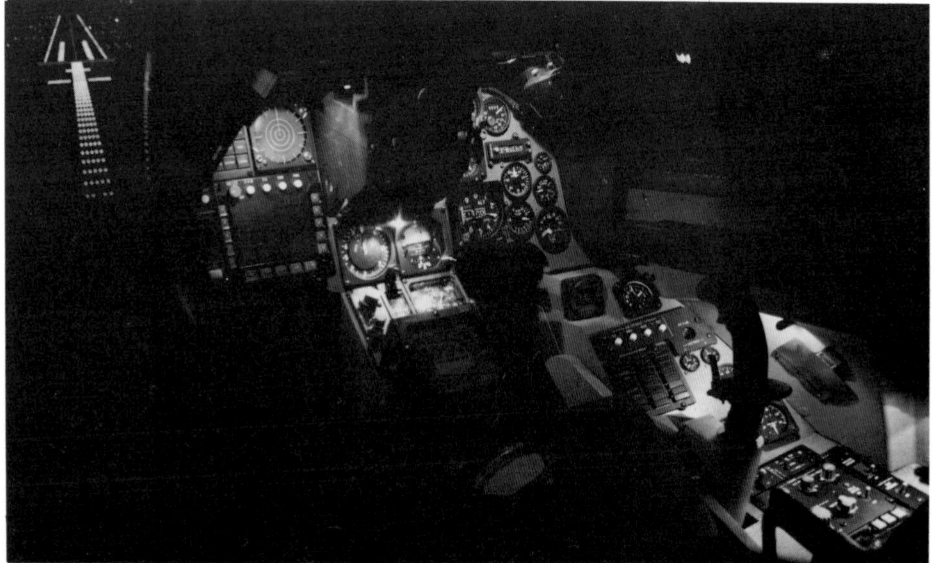

U.S. AIR FORCE
F-16

F-16

F-16

F-16

Left and below: **Sparrow air-to-air missiles are successfully launched from a prototype F-16 Multirole Fighter.**
Top left: **The radar-guided AIM-7F Sparrow ready for launch.**
Center left: **The missile achieves full thrust.**
Bottom left: **The missile guidance is activated and the Sparrow accelerates on a pre-programmed course.**
Below: **The F-16 is left in the wake of the missile.**

An impressive array of missiles in the foreground points to the F-16's development as a 'jack of all trades' and not to the planned lightweight fighter concept. Nine external store stations have a total carriage capacity of 15,200 lbs. The primary weapons are AIM-9 infra-red Sidewinders at the wing tips and a 6000 round-per-minute Vulcan 20mm M61 gun.

***Above:* A Grumman A-6E Target Recognition Attack Multisensor (TRAM).**
***Right:* The variable sweep wings of the F-14.**

Grumman A-6 Intruder

Manufacturer: Grumman Aerospace Corporation, Calverton, Long Island, New York.
Type: carrier-borne low-level attack.
Crew: two (pilot and bombardier/navigator).
Specification: A-6E.
Power Plant: two 9300 lb J52-P-8A/B.
Dimensions: wing span, 53 ft; wing span folded, 25 ft 4 in; length, 54 ft 9 in; height, 16 ft 2 in; wing area, 528 sq ft.
Weights: empty, 26,320 lb; gross, 60,400 lb.
Performance: maximum speed clean, 654 mph (Mach 0.86) at sea level; maximum speed at 36,000 ft, 625 mph (Mach 0.94); combat range clean, 2320 miles at 428 mph average at 37,700–44,600 ft.
Armament: five external (one fuselage and four wing) stations each of 3600 lb capacity for up to 15,000 lb of stores.

The A-6A was first flown in 1959. The A-6B was modified retaining full strike capability but had anti-radiation missiles for attack against surface-to-air missile sites. The KA-6D acted as a fair-weather bomber and refuelled other aircraft. The A-6C was configured with electro-optical sensors for strikes against non-radar significant targets. The A-6E incorporates the TRAM, Target Recognition Attack Multisensor, which provided an image of targets that were not detectable and was coupled with laser-guided weapon delivery.

Below: **Grumman F-14 Tomcat.**

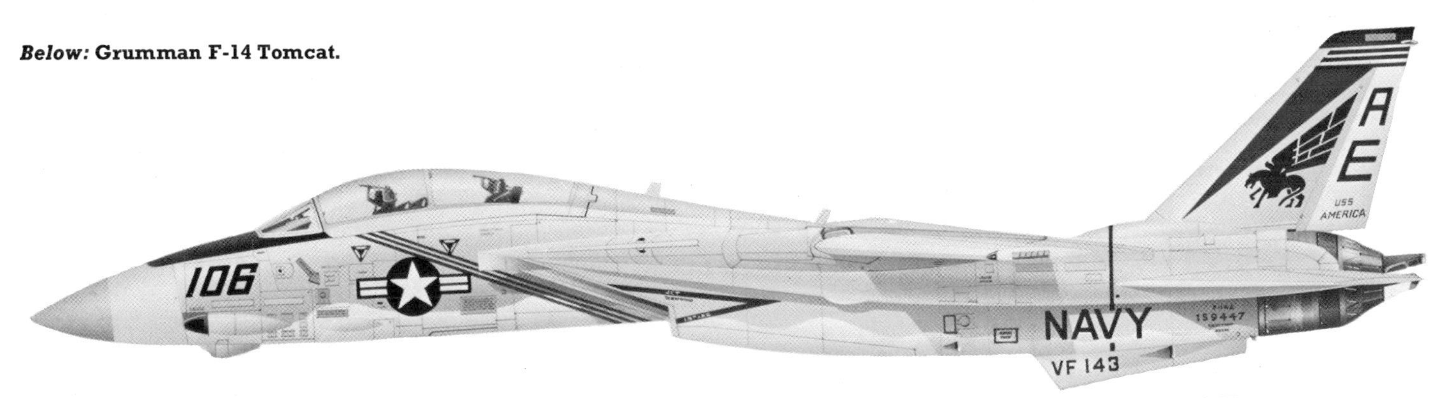

Grumman F-14 Tomcat

Manufacturer: Grumman Aerospace Corporation, Calverton, Long Island, New York.
Type: carrier-borne multirole variable wing fighter.
Crew: two (pilot and naval flight officer).
Specification: F-14A.
Power Plant: two 20,900 lb TF30 412A.
Dimensions: span 68° sweep, 38 ft 2 in; span 20° sweep, 64 ft 1.5 in; length, 61 ft 2 in; height, 16 ft.
Weights: empty, 37,500 lb; gross, 72,000 lb.
Performance: maximum speed at height, 1564 mph (Mach 2.34); maximum speed at sea level, 910 mph (Mach 1.2); initial climb at gross weight, over 30,000 ft per min; service ceiling, over 56,000 ft; range, 2000 miles.
Armament: one 20 mm M61-A1 multi-barrel cannon, four AIM-7 Sparrow and four or eight AIM-9 Sidewinder air-to-air missiles, up to six AIM-54 Phoenix and two AIM-9 maximum external weapon load in surface attack role, 14,500 lb.

In February 1969 the Navy asked Grumman to design a successor to the F-4 Phantom. The F-14 was the world's first operational air superiority fighter with a variable-sweep wing. The variable-sweep wing and the AWG-9 weapons control system make it a multi-mission fighter. The AWG-9 has a detection range of 100 miles.

Left: **The Tomcat in flight.**
Below: **The Grumman Tomcat over the USS *Constellation.***

10
410
NAVY
157502
04
NL
404
VY
00
NK
300
VY
NK
VY

LTV (Vought) A-7D, A-7E Corsair II

Manufacturer: Vought Systems Division of LTV, Dallas, Texas.
Type: attack bomber, A-7D, land-based; A-7E, carrier-borne.
Crew: pilot only.
Specification: A-7D.
Power Plant: one 14,250 lb TF41-1.
Dimensions: span, 38 ft 9 in; length, 46ft 1.5 in; height, 16 ft 0.75 in.
Weights: empty, 19,781 lb; gross, 42,000 lb.
Performance: maximum speed without external stores at sea level, 699 mph (Mach 0.92); maximum speed with 12,250 lb bombs at sea level, 633 mph (Mach 0.87); tactical radius with 12,250 lb bomb for hi-lo-hi mission at average cruising speed, 532 mph with one hour on station, 512 miles.
Armament: one 20 mm M-61A-1 Vulcan rotary cannon, max external stores, 20,000 lb.

The A-7 was derived from the same company's Crusader (see page 119) and the A-7A was first flown on 27 September 1965. The A-7D was first flown on 15 April 1968 and the A-7E on 25 November 1968. The A-7D was delivered into service in 1970-71. Although it did not take part in the Vietnam War until October 1972, it proved so effective and versatile that the 'SLUF' (short little ugly fellow), was accorded increasingly more responsible roles, including the demanding search and rescue mission. The A-7D had the lowest abort rate of any aircraft in a similar role in combat, losing only four aircraft to enemy fire in over 6000 sorties.

Four action shots of the A-7E Corsair II, a single-engine, single-seat attack and close-support aircraft with computerized navigation and weapon systems avionics.

AV-8B

McDonnell Douglas AV-8B Advanced Harrier

Manufacturer: McDonnell Douglas Corporation (MCAIR, St Louis), principal associate, British Aerospace (Hawker Aircraft, Kingston), UK.
Type: V/STOL light attack; ship-based air defense, reconnaissance and dual trainer/ multi-role.
Crew: pilot only.
Specification: AV-8B.
Power Plant: one 21,500 lb F402-RR-402.
Dimensions: span, 30 ft 4 in; length, 42 ft 10 in; height; 11 ft 3 in; wing area, 230 sq ft.
Performance: approximate maximum speed, 720 mph at 1000 ft, or Mach 0.95, (with typical external ordnance), 640 mph at 1000 ft, or Mach 0.85; VTO radius (with 1800-lb payload), 230 miles; STO radius (with 6000-lb payload), 460 miles, (with 2000-lb payload), 920 miles; ferry range, 2966 miles.
Weights: operational empty, 12,400 lb; maximum vertical take-off, 18,850 lb; maximum short take-off, 27,950 lb; maximum take-off, 29,550 lb.
Armament: two 30 mm cannon in ventral pod/centerline stores pylon; maximum external stores, 8000 lb; seven store stations for variety of bombs, flare launchers, rocket pods, AIM-9 missiles, guided weapons, and/or external fuel.

Higher performance version of the AV-8A in current service with US Marine Corps, incorporating a new wing having a supercritical airfoil for improved lift and cruise characteristics, far greater fuel capacity, use of graphite epoxy composite materials for new wing, ailerons, flaps and outrigger fairings to save weight, a new inlet engine design to permit greater engine thrust for VTOL and STOL and more efficient cruise, plus aerodynamic devices to improve vertical take-off capability. Other features include the Angle Rate Bombing (ARBS), being developed for the A4M Skyhawk.

The YAV-8B first flew on 9 November 1978. The AV-8B will enter service in 1984–85.

***Left and below:* The AV-8B makes its first flight on 9 November 1978.**

The AV-8B shows off its incredible hovering techniques at St Louis on 15 November 1978.

NORTHROP

One of two Northrop YF-17 development aircraft used in the Cobra program.

AMERICAN REVOLUTION BICENTENNIAL
1776-1976
71291

AF 74 084

Left: **A TF-15 decked out in bi-centennial garb during a flight in 1976.**
Below: **McDonnell Douglas F-15 Eagle.**

McDonnell Douglas F-15 Eagle

Manufacturer: McDonnell Aircraft division of McDonnell Douglas Corporation, St Louis.
Type: air superiority fighter (F-15A) and operational trainer (TF-15A).
Crew: (F-15A) pilot only.
Specification: F-15.
Power Plant: two 25,000 lb F100-PW-100.
Dimensions: span, 42 ft 9.75 in; length, 63 ft 9 in; height, 18 ft 5.5 in; wing area, 608 sq ft.
Performance: maximum speed, 915 mph at sea level or Mach 1.2, 1650 mph at 36,090 ft or Mach 2.5; tactical radius (combat air patrol), up to 1120 miles; ferry range, 2980 miles (with Fast Pack auxiliary tanks), 3450 miles.
Weights: empty equipped, 26,147 lb; loaded (clean), 38,250 lb; maximum take-off (intercept mission), 40,000 lb; max take-off, 54,123 lb.
Armament: one 20 mm M-61 cannon, four AIM-7 Sparrow air-to-air missiles, centerline pylon stressed for 4500 lb for 600 gallon tank, tactical payload or reconnaissance pod. Normal maximum external capacity, (FAST packs optional), 12,000 lb.

The F-15 Eagle was developed to bridge the gap in air superiority thought to have been gained, in 1967, by the MiG-23 and MiG-25, for the USAF.

The F-15A was first flown on 27 July 1972. The TF-15A was first flown on 7 July 1973.

Probably the best fighter in the world at time of going to press. Most maneuverable aircraft of its class on the current USAF inventory.

Left: **An F-15 climbs to altitude.**
Below: **An F5E Tiger II (foreground) and an F-15 Eagle.**

Above: **An F-18A Hornet, 18 November 1978.**
Below: **A Northrop YF-17 in USAF livery.**

McDonnell Douglas/ Northrop F-18 Hornet

Manufacturers: prime contractor; McDonnell-Douglas, St Louis, Missouri (forward fuselage, wings, tailplanes, landing and arrestor gear, avionics, crew station and flight control systems); associate contractor, Northrop Aircraft Division (30 percent of airframe development and 40 percent of airframe production).
Type: carrier-borne air combat fighter.
Crew: pilot only.
Specification: F-18.
Power Plant: two F404-GE-400 each rated at about 16,000 lb with afterburner. Internal fuel capacity, 10,860 lb; provision for two 300-US gal (1136-1) or 610-US gal (2309-1) drop tanks under wings and one 300-US gal (1136-1) drop tank on fuselage centerline.
Dimensions: span, 37 ft 6 in; length, 56 ft; height, 15 ft 3.6 in; wing area, 400 sq ft.
Weights: operating weight empty, about 21,500 lb; normal take-off weight (air-to-air, internal fuel only), 33,585 lb; maximum take-off weight (interdiction, two Sidewinder, four 1000 lb bombs, three tanks), 45,300 lb.
Performance: maximum speed, over Mach 1.8; minimum carrier landing speed, 131 kt; combat ceiling, 49,400 ft; combat radius (fighter), 425 nautical miles; combat radius (attack), 580 nautical miles; ferry range, 2000 nautical miles.
Armament: one M61 multi-barrel 20 mm cannon with 540 rounds; nine store stations—one centerline (bombs or tanks), two on fuselage (Advanced Sparrow or sensor pods), four on wings (AAMs, ASMs, bombs, tanks, etc) and two at wing tips (Sidewinder AAMs); maximum external load, 19,000 lb.

McDonnell Douglas Northrop F-18 was a derivative of the Northrop P-530 Cobra and YF-17 prototypes. The YF-17 competed against the successful GD. YF-16 competed in the LWF program (later ACF competition). However, the US Congress directed the US Navy to begin

***Above:* F-18A Hornet.**

studies of derivatives of the ACF designs to determine their feasibility for a multi-mission lightweight fighter. Northrop teamed with McDonnell Douglas and General Dynamics with LTV; in each case the latter companies well versed in Navy requirements, to produce the P-630 (later McDonnell-Douglas 267) and 1600 series respectively. The Model 267 was subsequently selected by the US Navy on 2 May 1975 to fulfill NACF requirement for a replacement of two dissimilar aircraft, the F-4 Phantom and A-7 Corsair.

The YF-17 was first flown on 8 June 1974. The F-18A was flown on 18 November 1978.

Rockwell XFV-12

Manufacturer: Rockwell International, Columbus, Ohio.
Type: fighter/attack technology development V/STOL aircraft.
Crew: pilot only.
Specification: XFV-12.
Power Plant: one 16,400 lb dry 28,090 lb reheat Pratt & Whitney F401-PW-400 turbofan.
Dimensions: span, 28 ft 6 in; length, 43 ft 9.5 in; height, 10 ft 4 in; wing area, 293 sq ft.
Weights: empty, 13,800 lb; maximum vertical take-off, 19,500 lb; maximum short take-off, 24,250 lb.
Performance: maximum speed, 990–1055 mph above 36,000 ft, or Mach 1.5–1.6; range (after 300 ft take-off roll), 1000 plus miles.
Armament: space for internal M61 cannon in lower fuselage; provision for missiles, with recesses in forward fuselage for two Sparrow missiles.

The Rockwell XFV-12 was developed in conjunction with the US Navy's Sea Control Ship studied during 1965–74 but subsequently abandoned through lack of funds. However, XFV-12 development continues, incorporating the main wing box and parts of the inlet ducts of an F-4 Phantom and the nose and main landing gears of an A-4 Skyhawk to reduce cost. The only prototype was flown on 26 August 1977.

***Top right and right:* The Rockwell XFV-12A fighter/attack technology prototype.**

Rockwell International B-1

Manufacturer: Rockwell International Corporation.
Type: strategic bomber and missile platform.
Crew: four.
Specification: B-1.
Power Plant: four 30,000 lb class F101-100.
Dimensions: span (15°), 136 ft 8.5 in; span (67°), 78 ft 2.5 in; length, 150 ft 2.5 in; height, 33 ft 7 in.
Weights: empty, about 140,000 lb; maximum loaded, 395,000 lb.
Performance: maximum speed at sea level (std day) about 646 mph (Mach 0.85); maximum speed at high altitude (prototypes) 1320 mph (Mach 2.0); service ceiling over 60,000 ft; range with maximum weapon load, 6100 miles.
Armament: 24 improved SRAM (AGM-69B thermonuclear missiles) internally, with provision for eight more externally; or 24 AGM-86A ALCM (air-launched cruise missiles) carried on the same mounts; 75,000 lb of free-fall bombs internally with provision for 40,000 lb externally.

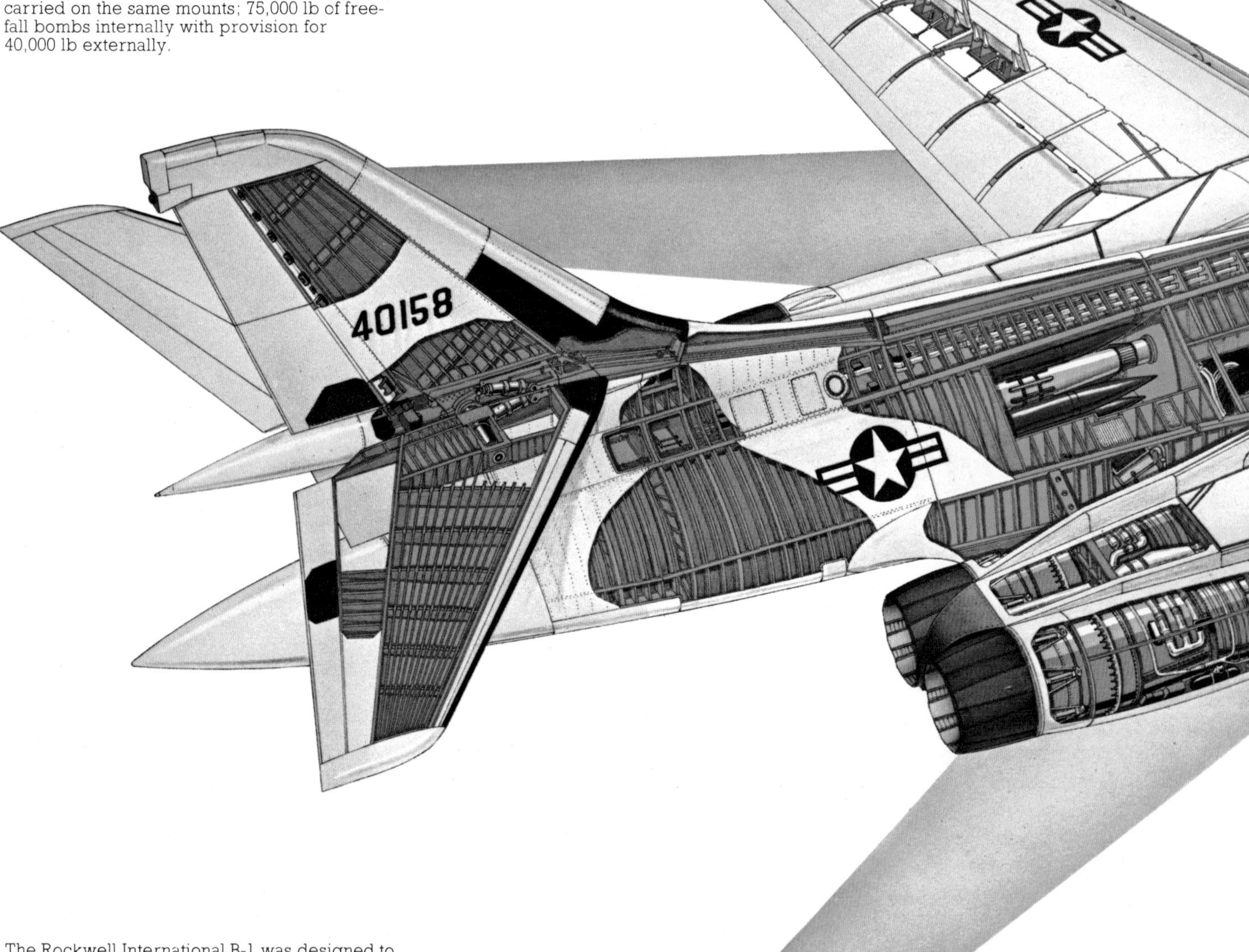

The Rockwell International B-1 was designed to supplant/supplement the B-52 with SAC.
The first flight took place on 23 December 1974.
This high-lift, variable-swept wing bomber, which can carry twice the weapon load of a B-52 at a greater distance and speed, is the most expensive combat aircraft in history. However, cost-inflation, a skeptical Congress and its use as an 'olive branch' in SALT negotiations together with President Carter's sanction, conspired to terminate the B-1 program, save for the prototypes.

Above: **The first B-1 prototype which flew for the first time on 23 December 1974.**
Below: **Rockwell International B-1.**

Below: **The first prototype B-1 comes in to land. In June 1977 the B-1 project was grounded for good.**

Sideview and underview of the YC-14, Boeing's entry in the AMST program.

Boeing YC-14

Manufacturer: Boeing Company.
Type: medium STOL tactical transport.
Crew: three; capacity for 62,000 lb payload, or 40 troops and six cargo pallets, or 150 troops.
Specification: YC-14.
Power Plant: two 51,000 lb CF6-50D.
Dimensions: span, 129 ft; length, 131 ft 8 in; height, 48 ft 4 in; wing area, 1762 sq ft.
Weights: operational empty, 117,500 lb; maximum take-off (STOL), 170,000 lb (conventional), 251,000 lb.
Performance: maximum speed, 504 mph at 30,000 ft, 403 mph at sea level; range cruise, 449 mph; tactical radius (with 27,000-lb payload), 460 miles; ferry range, 3190 miles; initial climb (at 160,000 lb, 6,350 ft per min; service ceiling, 45,000 ft.
Armament: none.

The Boeing YC-14 was one of two (the McDonnell Douglas YC-15 was the other) aircraft competing in the USAF advanced military STOL transport (AMST) program.
The first two prototypes flown on 9 August and 21 October 1976.

Lockheed C-5A Galaxy

Manufacturer: Lockheed-Georgia Company.
Type: strategic transport.
Crew: normally eight and accommodation for 83.
Specification: C-5A.
Power Plant: four 41,000 lb TF39-1.
Dimensions: span, 222 ft 8.5 in; length, 247 ft 10 in; height, 65 ft 1.5 in.
Weights: empty, 325,244 lb; loaded, 769,000 lb.
Performance: maximum speed, 571 mph; initial climb, 1800 ft per min; service ceiling at 615,000 lb, 34,000 ft; range with maximum (220,967 lb) payload, 3749 miles; ferry range, 7991 miles.
Armament: none.

The Lockheed C-5A Galaxy was modelled after its baby sister, the C-141 Starlifter to fulfill MAC's requirements for hauling very heavy loads from improvised short airstrips.
The first flight took place on 30 June 1968. Service deliveries began on 17 December 1969. Final delivery of production models took place in May 1973.
The Galaxy is, in most respects, the world's largest aircraft although later models of the Boeing 747 have surpassed it in power and weight. The C-5 carries virtually all types of the US Army's combat equipment, including such bulk items as the 74-ton mobile scissors bridge, from the USA to any theater on the globe. During trials the C-5 has dropped four 40,000 lb units in a single pass over a drop zone.

BOEING YC-14
U.S. AIR FORCE

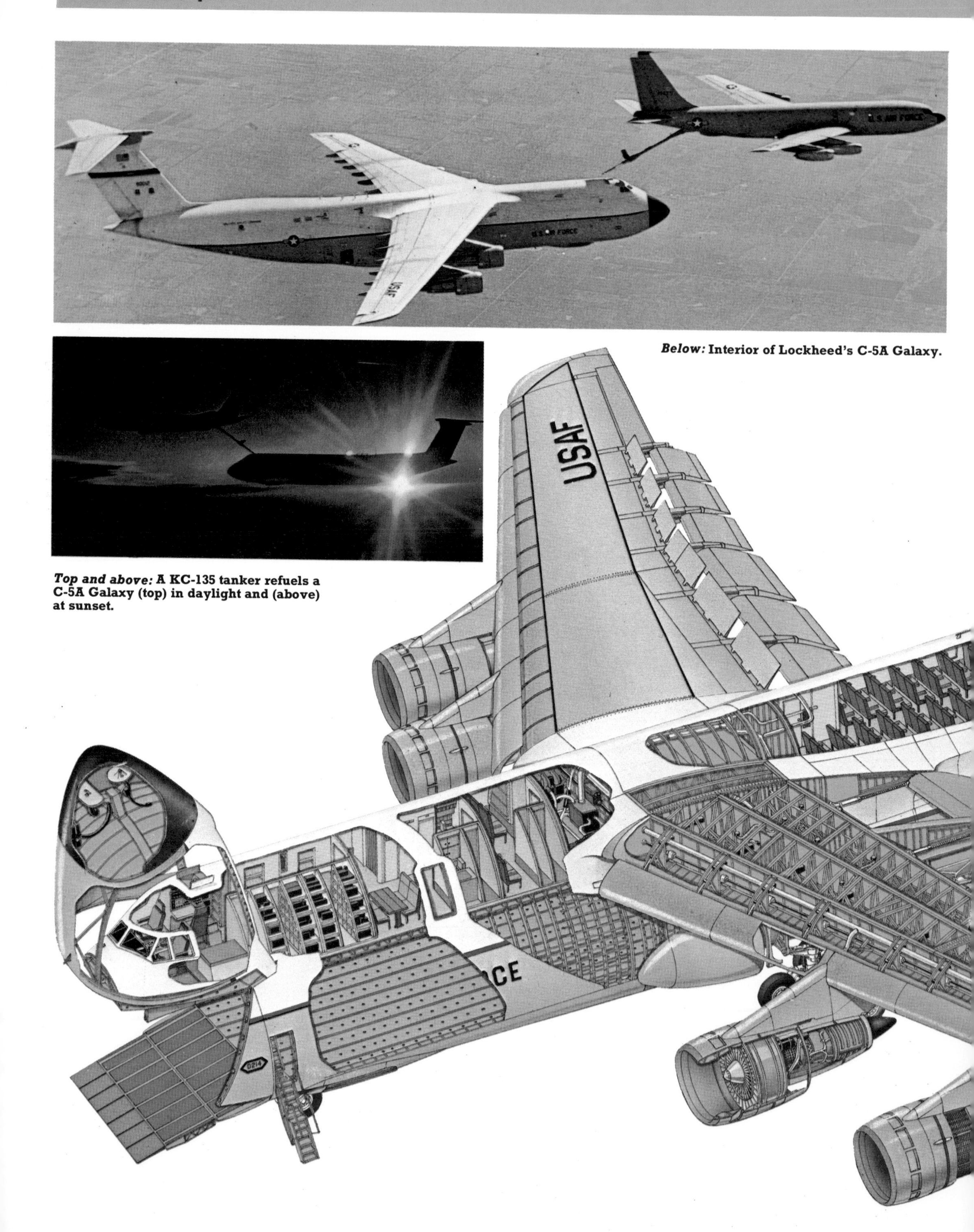

Top and above: **A KC-135 tanker refuels a C-5A Galaxy (top) in daylight and (above) at sunset.**

Below: **Interior of Lockheed's C-5A Galaxy.**

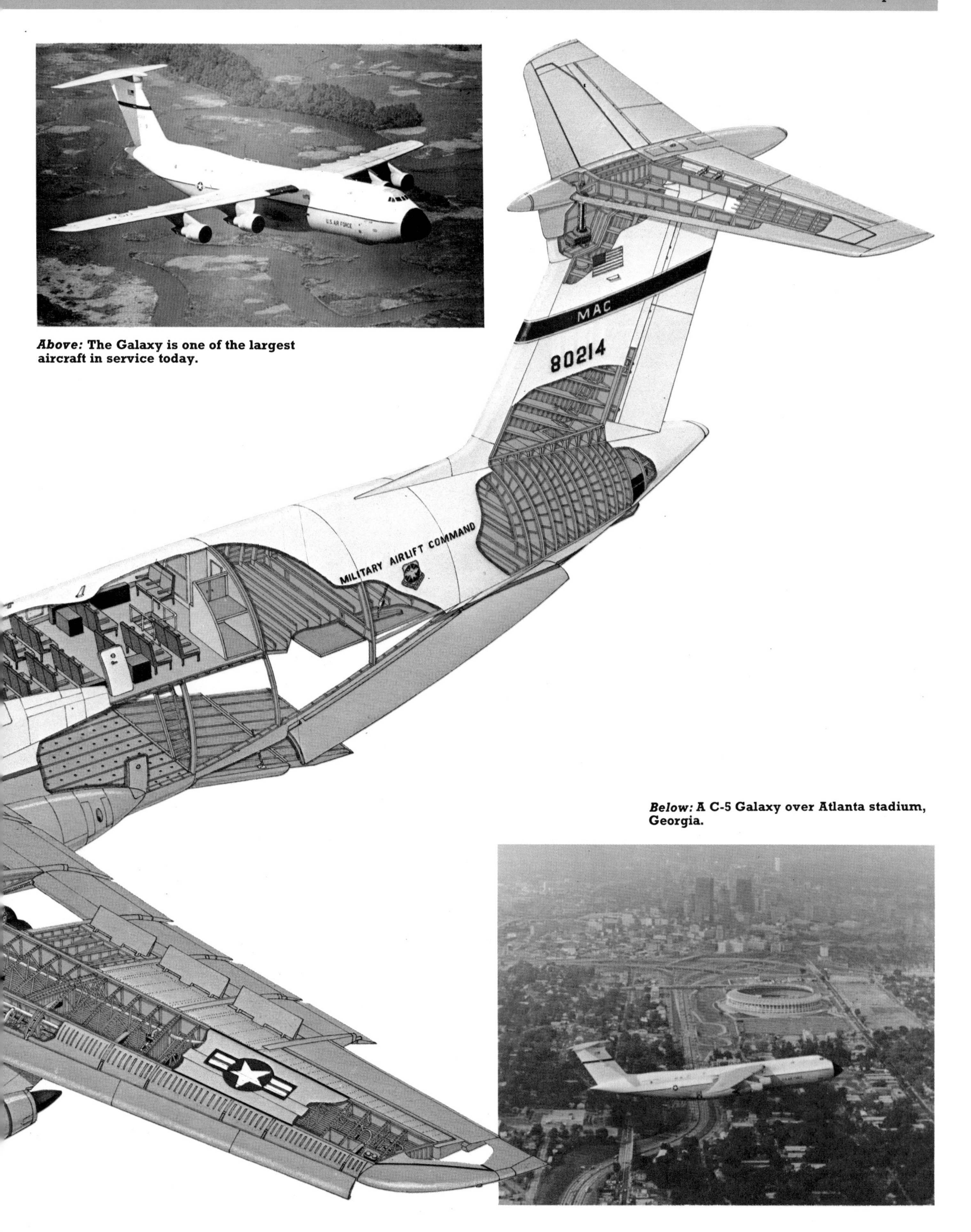

Above: **The Galaxy is one of the largest aircraft in service today.**

Below: **A C-5 Galaxy over Atlanta stadium, Georgia.**

C-5 'Fat Albert' and friend.

Lockheed YC-141B Starlifter

Manufacturer: Lockheed-Georgia Company.
Type: heavy military strategic transport.
Crew: flight crew of four; freight hold can accept a total of 13 standard 463L freight pallets totalling 59,800 lb in weight.
Specification: YC-141B.
Power Plant: four 21,000 lb TF33-P-7.
Dimensions: span, 159 ft 11 in; length, 168 ft 4 in; height, 39 ft 3 in; wing area, 3228 sq ft.
Weights: operational empty, 149,904 lb; maximum take-off, 343,000 lb.
Armament: none.

The body cross section in the C-141, which at 10 feet x 9 feet is the same as the C-130, was too small for ten percent of the US Army/USAF requirement. This led to development of a wider-bodied/stretched version, achieved by adding two 'plugs,' totalling 23 feet 4 inches, ahead and aft of the wing.

The Y-141B was first flown on 24 March 1977. The final test program was completed in July 1977.

Left: **A YC-141B Stretched Starlifter (left) next to a shorter, original model.**
Below: **A sideview of a YC-141 Stretched Starlifter in MAC markings.**
Bottom: **An aerial refuelling of the YC-141B Stretched Starlifter by a KC-135.**

McDonnell Douglas YC-15

Manufacturer: McDonnell-Douglas (Douglas Aircraft Company), Long Beach, California.
Type: STOL tactical transport.
Crew: three; capacity in hold for all US Army vehicles up to and including the 62,000-lb extended-barrel self-propelled 8-in howitzer; 150 fully-equipped troops may be carried.
Specification: YC-15.
Power Plant: four 16,000 lb JT8D-17.
Dimensions: span, 110 ft 4 in; length, 124 ft 3 in; height, 43 ft 4 in; wing area, 1740 sq ft.
Weight: maximum take-off weight, 216,680 lb.
Performance: maximum speed, 403 mph; tactical radius (with 27,000-lb payload), 460 miles; ferry range, 2992 miles.
Armament: none.

One of two competitors (the Boeing YC-14 was the other) in USAF advanced military STOL transport (AMST) program.

Two prototypes were first flown, No 1 on 26 August 1975 and No 2 on 5 December 1975.

Views of the YC-15. The fuselage of the YC-15 prototype contains 67 percent more cargo space than the USAF's biggest tactical transport (fuselage width: 18 ft).

YC-15
01875
AIR FORCE

YC-15
YC-15

Above: **A Boeing E4B converted from E-4A.**

Boeing E-4A and 747

Manufacturer: Boeing Company.
Type: airborne command post.
Crew/complement: 28–60.
Specification: E-4A.
Power Plant: four 45,500 lb F105-100.
Dimensions: span, 195 ft 8 in; length, 231 ft 4 in; height, 63 ft 5 in.
Weights: empty, probably 380,000 lb; loaded, 803,000 lb.
Performance: maximum speed, 608 mph at 30,000 ft; maximum Mach number 0.92; normal operational ceiling, 45,000 ft; normal unrefuelled range about 6500 miles.
Armament: none.

Currently the latest in a long line of airborne command posts started in the late 1950s. By 1965 the EC-135 had become restrictive and E-4As were developed to provide greater flexibility and capacity for a much larger staff in greater comfort. Boeing's commercial 747B airframe was adopted to carry the Advanced Airborne National Command Post (AABNCP) complete with unjammable communications.
The modified 747B, the E-4 was first flown in January 1973.

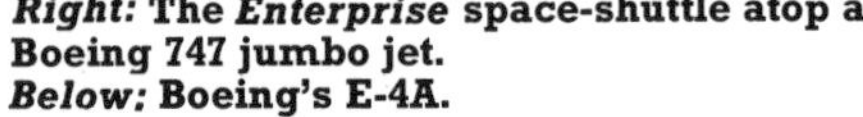

Right: **The *Enterprise* space-shuttle atop a Boeing 747 jumbo jet.**
Below: **Boeing's E-4A.**

Boeing E-3A (AWACS) Sentry

Manufacturer: Boeing Company.
Type: airborne warning and control system aircraft.
Crew: 17 (flight crew of four, systems maintenance team of four, a battle commander and an air defense operations team of eight).
Specification: E-3A.
Power Plant: four 21,000 lb TF33-PW-100/100A.
Dimensions: span, 145 ft 9 in; length, 152 ft 11 in; height, 42 ft 5 in; wing area, 3050 sq ft.
Weights: empty equipped, 170,000 lb; maximum take-off, 325,000 lb.
Performance: no details have been released for publication, but maximum and economical cruise speeds are likely to be generally similar to those of the equivalent commercial Model 707-320B (i.e., 627 mph and 550 mph respectively); mission requirement is for 7-hour search at 29,000 ft at 1150 miles from base; unrefuelled endurance, 11.5 hrs.
Armament: none.

Derivative of the Boeing 707-320B airliner and successor to earlier, basic, early-warning aircraft such as the Douglas EA-1 series and Grumman E-1B.

The EC-137D was first flown on 9 February 1972. It entered service in late 1977. American hopes that NATO countries would purchase and operate E-3As on a compatible basis were dented in 1977 when the UK announced its decision to convert Nimrods to AEW3s. In September 1978 a decision was still awaited on whether NATOs 18 E-3As still under consideration would be powered by Pratt & Whitney TF33 engines or GE(USA)/SNECMA CFM56s.

Except for the E-4A, the most expensive aircraft ever to enter military service. (As last reported the total cost to NATO for its 18 E-3As including support facilities and the re-vamping of its ground radar stations was estimated at about $2000 million.)

Below: **The Boeing E-3A (AWACS) Sentry surveillance system is equipped with the Westinghouse pulse-doppler radar.**

Grumman E-2 Hawkeye, C-2 Greyhound

Manufacturer: Grumman Aerospace Corporation, Bethpage, Long Island, New York.
Type: carrier-borne early warning surface surveillance and strike control aircraft.
Crew: five (flight crew of two and Airborne Tactical Data System team of three).
Specification: E-2C.
Power Plant: two 4910 hp T56-A-425.
Dimensions: span, 80 ft 7 in; length, 57 ft 7 in; height, 18 ft 4 in; wing area, 700 sq ft.
Weights: empty, 38,009 lb; gross, 51,900 lb.
Performance: maximum speed at 10,000 ft, 348 mph; maximum range cruise, 309 mph; maximum endurance at 230 miles from base, 40 hours; initial climb, 2515 ft per min; service ceiling, 30,800 ft; ferry range, 1604 miles.
Armament: none.

The E-2C Hawkeye is the latest Airborne Early Warning Command and Control aircraft built by Grumman and was test flown in January 1971. It is an all-weather carrier and land-based system designed for air defense of the fleet. Secondary mission capabilities include surface surveillance, strike control, search and rescue, air traffic control and communications relay. The E-2C has proved very impressive in service and has built-in advantages for land-based operations including excellent unimproved field capability along with compact size and storage. Economical twin turboprop power-plants make possible short-runway operations, low search speeds and long missions.

Below: **A Grumman E-2C Hawkeye from the USS *Constellation.* Its prime mission is detection and location of hostile aircraft but it also serves as a command and control station. The E-2C has been very successful in service.**

Grumman EA-6B Prowler

Manufacturer: Grumman Aerospace Corporation, Calverton, Long Island, N.Y.
Type: carrier-borne electronic warfare aircraft.
Crew: four (pilot and three electronic countermeasures operators).
Specification: EA-6B.
Power Plant: two 9300 lb J52-P-8A or -8B or -408.
Dimensions: span, 53 ft; length, 59 ft 5 in; height, 16 ft 3 in; wing area, 529 sq ft.
Weights: empty, 34,580 lb; gross, 63,177 lb.
Performance: maximum speed at sea level, 599 mph; average cruising speed, 466 mph; service ceiling, 38,000 ft; ferry range (external tanks), 2475 miles.
Armament: none.

The EA-6B Prowler tactical jamming system joined the US Navy in January 1971 and was first deployed to Southeast Asia in June 1972. The Prowler's primary role is to protect surface units and fleet aircraft by jamming enemy radars and communications. A derivative of the A-6 Intruder, the EA-6B is lengthened to accommodate a four-place cockpit.

Below: **Head-on view of a Grumman EA-6B Prowler showing the ALQ-99 high power jamming pods under the wings.**

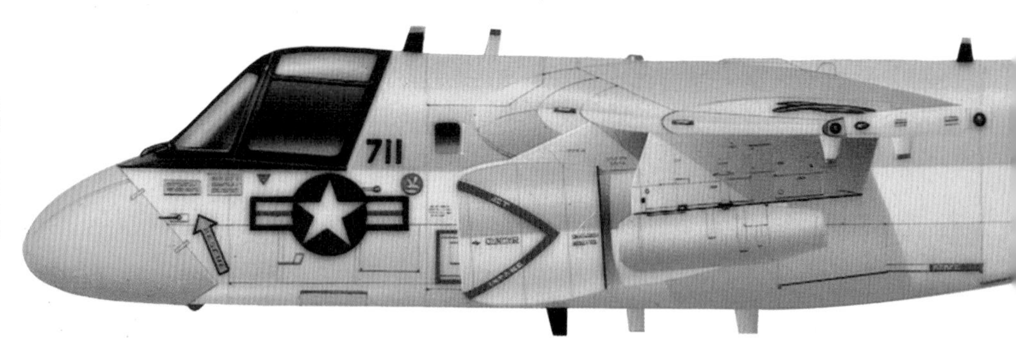

Top and above: **The Lockheed S-3A Viking was designed as a replacement for the perennial Grumman S-2.**

Lockheed S-3A Viking

Manufacturer: Lockheed-California Company, Burbank, California (in association with Vought Systems Division of LTV).
Type: (S-3A) four-seat carrier-borne anti-submarine aircraft; (US-3A) carrier on-board delivery transport.
Crew: pilot and co-pilot side by side on flight deck, with tactical co-ordinator and sensor operator in aft cabin.
Specification: S-3A.
Power Plant: two 9280 lb TF34-GE-2.
Dimensions: span, 68 ft 8 in; length, 53 ft 4 in; height, 22 ft 9 in; wing area, 598 sq ft.
Weights: empty equipped, 26,554 lb; normal take-off, 43,491 lb; maximum launch, 52,539 lb.
Performance: maximum speed, 506 mph at sea level; maximum cruise, 403 mph; typical loiter speed, 184 mph; maximum ferry range, 3500 miles plus; initial climb, 3937 ft per min; service ceiling, 35,000 ft; sea level endurance, 7.5 hrs at 186 mph.
Armament: Assorted combinations of bombs, depth charges, Mk-46 torpedoes and ASM's in internal weapons bay. Two underwing pylons can carry single or triple ejectors for bombs, rocket pods, missiles, tanks or stores.

The Lockheed S-3A Viking was selected by the US Navy in 1969 to replace the Grumman S-2 family.

The first R & D S-3A was flown on 8 November 1971. First carrier landings were made in November 1973 and service delivery began in February 1974.

Boeing Vertol Model 114 CH-47 Chinook

Manufacturer: Boeing Vertol Company; built under license by Elicotteri Meridionali and SIAI-Marchetti, Italy.
Type: medium transport helicopter.
Crew: normally two or three.
Specification: CH-47C.
Power Plant: two 3750 shp T55-L-11.
Dimensions: rotor diameter (each), 60 ft; fuselage length, 51 ft.
Weights: empty, 20,378 lb; maximum take-off, 46,000 lb.
Performance: at 33,000 lb; maximum speed, 190 mph at sea level; average cruise, 158 mph; maximum inclined climb, 2880 ft per min; hovering ceiling (out of ground effect), 14,750 ft; mission radius, 115 miles.

The Chinook is the US Army's primary transport helicopter but has also served with the armed forces of six other countries. Missions include the transportation of fuel, troops, ammunition, artillery and other cargo. The CH-47 became operational with a US Army unit 3.5 years after the company won the design competition in March 1959 for air-turbine helicopter to replace the Army's piston-engine aircraft. The first of the advanced B models were delivered in 1967 and this was followed by deliveries of the C model, capable of lifting 12 tons, in 1969. The Chinook has the capability of being operated in all types of environmental conditions. It has operated in arctic conditions (—70°F) and in both tropical and desert environments with temperatures as high as 125°F.

Below: **Two action shots of the Boeing CH-47 Chinook.**

Above: **A sideview of the Chinook. It is equipped with a multi-sensor nose installation.**

Hughes YAH-64 Model 77, AH-64 (to be named)

Manufacturer: Hughes Helicopters, Culver City.
Type: Tandem two-seat tactical helicopter.
Crew: two (pilot and co-pilot/gunner).
Specification: YAH-64.
Power Plant: two 1536 shp T700-GE-700.
Dimensions: rotor diameter, 48 ft; fuselage length, 49 ft 4.5 in.
Weights: empty, 9900 lb; primary mission, 13,600 lb; maximum take-off, 17,400 lb.
Performance: maximum speed, 191 mph; cruising speed, 179 mph; maximum inclined climb, 3200 ft per min; hovering ceiling (in ground effect), 14,600 ft, (outside ground effect), 11,800 ft; service ceiling, 8000 ft; maximum range, 424 miles.
Armament: Hughes XM-230 30 mm chain-driven cannon; 8 BGM-71A TOW anti-armor missiles (optional); 16 Hellfire laser-seeking missiles (also optional).

The Hughes YAH-64 won the US Army's AAH (Advanced Attack Helicopter) contest in late 1976. The prototype was first flown on 30 September 1975.

Hughes OH-6 Cayuse, 500M-D Tow Defender

Manufacturer: Hughes Helicopters, Culver City; (NH) BredaNardi, Ascoli, Italy; (369HM) Kawasaki, Japan, (RACA) RACA, Buenos Aires, Argentina; (Defender) South Korea under a co-operation agreement.
Type: light multi-role helicopter.
Crew: two, plus two additional seats.
Specification: OH-6.
Power Plant: one 420 shp 250-C20B turboshaft.
Dimensions: rotor diameter, 26 ft 5 in; fuselage length, 21 ft 5 in.
Weights: empty, 1295 lb; maximum take-off (internal load), 3000 lb, (with external load), 3620 lb.
Performance: (at 3000 lb) maximum speed, 175 mph at sea level; cruise, 160 mph at 4000 ft; maximum inclined climb, 1920 ft per min; hovering ceiling (in ground effect), 8800 ft, (out of ground effect), 7100 ft; maximum range, 263 miles.
Armament: provision for 4 TOW (Tube-launched optically-tracked Wire-guided) missiles; seven-round launchers for 2.75 in rockets, a 30 mm 'chain gun' or 7.62 mm 'chain gun' in extendible turret (all optional).

The Hughes OH-6 Cayuse was derived, via civil 500D, from the OH-6A US Army observation helicopter.

Sikorsky S-70, UH-60A Black Hawk

Manufacturer: Sikorsky Aircraft Division of United Technologies, Stratford, Connecticut.
Type: multi-role tactical combat assault/transport helicopter.
Crew: capacity for 11 fully equipped troops/80001 slung load.
Specification: S-70.
Power Plant: two 1543 shp T700-GE-700 turboshafts.
Dimensions: rotor diameter, 53 ft 8 in; fuselage length, 50 ft 0.75 in.
Weights: gross, 16,500 lb; maximum take-off, 22,000 lb.
Performance: maximum speed, 224 mph at sea level; cruise, 166 mph; vertical climb rate, 450 ft per min; hovering ceiling (in ground effect), 10,000 ft, (out of ground effect), 5800 ft; endurance 2.3–3.0 hrs.
Armament: none.

The Sikorsky S-70 Black Hawk won the US Army UTTAS (Utility Tactical Transport Aircraft System) competition.
The prototype YUH-60A was first flown 17 October 1974.

Sikorsky S-70L, SH-60B

Manufacturer: Sikorsky Aircraft Division of United Technologies Corporation, Stratford, Connecticut.
Type: shipboard multi-role helicopter.
Specification: S-70L.
Power Plant: two 1630 shp T700-GE-400.
Dimensions: rotor diameter, 53 ft 8 in; fuselage length, 50 ft 0.75 in.
Weights: mission loaded (ASW), 19,377 lb, (anti-ship surveillance), 17,605 lb.
Performance: (estimated) maximum cruise, 172 mph; maximum vertical climb rate, 450 ft per min; ceiling, 10,000 ft; time on station at radius of 57 miles, 3 hrs, (at radius of 173 miles 1 hr.)
Armament: two homing torpedoes, 25 sonobuoys.

The Sikorsky S-70L derived from the UH-60A Black Hawk and winner of the US Navy LAMPS (Light Airborne Multi-purpose System) Mk III helicopter competition.
First flown in December 1978. Deliveries expected to commence in 1981.

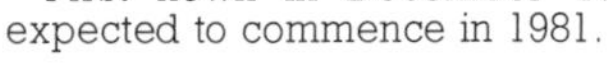

Beechcraft T-44A (Beech King Air)

Manufacturer: Beech Aircraft Corporation, Wichita, Kansas.
Type: multi-engine pilot trainer for the US Navy.
Crew: two with provision for two students, one instructor and two additional passengers.
Specification: T-44A.
Power Plant: two 550 or 620 hp PT6A turboprops.
Dimensions: span, 50 ft 2 in; length, 35 ft 6 in; height, 14 ft 2 in.
Weights: basic, 6326 lb; maximum take-off weight, 9650 lb.
Performance: maximum cruise speed, (KTAS at 15,000 ft) 240.
Armament: none.

The Beechcraft T-44A was a replacement for the Grumman TS-2A and 2B derived from the civil King Air.

Bottom left: **The Beechcraft T-44A.**
Right: **A Beechcraft C-12A of the USAF in formation with a C-12A of the US Army.**

Beechcraft C-12A (Beech Super King Air)

Manufacturer: Beech Aircraft Corporation, Wichita, Kansas.
Type: pressurized transport.
Crew: pilot and co-pilot and up to 8 passengers.
Specification: C-12A.
Power Plant: two 750 hp PT6 engines.
Dimensions: span, 54 ft 6 in, length, 43 ft 10 in; height, 15 ft 5 in.
Weights: empty, (basic), 7821 lb; maximum at take-off, 12,500 lb.
Performance: cruising speed, 287 mph at 12,000 ft; 274 mph at 21,000 ft.
Armament: none.

Latest member of the Beech King Air family of turboprop aircraft. Off-the-shelf purchases were made by both the US Army (as the C-12A Huron) and the USAF for deployment among the Embassies, Attaches and Military Missions throughout the world. RU-21J is a severely modified electronic platform version.

***Below:* Beechcraft T-44A of the US Navy.**

USAF
US AIR FORC

***Left and right:* The Boeing T-43A Airborne Navigator trainer of the USAF.**

Boeing T-43A and 737

Manufacturer: Boeing Company.
Type: navigational trainer.
Crew: T-43 crew plus up to 12 trainee navigators, four proficiency students and three instructors.
Specification: T-43A.
Power Plant: two 14,500 lb JT8D-9.
Dimensions: span, 93 ft; length, 100 ft; height, 37 ft.
Weights: empty, about 62,000 lb; maximum, 115,500 lb.
Performance: maximum speed, 586 mph; maximum cruising speed, 576 mph at 22,600 ft; economical cruise, Mach 0.7 at 35,000 ft; initial rate of climb at gross weight, 3750 ft per min; range with military reserves, 2995 miles; endurance, 6 hours.
Armament: none.

The Boeing T-43A was a derivative of the Boeing 737-200 commercial airliner and is the world's most advanced navigational trainer. Computers and an increase in trainee-carrying capacity has enabled the Navigator Training wing at Mather AFB to replace 77 Convair T-29s with just 19 T-43As.

Boeing Model 1041-133-1

Manufacturer: Boeing Aerospace Company.
Type: V/STOL ship-based multi-role aircraft; especially ASW and AEW missions.
Crew: two.
Specification: 1041.
Power Plant: two 8080 shp XT701.
Dimensions: span, 41 ft 3 in; length, 48 ft 1 in.
Weights: about 15,000 lb; empty and 30,000 lb loaded.
Performance: maximum about Mach 0.8; ceiling over 40,000 ft.
Armament: suitable for ASW, (AEW) none.

The success of the Harrier/AV-8A led to a US Navy study of how jet-lift technology could be applied to ship-based aircraft.

The study took place from 1975–77 with an anticipated service delivery by 1984.

***Below:* The V-530, Vought's proposed V/STOL aircraft, was developed from the TA-7C.**

LTV TA-7C Corsair

Manufacturer: Vought Systems Division of LTV, Dallas, Texas.
Type: combat crew trainer and instrument trainer.
Crew: instructor and student pilot.
Specification: LTV TA-7C.
Power Plant: one TF30-P408.
Dimensions: span, 36 ft 8 in; length, 48 ft 6 in; height, 16 ft 5 in.
Weights: empty, 19,180 lb; take-off with no military stores, 31,982 lb.
Performance: maximum speed, 582 knots at sea-level.
Armament: six wing and two fuselage weapons stations; the M61 20 mm cannon with 500 rounds of ammunition provides full weapons systems training capability.

Although converted from earlier Navy A-7s the TA-7C is carrier-suitable and is easily adapted for carrier-borne and land-based combat operations. Although similar in appearance to the A-7 a 16-inch section in the forward part of the fuselage has been added and a further stretch of 18 inches made at the trailing edge of the

TA-7C
NAVY
154544

VOUGHT
TA-7C
NAVY

wing. The tail has been increased by four inches and despite the addition of a second cockpit internal fuel capacity remains about 1500 gallons; the same as the A-7E. The aft fuselage was modified by an upward cant of little more than one degree, thus allowing approach and landing attitudes identical to the A-7E. The rear-seat is elevated to provide the instructor with exceptional visibility.

The first production TA-7C was test flown in December 1976 and deliveries to US Navy began January 1977.

Left, top and bottom: **The TA-7C two-seat trainer can be adapted for combat to operate from carriers or land on runways.** ***Below and bottom:*** **The Talon is in service primarily with the USAF and the Luftwaffe.**

Northrop T-38A Talon

Manufacturer: Northrop Corporation, Norair Division, Hawthorne, California.
Type: supersonic basic and advanced trainer.
Crew: pupil and instructor in tandem.
Specification: T-38A.
Power Plant: two J85-5 rated at 2680 lb thrust dry and 3850 lb with maximum after-burner.
Dimensions: span, 25 ft 3 in; length, 46 ft 4.5 in; height, 12 ft 10.5 in.
Weights: empty, about 7164 lb; maximum loaded, 12,093 lb.
Performance: maximum speed at 36,000 ft, 812 mph (Mach 1.23); initial climb, 30,000 ft per min; service ceiling, 53,600 ft; range with maximum fuel (all internal), 1093 miles.
Armament: none.

The Northrop T-38A Talon was evolved from Northrop's study for a lightweight fighter which led to the F-5 development.

The first flight took place on 10 April 1959 and it was operational in March 1961. Final deliveries were made in January 1972.

When delivery of this first ever supersonic trainer for the USAF finished in January 1972 over 1187 had been built. This is exceptional for a supersonic aircraft of one design but despite a high reliability and safety record it is adjudged to have been a mistake. Outside the USA only the Luftwaffe bought the T-38, retaining US markings on all 46 aircraft. However, in parallel with the T-38, Northrop developed the F-5 as a private venture. Five Talons were bought by the US Navy and 24 by NASA for Astronaut practice.

Appendi

Mi

siles

The B-52H in flight shows to excellent advantage the eight underwing AGM-69 Short-Range Attack Missiles (SRAM) which can be launched at subsonic or supersonic speeds, from high or low altitudes and are capable of changing direction.

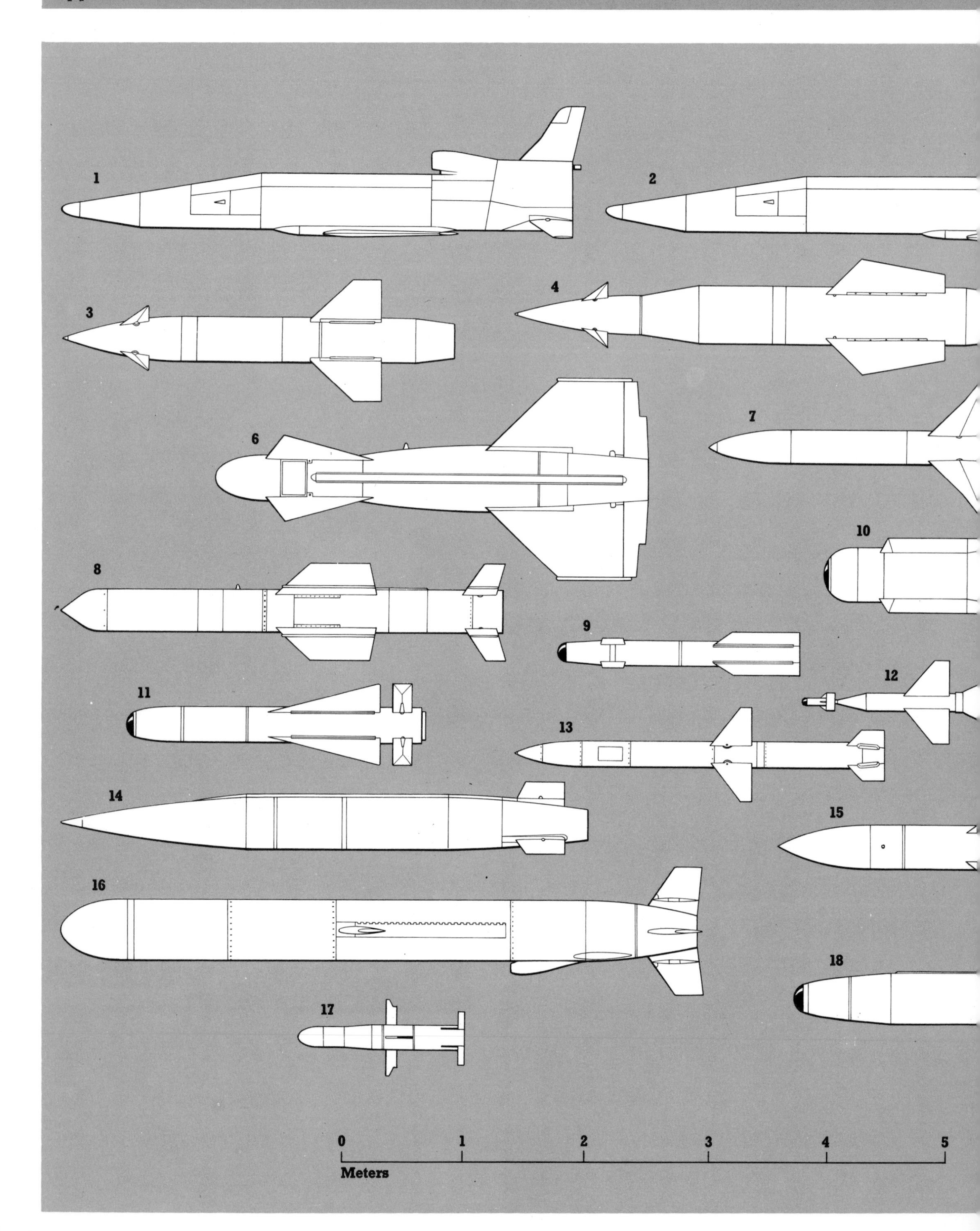
1
2
3
4
6
7
10
8
9
11
12
13
14
15
16
18
17
0
1
2
3
4
5
Meters

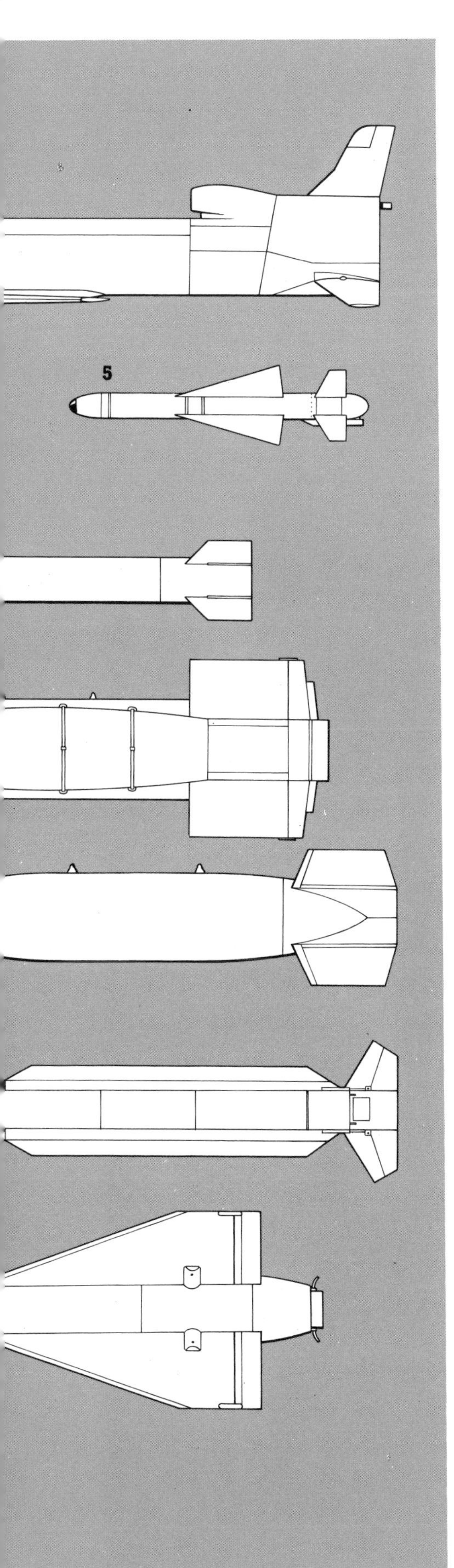

Air to ground missiles (left)

1 ALCM (Boeing), Air-Launched Cruise Missile AGM-86A.
2 ALCM B (Boeing), Air-Launched Cruise Missile AGM-86B, improved and enlarged version with a range in excess of 1300 nautical miles.
3 Bullpup A (Martin Marietta Corp), radio-command guidance tactical missile, high explosive warhead, range 7 miles.
4 Bullpup B (Martin Marietta Corp), enlarged and improved version with H E or nuclear warhead, range 10 miles.
5 Condor (Rockwell International), tactical missile, command guidance from launch aircraft with TV data link, range about 50 miles.
6 GBU-15 (Rockwell International), glide bomb with self-contained radar guidance.
7 Harm (US Naval Weapons Center), anti-radar missile, passive broad based RF radiation homing.
8 Harpoon (McDonnell Douglas), radar homing anti-ship missile.
9 Hellfire (Rockwell International), laser homing 'fire and forget' battlefield anti-armor missile carried by attack helicopters.
10 Hobos (Rockwell International), electro-optical guided homing bomb.
11 Maverick (Hughes), tactical or battlefield missile available in laser guided or TV homing versions, designation – AGM-65.
12 Paveway (Texas Instruments), laser-guided series of homing bombs.
13 Shrike (US Naval Weapons Center), tactical anti-radar missile, passive radar homing.
14 SRAM (Boeing), Short Range Attack Missile AGM-69A, programmed inertial guidance, nuclear warhead.
15 Standard ARM (General Dyanamics), AGM-78, anti-radar missile passive radar homing.
16 Tomahawk (General Dynamics), AGM-109, Air-Launched Cruise Missile, tactical version has range of 300 nautical miles, strategic version 1300 miles.
17 TOW (Hughes), automatic optical tracking battlefield or anti-armor missile, carried by attack helicopters.
18 Walleye (Martin Marietta Corp), automatic TV tracking homing bomb.

Below: **Hughes Aircraft AGM-65 Maverick.**
Bottom: **Boeing AGM-69 SRAM.**

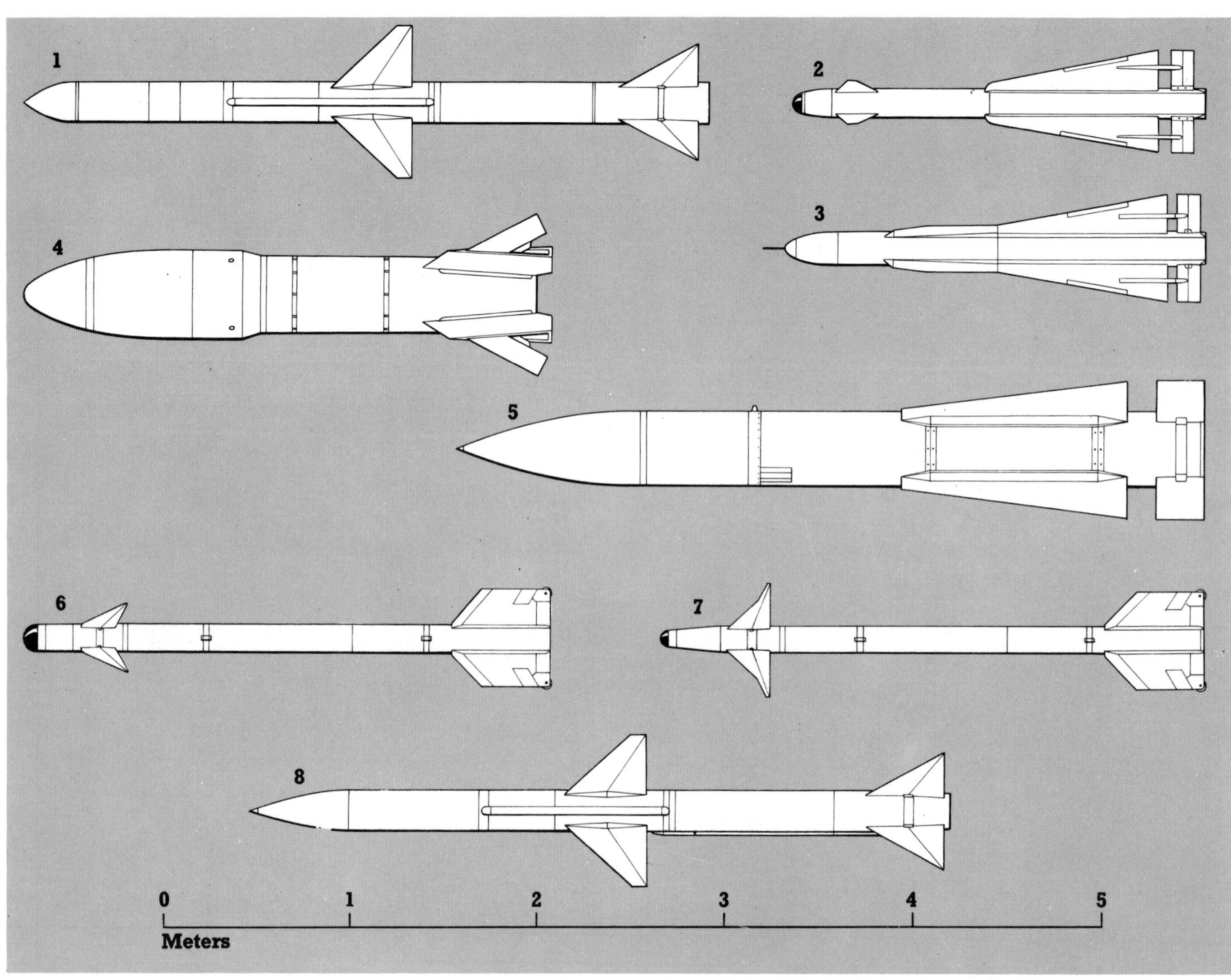

Air to air missiles (above)

1 Brazo (Hughes) based on Sparrow airframe, broad-band RF homing anti-radiation missile.
2 Falcon (Hughes) AIM-4D, infra-red homing missile speed Mach 4, range 6 miles.
3 Super Falcon (Hughes) AIM-4G, improved version available with either infra-red or semi-active radar guidance, greater range and improved accuracy.
4 Genie (McDonnell Douglas) AIR-2A, unguided, gyro-stabilized missile with nuclear warhead designed for the threat of large bomber formations.
5 Phoenix (Hughes) AIM-54A, long-range, 70–100 miles, active radar homing missile, can be launched from F-14 Tomcat aircraft in salvoes of up to six missiles against independent targets.
6 Sidewinder (US Naval Weapons Center), basic dogfight missile with infra-red homing, range 2+ miles, speed Mach 2.5.
7 Improved Sidewinder (US Naval Weapons Center), infra-red homing of increased accuracy, range improved to 5–9 miles.
8 Sparrow (Raytheon) AIM-7, all-weather radar homing missile range 24 nautical miles, speed Mach 3.5.

Top right: **The AIR-2A Genie.**
Right: **Raytheon AIM-7 Sparrow III.**

U S AIR FORCE

1337-179-9203
ROCKET MOTOR, MARK 52 MOD 2
DO NOT ROLL, TUMBLE, OR DROP

Index

Acknowledgments

Aviation Photo News: 10/11 (bottom), 16/17 (bottom), 42 (top), 47 (bottom), 63 (top), 74 (top left), 78 (bottom), 81 (center), 83 (bottom). 86/87 (top left and top center), 91 (bottom right), 99 (top right), 116 (top), 117 (bottom), 130 (center), 132 (bottom 2), 135 (top), 137 (bottom).
Michael Badrocke: 39 (right, second from top), 42/43, 46 (top), 50/51, 54 (top), 55 (bottom), 62 (bottom), 70 (center right), 74/75, 83 (top right), 94 (top), 98/99, 103 (2 drawings), 107 (bottom), 110 (bottom), 111 (top), 113 (bottom), 120/121, 128 (bottom), 146/147, 151 (bottom right), 159 (bottom), 162 (bottom), 196/197, 200/201, 209 (bottom), 218/219, 220 (top).
Beech Aircraft Corporation: 82 (both), 83 (center lower), 139 (upper center and bottom left), 210/211 (all 3).
Belgian Air Force: 14/15 (bottom).
Bison Picture Library: 37 (top), 49 (bottom), 50 (bottom 2), 55 (top), 58 (center), 62 (center left), 66/67 (bottom), 70 (top), 72/73 (center top), 77 (top), 78 (center), 81 (top).
Boeing: 6/7, 17 (top), 26/27, 33, 34/35, 47 (top and center), 48/49, 52 (top), 84, 100, 104 (bottom), 106/107 (4 photos), 108 (top), 109 (bottom), 129 (both), 130, (top), 164, 198/199 (both), 206 (top), 209 (center right 2), 213 (top right), 216/217.
Martin Bowman: 128 (center), 159 (top right).
Cessna: 83 (center near top), 85 (both), 139 (lower center), 140/141, 168/169 (center 2 and right 2), 170/171.
Confederate Air Force: 95 (top right), 116/117 (center).
Convair: A Division of General Dynamics: 90 (top left), 105 (top), 110 (top), 111 (bottom and center right).
Dutch Defense Department: 154/155 (center and top center).
General Dynamics: 1, 2/3, 25 (top), 146 (top left), 148/149, 174/175, 177 (top and center), 178/179 (all 4 but top left), 180/181 (all 5).
Grumman: 28 (top), 68 (bottom left), 69 (top right), 70 (bottom left), 77 (center and bottom), 115 (bottom), 117 (center right), 118 (both). 124 (top), 124/125 (bottom), 158/159 (top), 182 (top), 183 (center), 207 (center), 208 (bottom).
Imperial War Museum: 48 (bottom), 58 (bottom left), 59 (center 2), 61 (both), 62 (top), 65 (center), 68/69 (top center), 71 (center), 72/73 (bottom).
Italian Air Force: 32 (bottom), 39 (center), 40 (bottom), 45 (center), 83 (top left), 86 (bottom), 92/93 (bottom), 104 (center).
Archie Jones: 54 (bottom).
Lockheed: 12/13, 14 (top), 20/21 (both), 30/31, 37 (center), 38 (bottom 2), 39 (bottom), 53 (top), 60 (top), 81 (bottom RIGHT), 91 (upper right), 92/93 (top 3), 105 (bottom), 126/127, 128 (top), 133 (top), 134 (top and center 2), 135 (bottom 2 and center), 142, 156 (bottom), 158/159 (center), 201 (bottom right), 202/203 (all 4), 208 (top).
McDonnell Douglas: 22/23, 28/29 (bottom), 56 (both), 57 (bottom and center), 67 (top right), 68/69 (center), 80/81 (all 4), 88/89, 94 (bottom), 112 (bottom), 114 (both), 115 (top), 122 (both), 123 (bottom left), 131 (bottom), 133 (top), 143 (top), 144/145, 150/151 (center bottom), 151 (top right and center), 152/153, 156/157 (top), 157 (right 2), 161 (right 2), 186/187 (both), 188/189, 192 (both), 193 (center right), 194 (top).
Dave Mayor: 41 (top), 87 (top right).
National Archives: 8/9, 63 (center).
National Maritime Museum: 70 (bottom right).
Wiley Noble: 76 (center).
North American Aviation: 40 (top), 41 (bottom), 64, 65 (top), 96 (top), 101 (top and center), 123 (top).
North American Rockwell: 173 (top).
Northrop: 11 (top), 44 (bottom), 103 (bottom), 154/155 (bottom 2), 190/191, 193 (center), 215 (bottom).
Stephen P Peltz: 36 (bottom).
Pilot Press: 32 (center), 36 (top and center), 39 (top right), 43 (center), 44 (top), 45 (top left), 46 (center), 51 (bottom), 57 (top left), 58 (top), 59 (top), 60 (center), 63 (bottom), 65 (bottom), 66 (all 3), 68 (top), 70 (center left), 71 (bottom), 72 (top left), 75 (right), 76 (bottom), 78 (top), 79 (bottom), 87 (bottom right), 93 (top right), 99 (bottom), 103 (center), 113 (top), 116 (bottom), 124 (center left), 125 (top right), 134 (bottom), 139 (top and bottom right), 147 (bottom), 150 (bottom), 154 (top), 163 (top right), 165 (bottom), 176/177 (bottom 2), 183 (top), 193 (top), 208/209 (near top).
Rick Rockiki: 183 (bottom).
Rockwell: 162/163 (top), 194/195, 195 (top).
Royal Netherlands Air Force: 96/97 (bottom), 98 (top right), 103 (center).
Royal Norwegian Air Force: 76 (top), 97 (top), 98 (bottom left), 104 (top), 132 (center), 137 (center), 158 (bottom left).
United States Air Force: 38 (top), 43 (bottom), 45 (top right and bottom), 46 (bottom), 51 (top 2), 52 (bottom), 53 (bottom), 55 (center 2), 57 (top right), 59 (bottom 2), 60 (bottom), 62 (center right), 67 (top left), 71 (top), 79 (top), 90/91 (center 2), 95 (bottom), 101 (bottom), 102, 108 (bottom), 109 (top), 112/113 (center 3), 130/131 (bottom), 131 (top right), 133 (bottom), 136 (top), 143 (bottom 2), 150 (center left), 150/151 (top), 155 (right hand 2), 160/161 (both), 165 (center), 166/167, 168 (bottom left), 173 (bottom), 176 (center), 193 (bottom), 197 (both), 200 (top 2), 201 (top), 206 (center and bottom), 212, 215 (top), 219 (both), 220/221 (bottom), 221 (top).
United States Marine Corps: 4/5, 119 (bottom), 138 (top and bottom), 172 (both).
United States Navy: 18/19, 24/25 (bottom), 68/69 (bottom center and right), 86/87 (center bottom), 117 (top), 121 (center right), 125 (top and bottom right), 138 (center), 151 (bottom left), 159 (center right), 162 (center), 163 (center left), 182 (bottom), 184 (bottom), 185 (top).
Vought: 72 (top right), 87 (center), 119 (top), 121 (top), 123 (bottom right), 184 (top), 185 (bottom), 213 (bottom right), 214 (both).
West German Air Force: 163 (bottom and center right).
Westinghouse: 178 (top), 207 (bottom).
Westland: 136 (bottom).